JAMIE BOWLBY-WHITING

The Boy Who Was Afraid of the World

Published by Jamie Bowlby-Whiting
Printed by CreateSpace

First Edition

Author's Note

This is a true story. All of the events recounted in this book are authentic. To protect the identities of various crazies across the planet, names have been changed and in order to make a more pleasant reading experience, some minor events appear in a slightly incorrect chronological order. In an effort to involve the reader in the experience, much of the story is told through dialogue and while it's not verbatim, conversations have been reconstructed to both articulate actions and to remain true to actual discussions. Many locations and innumerable occurrences were omitted for brevity: after all, it's a story, not a diary. And just in case you were wondering who that terrified child is on the cover of the book, well, that's me.

For you,
who has been afraid,
yet dares to dream.

Contents Page

JAMIE BOWLBY-WHITING

The Boy Who Was Afraid of the World

Prologue

I'm three years old and I can barely breathe. Where is my mother? Why has she left me alone with these strangers? I see the door that she left by and I start running. I run as fast as I can so that no one can stop me. Please, please don't stop me.

I'm four years old and I'm shaking. My father is driving, it's late at night, and we have run out of fuel next to a large forest. I don't want to know what monsters are lurking in the darkness. Hot tears run down my face. Is that me screaming?

I'm five years old and I can't get to the door. I can't get out of my bed, I can't move, I can't roll back the bedsheets. A dinosaur is lurking outside my bedroom and it is going to eat me. My mouth is so dry, I can't even call for help. I need somebody to save me.

I'm six years old, dressed in a white karate robe. I stand on the stage in front of my whole school and their parents. Everybody is watching me because I am Angel Gabriel. I have fifteen words to say, but I can't even remember my own name. I do not want to do this anymore, I do not want anyone to watch me. I do not want to be Angel Gabriel.

I'm eight years old and it's my first day at a new school. Five hundred children. I don't think I've met five hundred people in my whole life. I bet they all know each other, I bet they are cooler than me, I bet they don't like me. I don't want to be here, I don't want to speak to anyone, I want to go home. I am a little fish and I am drowning.

I'm sixteen years old and a girl in my class tells me that she has never heard me speak during five years of high school. I can speak, of course I can speak. I open my mouth, but no words come out. I shrug my shoulders and smile apologetically, hoping she leaves me alone. What is it that people even talk about anyway?

I'm seventeen years old and I don't know what to do with my life. I don't know which university to go to, I don't know which course to apply to, I don't know anything. I don't want to think about it, I don't want to have to think about it, I don't don't don't. Life should be simple, like computer games.

I'm twenty-three years old and my back is broken. The doctor asks me to wiggle my toes, checking for paralysis. He says I can't play sport for at least a year. My panicked breaths are so laboured that they are causing me further pain. I wish I could wake up from this nightmare.

I am falling. It's that feeling you get just before you hit the ground. Except that I am not going to hit the ground, I am not going to stop falling. It just goes on and on and I beg for it to stop because it is the worst feeling in the world and I don't even know what is causing it anymore.

I am twenty-five years old.

1. Hold Tight

It's not that I'm scared. It's just that I don't really know if this is what I want to be doing.

I mean, look at me. Twenty-five years old on the side of the road with my thumb out. That elderly couple in the red car keep looking at me. If I wasn't standing here in this old t-shirt and these borrowed hiking boots, they wouldn't be looking at me like that. If I was wearing a suit and driving a nice car, they wouldn't be poring over me with pitying eyes. If they knew I had a Masters degree in Mathematics… they'd probably ask me why I am standing on the side of the road trying to catch a free ride.

I pull my phone from my pocket and look at the time. Nearly ten minutes have passed since my mother dropped me at this petrol station. By now she will be halfway back to our little English village, my home for over eighteen years before I started university.

"Just call me if you change your mind," she said before driving off. If I call her now, maybe I could start again tomorrow. Maybe I could say I never even started at all and that it was just a silly idea that I never really intended to follow through on. Yes, that sounds right. It was all a joke. I never really intended on hitchhiking into Europe by myself. Surely nobody took me seriously when I first proposed this idea.

Besides, what have I got to prove anyway? It's not as if I will receive a bravery award for hitchhiking by myself. Thousands and millions of people have done it before. Yes, I think that this was a silly idea. It's time to go home and start thinking about what I am going to do with my life. I can go back to my village and I can make a new plan, a sensible plan.

Standing on the unkept slip road that leads to the dual-carriageway, brambles clutch at the tarmac so that I have to stand in the road.

I am impossible to miss, but none of the passing cars have even made eye contact with me yet.

An old, white Ford Transit pulls out of the run-down service station and I gingerly hold out my thumb. The reflections on the windscreen stop me seeing inside the vehicle. I bet the passengers are all looking at me, laughing, thinking that I look ridiculous. Look at that kid standing on the road, trying to catch a ride.

Nobody is going to pick him up.

As my hand falls back to my side, I'm defeated. This is too embarrassing to go on, I don't want people to look at me anymore. I should call my mother.

The van has pulled up next to me.

Joy! I open the door and scramble to throw my overladen backpack into the cab. I can hardly believe it, this van has actually stopped. I am a hitchhiker, a solo hitchhiker.

On a typical English day, miserably grey and overcast, clouds from horizon to horizon, I am on my way. This might be the best thing I have ever done in my life.

"Hi, I'm Jamie," I excitedly tell the driver. He is about thirty with long black hair that has either been straightened or recently washed. Without a word, he looks into his side-view mirror and pulls away at speed. I wait awkwardly for him to break the silence. Is it inappropriate to speak in this situation? One of us has to say something...

"Hi Jamie, I'm Rich," he finally says once we're moving with the flow of traffic. I breathe a sigh of relief. "Where are you heading?"

"Sweden, hopefully. It's nearly midsummer and I want to experience perpetual sunlight."

"I can't take you to Sweden, but I'm going as far as Newmarket. Is that alright?"

"Yeah that's great, it's the right direction so I'm sure I'll get there eventually." Growing up in rural England, there aren't many towns around so I know exactly where Newmarket is.

"How long have you been trying to get a ride?"

"At that fuel station? About ten minutes. My mother drove me out from Castle Acre this morning, but you're the first ride I've got." Rich flicks a glance in my direction, a few more seconds of silent contemplation. His face is expressionless and I can't read what he's thinking, but I see his brilliant blue eyes for the first time. They give nothing away.

"You're lucky I was going past," he tells me, thinking carefully about his words, "most people aren't like me. People don't like picking up strangers." I try to smile. "You know, you ought to be careful, not everybody is as nice as me. Have you got anything for safety?"

"Just my wits," I joke. Rich doesn't find this funny and continues as if I haven't spoken while the world whizzes by.

"You need to be careful of some people. They might like the look of a young boy like you standing on the side of the road. You look like you've just come out of high school, how old are you?"

I confess that I'm twenty-five. Clearly surprised, Rich tells me I don't look twenty-five. Since cutting my hair off, I struggle to buy a beer in England without having to show my ID.

"Why are you travelling alone?"

To see if I could, to push myself… because no one else wanted to come with me. I don't actually know. I intended to start this journey with two of my brothers, but they bailed at the last minute. "I like travelling alone." Lies! I have never travelled alone, not like this anyway. This journey should have started two days ago, but I put it off because of bad weather. Oh, the weather is bad, I'm just going to do something else with my life for the next few months. What kind of a half-hearted pathetic excuse is that? It's like the times I used to skip school because I sent myself into such a frenzy that I physically felt sick.

"Where are you sleeping tonight?" Rich asks, moving quickly and passing cars in the outside lane.

"I'm staying with a guy in Brussels for a couple of days before visiting my cousin in Holland."

"A guy? Is he a friend?"

"Sort of. Well, not yet." I shift uncomfortably in my seat, explaining that I am experimenting with a website called Couch Surfing where travellers offer other travellers a place to stay for free. "It's cheaper than a hostel and I get to stay with locals. I want to know what it feels like to be in a foreign place and interact with people who live there every day." Disdain spreads across Rich's face for a fraction of a second. It's the first emotion he has shown me.

"That doesn't sound very safe. Have you done this sort of thing before?"

"No," I confess, "but I really like the idea of it." I'm not really sure if I do like the idea of it. Going into the home of someone I've never met, sleeping in their private space and talking to them. What if I don't like the person? What if they are a weirdo or have certain expectations of me? What if they don't like me?

"Well I wouldn't do it. What if things go wrong? Have you got enough money to get a hotel for the night?" I shrug, uncomfortable with talking about money. It's something everybody thinks about and spends their life obtaining, but by removing myself from a working environment, I had hoped to distance myself from the money orientated world.

"Money is water in my hands. I worked as an English teacher for the past year in South Korea, but I had to pay off some debts from university and the couple of years since I graduated. I don't want to be dependent upon others and as long as I don't have to pay for transport or accommodation, I have enough to buy what I need for the next month or two. Besides, I like the idea of trying to survive without much money for the time being because I've become too comfortable and I want to push myself. I simply have what I have and I'll do what I can with it." I don't believe that money should be a limiting factor to what any of us can do in life.

"It sounds like a crazy idea to me."

Is it a crazy idea? Are my words the covering spiel of a lost soul who doesn't know what to do with himself? I can't even remember what I believe anymore. Maybe I have fooled myself into thinking that I should do this. Best not to think of such things. Best to stop thinking of anything at all and just keep going.

I watch the world as we drive in comfortable silence for a few minutes. Rich is deep in thought, presumably assessing everything that I have just told him.

Here I am, on the road, hitchhiking. It is actually happening. I think back to all my time spent poring over maps during the evenings in South Korea, the notes I made and the daydreams I had as I thought about where to go. I had so many round-about conversations until one day I decided that perpetual sunlight was what I would search for and everything else was thrown out the window. Then I said it out loud and for better or worse, I committed myself by doing so. Next time I will keep my big plans entirely to myself. Next time I will be sure of what I'm doing before I open my mouth.

Yet sometimes, the excitement is too much not to share. There is a glorious feeling when sitting over a map, imagining the great treasures that await you on the open road. And there is a part of every journey in which you realise that all planning and preparation is done and that the journey has begun, so that all that matters is the here and the now. That moment is happening, my journey has begun. I am here and I am now and there is no going back.

My heart races a little, my throat tightens. No going back? No get out of jail free card? No, I can always catch a bus, go home, pretend it never happened. I had pictured blue skies and sun kissed hippies, but my reality is grey skies and an old van. It's so anti-climatic that I could pretend it never happened and I wouldn't even have a story not to tell.

No pop, no crackle, no fizz.

"Do you know what a gypsy is?" asks Rich, breaking the silence. He is staring at me intently and the question seems like a challenge. I think hard before answering.

"A Gypsy," I stumble, "is a group of travelling people…" I stop before I say the wrong thing. Across the UK, the term Gypsy has been misapplied to any group of people who live in caravans, steal things, and start fights. I know that these are not real Gypsies, but Rich's question is loaded and he seemingly wants me to fall into a trap.

"I'm a Gypsy," he announces, his voice tinted with pride and sorrow. "The Gypsies are a race of people who have been persecuted for hundreds of years, like the Jews. But unlike the Jews, we have no homeland, so we move from place to place and no one welcomes us. I bet you don't know what it feels like to be persecuted for being yourself and doing nothing else except trying to live each day."

"I don't."

"Are you scared?" Another challenge.

"Am I scared?"

"Yes, are you scared? You're in a vehicle with a Gypsy. Alone."

"No, I'm not scared. Should I be?" I shift nervously in my seat once more, trying to force a casual smile. My face implies that I am eating something vile, but I pretend that I like it for the sake of being polite. Someone once told me not to cower before a ferocious dog because he will sense your fear. I do not want him to sense my fear.

A hammer shatters the ice cold atmosphere in the van as Rich breaks into his first smile. A weight is lifted from my chest. "No, you don't need to be scared. I'm a good person, but you just need to be careful. Not all people out there have good intentions. I know what it feels like to be persecuted for who you are and I get persecuted twice as much as everyone else because I'm a Gypsy and I'm gay. It's not a nice feeling. You're a young boy with a nice face and I just want to warn you to watch your back."

"Thank you." The compliment and advice seem genuine enough. Behind Rich's brilliant blue eyes is a world of hurt and rejection.

Looking around, I see that we're entering Newmarket and I know that my first ride is coming to an end. We've left the dual carriageway and I need to find a way back onto it. "Are you stopping somewhere around here?"

"Yeah, I am. I'll take you to the other side of town so that you can get a ride back onto the main road."

"Thank you, I appreciate it."

As Rich drops me off, he tells me again that he likes my face and echoes his words of warning about the world and the bad people in it. I like him, but I try to shut out everything negative that he has said to me: I already have to deal with my own internal monologue, constantly pounding my brain.

Farewell Rich. He spins his van around in a driveway as I shoulder my backpack, regretting how much stuff I brought with me. My pack weighs an excessive twenty kilograms. Even with my tent and sleeping bag, it should only be about half of what it is.

I walk along the pavement, looking for a place where cars can pull over safely to pick me up. After a few minutes, the only suitably safe location that I can find is a bus stop leading away from the town. Once more I put out my thumb and I wait. A car beeps its horn at me. The young guys inside are laughing. I hop from foot-to-foot as awkward minute after awkwarder minute tick by. The second ride is little easier than the first.

Innumerable cars pass me, but no one even contemplates stopping. Allowing it to pass, I put my thumb down as a National Express coach pulls into the bus stop where I stand. The driver appears at the door, a short, stocky man with a shaved head.

"What are you doing?" he yells at me over the passing traffic.

"Hitchhiking."

"Hitchhiking?"

"Yes, hitchhiking."

"Hitchhiking doesn't work, it's not the sixties anymore."

"It might work." I hope it works. In my peripheral vision, I see an almost full coach load of people watching our exchange and trying to listen to what we are saying.

"Where are you going?"

"Belgium."

"Belgium? I'm going to London, I can give you a lift there if you like?"

"I guess that London is closer to Belgium than Newmarket is. How long will it take?"

"It depends on traffic, but probably a couple of hours."

I tell him that I would like a lift and immediately speculate on what other vehicles I could get rides with. Would someone on a horse ever stop to pick me up?

The driver climbs out of the coach and opens the luggage hold where I store my pack. "Don't tell anyone about this, I'd get fired if my bosses knew what I was doing." As I climb onto the coach and take one of the only empty seats near the back, I am met by a mixture of curious and suspicious glances. I can't help but think that of all the people on this coach, I am the least likely to tell his superiors about my free ride. Presumably, any one of the forty-something paying passengers may have more to say on the issue than I.

We pull away and my head fills with terrors. What if the passengers say something, what if they confront me? What if they call the National Express office? What if the police are waiting for me and make me pay? Can I be made to pay if the driver let me on for free? What if... no. Stop thinking. I close my eyes and put my headphones on, trying to return to a happy place.

Approaching London, I decide to get off as soon the bus stops. London is a sprawling city of close to ten million people and it is orbited by a congested ring road, the M25. If I go inside this orbital, I will be stuck and lost.

I look through the window with regret as we cross the M25 without stopping, rain beating against the windows. It's the sort of weather for which ducks might get excited and if I was a duck, I too might feel excited. But I am not a duck. I am a boy and I packed for summer and I am dreading the rain already. Another gloriously wet June day in England.

I climb out of the bus at Stamford, a place I have never heard of. All I know is that I am somewhere inside London's orbital. Why did I say yes to that ride? I'm such an idiot. I walk into a newsagent, bashing the shelves with my backpack as I try to navigate the narrow aisles.

"Is there a road out to Dover from here?" I ask the guy on the counter. Dover is the closest port to France and from there, I hope to cross the English Channel.

"No clue mate, no clue."

Brilliant.

I put on my flimsy rain jacket and walk into the wetness. Despite being known as a rainy city, London actually receives less rainfall per year than a lot of major European cities. However, it rains often and is miserably overcast for the majority of the year. It's that soft, miserable misty rainfall that lasts all day, keeping everything damp without fully soaking it. Berating our country's uninspiring weather is a popular English past-time and a delightful source of melancholy throughout the year. One day we English people will accept that our weather is not that great and move somewhere sunny, only to discover that we have nothing left to talk about.

Today however, is not a normal pitter-patter rainy day. Today is one of the rare days in England when it is truly and unequivocally, raining. It is one of the few days in this country that I can say it is raining cats and dogs. In fact, it is raining hippos and elephants.

I zip my rain jacket all the way up and pull over my hood. Inexplicably, water still manages to seep in from some unknown location. The neck of my t-shirt is getting very wet. I walk the streets of London, looking for a sign pointing me in a familiar direction. Except that I don't know anywhere in London. If I had a map it would help. Or a smart phone. It seems curious that I have known about this journey for months and in twenty kilograms of belongings, I don't have any form of navigation with me, not even a computer print-out.

Oh, thanks for the offer Mother, but I won't need a map. I'll just know where I am going.

No, no, no! I don't know where I am going and I don't know where I am and all I know is where I want to be and where I want to be is not here. I am a fool. Maybe I won't take clothes next time, maybe I'll just take nothing at all, maybe I'll just carry a desk lamp because I'm sure that it will be hugely useful to travel around Europe with and everybody can look at me and say oh look at that idiot with the desk lamp and no clothes, travelling around Europe, how happy he must be.

And breathe.

Think blank thoughts.

Try to be calm.

I like the rain. I like playing football in the rain, I like swimming in the rain, I like walking through the forest in the rain.

I do not like the rain today when I am trying to stay dry.

It's been an hour and I haven't seen a single place name I recognise. As it turns out, my waterproof jacket is not waterproof. It is simply splash-proof. My t-shirt is soaked, my shorts are soaked, my underwear is soaked, even my socks are soaked. As I walk, I wave at every passing car. Surely someone, anyone will help me out.

As a car finally stops, I run to it, delighted. It speeds away just before I reach it, spraying me as it races through puddles. I'm so wet that it doesn't even matter, but why would someone taunt me like that?

This was a really bad idea, it isn't at all the summer adventure I had planned in my mind. This miserable city, this pointless journey. This is rain hiking in the urban jungle with a heavy backpack that doesn't contain anything useful. And what's worse, I'm now too far from home to go back and say I never started. To go back now would be to fail. Even if I only make it to France, I must keep going, I must be able to say that I made it into mainland Europe.

Another hour rolls by. Then another. Car after car pay me no heed and after nearly five miserable hours of walking in the hippo and elephant rain, I am broken. I do not think England has ever seen so many hippos and elephants in one day.

I am jealous of the dry people in their dry cars who have a dry bed to sleep in tonight. I am jealous of the people who are not lost and who are spending the evening with their friends. A matter of weeks ago, I had a stable job, a steady income, a warm bed, and everything else that all these people have now. Why have I left this behind?

Incessant whining, ya ya ya.

Hush, mind!

In front of me is an Underground station. It is a sign.

My shoulders slump, my head drops. I am crushed.

I drag my wet feet into the station and approach a bored looking man in the ticket booth. Europe or home? Where am I going?

"Can you help me please?" The man looks up, uninterested. I have no idea what I'm about to say. "I need to get to… to Dover. Do you know how I can get to Dover please?" He taps away on his computer for a few seconds.

"Liverpool Street."

"Can I buy a ticket please?"

Sighing and heaving his shoulders as if I have just ruined his day, the man points at the automatic ticket machine a few metres away. I walk away without thanking him and buy an Underground ticket.

At Liverpool Street Station I walk to the road, hoping for some hint of Dover. Red buses, streets, signs to places I don't know. Nothing that suggests Dover. I am left with two choices: give up or carry on. I want to give up, I want to go home, I don't want to be wet and lost anymore. But I must get to France first. Even if I'm wet and miserable and have to cry all the way there, I will make it across the Channel.

Boarding a train to Dover, I know that I am a fraud. In a matter of hours and because of a little rain, I have folded on my plans. Hitchhiking around Europe? I have hitchhiked less than a hundred miles. Oh, look at me, the guy who hitchhiked a bus to the train station. I don't ever want to tell anybody about this. I hope they never ask.

On a dry train seat, I change my wet t-shirt. My wet shorts don't get changed because I only have one other pair of dry bottoms.

In exhausted sleep, I hug my backpack all the way to Dover.

Getting off the train, the sky is a glorious blue, my clothes have begun to dry, and the core of my soul is thawing out. How can the world have changed so much in only a couple of hours? Today must have been a test and this is my reward for not giving up. Bring it on world, I'm still going to France!

"Excuse me, can you please tell me how to find the ferry port?" I ask a passer-by. The White Cliffs of Dover, the symbolic guardians that have stood tall against so many invasions at the narrowest part of the English Channel, they are what I am looking for. On a good day, you can see them from France and that is where I will find my ferry to enter Europe.

"You see that roundabout?" he gestures. "Take a right at that, left at the next, then keep walking straight. You can't miss it. Where are you headed?"

"Sweden," I say proudly. "I'm hitchhiking there to experience perpetual sunlight." Under the blessing of the sun, I've almost forgotten that I have in fact, only obtained two rides before giving up and taking a train. But just for a moment, I am a fearless hitchhiker.

"Ooo!" he says. "You're lucky, I wish I was doing that, but I'm stuck here now. Work and job, you know? I went to Hungary last year and it is one of the best countries I've ever been to. If you get the chance, go there. Great food, great drinks, great people, and it costs nothing." The man then proceeds to tell me all about the delights of Hungary and by the time we walk away from one another, I'm sold. If I get the chance, I will go to Hungary. In fact, I'll go everywhere. The world is my oyster and I am the king of it and even my pants have nearly dried.

I have only hitched two rides.

Cars and lorries buzz around the ferry terminal and inside, every ticket desk is closed. An information booth tells me that I have missed the last ferry of the day that accepts foot passengers. I must wait until tomorrow. Outside the terminal, I climb the winding path that leads to the grass atop Dover's white cliffs, the world smelling anew. The rain has fallen and washed away all the badness of the past few hours and I am both looking forward to and terrified of the idea of camping alone on these icons. I am in Dover, tomorrow I will be in Europe. That's where my adventure really begins.

I look back down at the cars passing by. If I had a car, I could get on the ferry tonight. I should text the guy who invited me to stay at his house in Brussels and tell him that I won't be there until tomorrow. But wait, is that a hitchhiker? Delighted, I run back down the slope and find that it is in fact someone trying to catch a ride onto the ferry for free. He is standing right outside the small police office, but no one seems to mind him being there.

"Are you trying to hitchhike to France?" I ask. The guy is in his twenties and doesn't have any luggage.

"Yes I am. I need to get back home by tonight."

"And it's OK to hitchhike here?"

"Five people went before me. I'm at the back of the queue. Why don't you try over there?" He points to where vehicles are entering the port. It's not a good place to hitchhike, but being second in line means I get second choice.

"OK, I will. Thanks and good luck."

"You too."

I trot away to my new hitchhiking spot and sit on the floor to eat a sandwich. My mother made it before I left and it's the last delicious food I am guaranteed for the time being. Creamy goat cheese, sun-dried tomatoes, seeded bread. It tastes like the sunshine that has revealed itself to me. Being a lover of food, I am not keen on the thought of simple eating during my days on the road. I packed a small gas stove so that I can at least try cooking when I get the opportunity.

Sandwich gone, I try for my last ride of the day. Just one person. One person is all that I need to get to Europe. One person and I can be happy with my first day.

Despite my poor location between two roads and security fencing, a heavily loaded estate stops for me. The owner, a short man with a friendly face and grey hair, jumps out and begins moving paintings out of the passenger seat.

"Sorry about the mess, we're moving to France." Immediately I like the driver, possibly because he reminds me of my dad. His car is so full that I wonder if he'll even be able to fit me into it.

"Thanks very much for the ride." With the paintings out of the way, I jump in without introducing myself. What I realise from my ride with Rich, is that a name tells you nothing that you need to know about a person. Despite his expressionless persona, his over the top compliments, and the misery of his persecution, I liked Rich. We talked, but more than that, we communicated. He listened to what I said, thought about it, and responded. Most of the world talk without speaking, listen without hearing, and look without seeing. It makes for a very lonely world when there is no communication.

As we drive past the other hitchhiker, I avert my eyes, guiltily grateful that I caught a ride before him. Should I get out the car and offer the ride to him? No, I'm not big enough to do such a thing.

"Look, another hitchhiker," I say innocently.

"No more room for him unfortunately. So, where to?"

"Sweden, I hope. But Belgium today. I'm meant to be staying with someone in Brussels."

"You're in luck, I'm driving past Brussels so I can drop you off on the way through."

When we get to border control, they let us pass with no more than a flash of our passports and I know without doubt that I am on my way to Europe. One day and I made it out of England. That, however small, is success. Delicious, heart-warming, train-aided success.

Sitting in a long line of cars, I talk with my new driver about hitchhiking. It seems everybody loves this topic when picking up hitchhikers. Easy, relevant material.

"I used to hitchhike a lot," he tells me, "but I didn't think that people did it anymore. Everyone has started to believe that the world is a dangerous place and that it can only end badly."

"I know. You wouldn't believe how many of my friends have told me that I'll get mugged at best. Most think I'm more likely to get abducted or killed and one friend asked if I wanted to get sold into the male sex trade! I think people watch too many wild news stories and scary movies." I laugh as if none of these stories have any effect on me. Surprisingly, I have no desire to be mugged, abducted, killed, or sold as a male sex slave. I quite enjoy my body and few possessions being solely my own and in full working order.

"Use your common sense and you'll be fine."

"Thank you. You are one of the first people out of hundreds who has actually supported this idea."

"We all have to try and do what makes us happy. How did it start though?"

"The short answer is Japan. I can give you a longer one if you want to hear it?"

"We're not going anywhere soon," he says, gesturing ahead. The queue for the ferry hasn't moved since we arrived and cars are still being unloaded from its recent arrival.

"Alright, here goes. About a year ago, maybe less, I was working as an English teacher in South Korea and we had been granted a five day weekend due to a national holiday. This is rare in Korea because they don't really believe in holidays, so to make the most of it, six of us took the ferry to Japan for a couple of days. We were in this fantastic town called Kyoto, beautiful old temples mixed with nature, all set amongst a city more modern, clean, and developed than I have ever

14

known. It had everything in one place and we were all so happy to be there and to not have to go to work for a few days. On our last day there, we were supposed to be catching a bus at seven in the morning, so everyone had gone back to the hostel to catch a few hours sleep. Everyone except myself and my American friend. We discovered, like so many before us, that pretty girls are the downfall of men across the world. As the sun rose, we were at a bar enduring stuttering conversations with two attractive Japanese girls. Neither of us had phones or watches so it wasn't until someone told us the time that we realised how close we were to missing our bus. We jumped out of our seats and started running back to the hostel. Never before have I left a bar without paying for my drinks, but our sake-clouded minds were so panicked that we were incapable of thinking clearly about our actions.

"We ran up and down the streets because we couldn't remember where we were staying and all the street names were in Japanese. By the time we got back to the hostel, all our friends had gone. If we hadn't got so lost trying to find the hostel, we might have made it back before they left. We grabbed our bags, jumped into a taxi, and headed for the bus station. We literally missed the bus by a matter of minutes because we were in the wrong terminal. If we had spoken Japanese, we'd probably have been able to ask for the right terminal and made it there on time. We walked over to the train station and found out that the train would cost us nearly two hundred pounds. Rather than paying two hundred pounds for a train, we went for breakfast. A sit down and some food always makes things better. Not that we needed it, but we ordered another beer too. By the time we finished breakfast, it was nearly nine in the morning and we decided that the best way to get to our next destination, would be to hitchhike. It was one of those mind clouded ideas that most people forget about, but we had to follow through on it because we didn't want to pay for the train. We asked every policeman, every passer-by who'd stop for us, every everyone where we should go. Eventually we found our way to a set of traffic lights and caught a ride with a friendly young Japanese couple.

"Not knowing what would happen or if we would make it was so exciting. I didn't want it to end. But of course, we had jobs and lives to return to. The next evening, I took my notebook and I wrote down that I wanted to hitchhike, without plans, without an end date. And here I am. Except that no one wanted to come with me when they were sober. If I hadn't missed that bus, none of this would have happened."

"That's quite a big idea."

"Maybe. I like to write all my ideas down in my notebooks so I don't forget them. Most of them will never happen, but sometimes they do."

The cars in front of us begin to move and we start up the engine and drive onto the ferry.

By the time we arrive in France, I'm so tired that I struggle to keep myself awake.

"The badgers don't want anymore ice cream."

"What?"

"The badgers don't… oh. I must have been dreaming." I wipe the drool from the side of my face.

"Don't worry about it, you can sleep if you want to."

In what feels like seconds later, I am woken up and dropped on the outskirts of Brussels. "If you ever come to the Alps, drop me an email. My name is Steve." I shake Steve's hand, thank him for the ride, and take the piece of paper carrying his email address. Then he is gone.

I have no idea how big Brussels is, but I am by a sign that indicates the start of the city and it is four o'clock in the morning. My mind itches. I'm exhausted and I can't turn up at a stranger's house at this time. I'll have to find somewhere else to sleep. In a city, without a bed, I'm going to have to sleep outside. I have never, ever done this before. I don't know what it's like to not know where I'm going to sleep at night.

I wish I had someone with me.

I walk into the city, find nothing, then walk back to the outskirts. Next to the motorway is a big field. I struggle to wade through the waist high grass until, like an upturned tortoise, I find myself lying on my back. This is ridiculous. I cannot pitch my tent in this long grass.

I roll to my feet and climb back out of the field. The best place I can find to sleep right now is the pavement and someone would surely find me in the night and do terrible things to me. I must hide.

I walk back towards the city, this time on a different street, until I find an abandoned building. It's large and gloomy, every window boarded up. The whole place freaks the hell out of me and sends shivers down my spine. If I was a child, it's the sort of place I would have dared my friends to go into, but never dared enter myself. As an adult, I slip into the garden, my heart racing, wondering if anybody saw me.

I don't want to be here, I really don't want to be here, but I don't have anywhere else to go.

I pitch my tent in the shadows of the house and sit on a log to eat a few pieces of dried fruit. When I finally stop looking over my shoulder every ten seconds, I crawl into my tent, curse myself for pitching the tent on sharp gravel, and bury my head inside my sleeping bag.

Wrapping my arms around my knees and shutting my eyes tight, I rock myself to sleep, echoing the same mantra over and over again.

Hold tight, tomorrow will be another day.

Hold tight, tomorrow will be another day.

2. Passion

My body is stiff.

Where am I?

It feels like I've been sleeping on gravel.

I have been sleeping on gravel, how very unpleasant. In future, I will try to sleep on lush, soft ground. That seems far more appealing than a bed of pointy stones. Equally, a tent in which I could fully stretch out would be greatly appreciated. Despite the manufacturer's claims that my tent is two hundred and ten centimetres, I at one hundred and eighty-three centimetres, claim that the tent is one hundred and seventy centimetres at best. Curse you, world.

I zip open the front flap of my tent, merging my little bubble with Belgium. I had almost forgotten that I was here.

That precious place between slumber and wakefulness is where everything and nothing are real and dreamlike all at the same time. It's a crazy land of possibility and disappointment for all you've had, lost, and never experienced. Happy in that place, I struggle to re-enter the land without dreams.

In daylight, with the returned gift of sight, I realise that the abandoned building by which I have been sleeping is in fact an uninhabited building, currently undergoing the process of renovation. A group of builders are busy with materials as I pack up and scuttle past them. Thank you for not disturbing me.

My mantra from the night before has seen me through. I held tight and today is a new day. I feel alive and awake and that I never have to worry about where to sleep ever again. I can turn up, pitch my tent, and lay my head wherever I find myself as darkness falls. The fact that I have only ever done this once and had to hug-chant myself to sleep is neither here nor there now that the sun is shining.

I love you sunshine.

After a long walk to the city centre, I store my backpack in a locker and walk through the streets of Brussels, happy to be free of the excess weight. I find myself on La Grand-Place, a large open area that is common in many European cities. The square, which is actually a rectangle, is adorned with elaborate architecture. Innumerable pillars, stone spiderwebs, and windows wearing wedding hats. After my year in South Korea I am immediately reminded why European cities are touted as some of the most beautiful in the world. The front of every structure has been intricately carved and decorative turrets spring from the rooftops of the already multi-storey buildings. This is human architecture without the need for financial restraint, where beauty takes precedence over function, the way all cities should look in a perfect world. If aliens ever come to investigate our societies, I hope they find our old European cities before they find anything else.

I am not the only one pleased with the European architecture. Across the square there are hundreds of people, just like me. Tourists from every country, all admiring the buildings that adorn the open space, all of them searching for that perfect picture. People walk onto the square and start taking photographs before they've even looked at what is around them. Some tourists spend more time looking through their camera screen than at the world before them. Like a colony of ants they work individually, but all serving the greater purpose: documentation of their holiday. Far above us, the sky is full of cumulus clouds and I can't help but feel that we part time photographers are fighting a losing battle.

Our photos will never look as good as the postcards.

But the people. The people are more fascinating than the buildings. So many of them busying away, taking photographs.

I take a seat on some stone steps right outside a big wooden doorway and reach for my camera. I have a brand new digital SLR with a zoom lens, the financial prize of all my worldly possessions. Pointing it across the square, I locate an elderly man in a baseball cap through the viewfinder. He is holding a small camera at arm's length. Snap. A woman crouched to the floor, pointing her camera upwards. Snap. A girl with long dark hair, facing away from me. I can only see her back as she holds a camera phone above her head. Snap, snap. Shot after shot, everywhere I point the camera, someone else is taking a photo. And I am taking a photo of them.

Then my camera reveals another secret. Not only are people taking photos, they are engaging in all manner of actions. A nameless bride on the most precious day of her life, hand in hand with the man she loves. A child with a balloon, watching it dance as he waves it in the air. An old man, carefully unwrapping a sandwich and tenderly sharing it with his wife. A lady with a lollipop, savouring the taste. A family chatting, laughing, walking. A young couple, possibly teenagers, holding each other so very tightly. I think the boy is crying. Smiles, grimaces, happiness, and sadness. Running, skipping, skateboarding, drinking, looking, being. Everybody is doing something. Somebody is doing nothing. Even nothing is something.

I take my last photograph, an image of a man photographing his friend, then lower my camera. Hanging out of a window above me, I see a young man pointing a camera at me. He was taking a photograph of me taking a photograph of a man taking a photograph of a friend. Before I can think to wave, shout, or point the camera back at him, he slips out of view and the window silently closes. So much for original ideas.

Camera away, I walk the streets, admiring the street art, noticing the colour of the walls, the flaking paint from a door. Directionless, I pass nameless street after street, nameless person after person. Where I would have seen nothing before, there is so very much going on. On a normal day in a foreign town, I would head straight to a museum or an art gallery, skipping everything in-between. Not having a final destination, I find pleasure in what I have before me.

I look with both of my eyes and listen with both of my ears. It's such a big world that it's easy to miss. There are wondrous findings, all of the time, right in front of us, but we look without seeing. How can there be so many wondrous findings if we don't take the time to find them?

The more I look, the more I see.

Before I know it, the evening has arrived and I make my way to the apartment of my host. He lives on a residential street, somewhere between the centre and the suburbs.

Apartment 39, I count as I walk. 33, 35, 37. This is his place. I know nothing of this person I am about to meet except that his name is Daniel and he is Belgian. I stand before his door and look at the array of buzzers. Number 6. This is his flat. All I have to do is press the button.

Number 6.

I take a deep breath.

I still haven't pressed the button.

A little wave of emotion tingles in the bottom of my feet. Then it spreads to my ankles and before I know it, I'm walking down the street, away from the door.

39, 41, 43, 45, 47, 49, 51, the end of the street. I walk around the corner and put my backpack on the floor. That small child in me, the one that was terrified of everything, especially embarrassing himself in front of people, is so very close to the surface. Why are interactions so very overwhelming?

I sit on the floor for a minute and take a sip of water.

We are all people, one and the same.

Another sip of water.

This is normal.

Last sip.

Go.

I get up, shoulder my backpack, and march back down the street. 51, 49, here I go, 47, 45, don't stop, 43, 41, maybe I will turn around, 39, got to press the button. I put my bag down. Another sip of water. I can't stand here all evening. I hold my breath and reach out... a long blink... Buzz!

I let out a long, deep breath.

"Oui?" sounds a distorted voice over the intercom.

"Hello, Daniel? It's Jamie. I spoke to you on Couch Surfing."

The intercom buzzes and the door clicks open.

Here I go.

I pull open the door and walk slowly up the staircase. By the time I reach the top, my host is waiting for me.

"Hello Daniel," I say, smiling and offering my hand, "it's a pleasure to meet you."

"Hi, please come in."

Daniel is taller than I with short fair hair and a well kept appearance. I follow him into his open-plan apartment. It has high white ceilings, a large fireplace, and marble work surfaces that when considered together, suggest a successful individual. Minimalistic and clean, this is a really lovely apartment.

"Would you like a drink?"

"Sure." Is it acceptable to accept a drink from someone who has just offered you their home for the night?

"What would would you like?"

"Anything cold will be fine. Tap water maybe?"

"How about a beer?"

"That sounds much better." I like this guy immediately. "I'm just going to put my shoes outside."

"Please, just put them on the doormat inside."

"Please, I'd like to put them outside. I've been wearing them for two days, mostly wet."

"I insist."

"I insist."

"You really mustn't leave your shoes outside."

"OK." I hope he doesn't smell my shoes. I can smell them already. Maybe I should put them outside when he isn't looking. My socks smell just as bad and I stuff them into my hiking boots in the hope that no odour will come out. At the kitchen counter I pick up the cold beer he has opened for me. "You have a really nice apartment."

"Thanks. But I forgot to mention, I don't live here alone." The apartment has just two rooms: a bedroom and an open plan living, kitchen, and dining area. There is a large leather sofa that wraps around the corner of the room, but apart from that, I don't see anywhere else to sleep. "Let me introduce you to my flatmates. Cake?"

"Thanks." I take the small plate and follow him out the back door. Confusingly, despite living on the first floor, Daniel has a garden. I sometimes forget that the world isn't as flat as the farmland I grew up in.

In the garden are two pretty, young cats, white with splashes of grey. These I realise, are his flatmates. Fortunately that means I have the sofa all to myself.

"This is Hector and this is Elizabeth. They are brother and sister." I stroke them both in turn and say hello as they purr loudly. They are as happy to see me as I am to see them.

Animals are a great distraction from conversation. As are babies, food, and drink. When I run out of conversation, I invariably say something, anything, to an animal or a baby. It works wondrously because other people will just watch in silence, a simple smile plastered upon their face. If there isn't an animal or a baby to hand, eating something or drinking something buys a precious few seconds. Cat caressing over, I take a sip of my beer and a bite of cake. I must now say something, anything unrelated to the obvious topics of hitchhiking or Couch Surfing.

We both watch the cats.

"You're actually the first person I have ever Couch Surfed with."

"Oh, really?"

"Yes, really. And I hitchhiked here." Damn my simple mind.

After the beer, Daniel whirlwinds me from his apartment to a bar. I meet person after person, all of whom speak perfect English and before I know where I am, I'm dancing the night away in the centre of town with a group of people I just met.

I'm not entirely sure how we got here. We dance, we leave. The sun is threatening to rise. Where did all that time go?

Back at the apartment, I slump onto the comfy sofa, grateful not to be sleeping on gravel or in the garden of an abandoned building.

This, I realise, is Couch Surfing. I have spent a handful of hours in the home of a stranger, interacted with him continuously, and I no longer feel the need to talk about Couch Surfing or hitchhiking.

"Goodnight," I shout, drifting into sleep before I have time to hear a response.

My waking sight is Daniel walking through his bedroom, naked. I avert my eyes and concentrate on getting myself up and ready to go.

Despite my next destination being in Holland, Europe is conveniently small. It's little over a hundred miles to my cousin's house in Den Haag, but I promised that I would arrive today.

A couple of hours after leaving Brussels, I'm on the outskirts of my target city. Except that I don't quite know where to go. Street names surround me which indicates that I am somewhere within the city's limits. The only writing that makes sense to me is a piece of graffiti that has been sprayed on an exterior wall, overhanging a narrow river. In capital letters it says, 'LOST.' How very appropriate.

A well-kept pavement sandwiched between a well-made cycle route and a smooth road. Everything in Holland seems to have been done very well. I message my cousin telling him where I am and within minutes, he picks me up.

"Si, it's great to see you." I hug both him and Lisa, his heavily pregnant wife. "I'm so sorry I missed your wedding. I heard it was fantastic." Lisa and Simon's wedding had been a few months after I had started working in South Korea. To my great disappointment, I had neither the money nor the vacation time to be capable of returning to Europe for it. On the special days that they were celebrating, I was going to work, living through days that were no more or less significant than any other. Not having the freedom to live life as I pleased had been a motivating factor in my decision to try and step away from a job which controlled me.

We drive back to their apartment and once again I find myself thrown into a whirlwind of activity. I'm being shown to my room then I'm in a bar watching football, the European Championships. We eat dinner, sleep, go out for breakfast, and tour the city, but I hardly remember what it looks like. What was its name again?

"Where are you heading next?" Lisa asks me.

"I don't know. Is there anywhere nice around here that you would suggest?" Lisa was born in Belgium and I imagine her to have good taste in cities.

"You should try Gent, it's where I'm from. Of course Brugge is nice too and if you get the chance, I think that you would like Maastricht. It's a friendly little university town just inside Holland, but it's filled with people from all over Europe." I look up the three places on a map. I've only ever heard of Brugge because of the film, but the other two are new to me. I don't know anything about these places, but I have made a promise to myself for the past few years: say yes more. So without thinking too much, my next few destinations are planned for me.

And then I'm hugging them both goodbye.

"Great to see you guys. Best of luck with the baby."

"Thanks. Enjoy your journey. Not tempted for a baby yourself?" Si jokes. I shrug and put my arms wide.

"Maybe tomorrow."

As quickly as I arrived, I am gone.

Thumb out, smile. Wave occasionally. Make eye contact.

A white estate swings out of the fast moving traffic. "Get in, this isn't a good place to stand," a lady shouts from the window.

"I know, thanks…" I stop for a second as I realise there are already six people in the car. Two parents in the front, two young girls in the middle seats, and two even younger girls in the rear two seats. Tall and slender with fair hair, physically the six of them are the perfect Dutch family. The boot is piled high with belongings and I have no idea where I'm going to sit. In a practised motion, the mother swings around from the driver's seat and shuffles the children and belongings around. Within seconds, a seat is free.

As I close the door, my backpack on my lap, the four young girls stare at me, curious but nonplussed. They are inquisitive as to why I am there and the ten year old, the eldest of the four, plucks up the courage to begin questioning me in Dutch. I admire her lack of concern. At her age I would have started crying if a stranger sat next to me.

What I see before me is a child who has not built up scepticism and walls of self-defence towards strangers. Why wouldn't an unknown man get into her parents' car for a lift? This untarnished mindset is one of the reasons I first decided to spend time teaching children for a year. Young children do not second guess your motives and they do not pre-empt your reaction to their behaviour: they simply be themselves and do as they please which is refreshingly heartwarming when accustomed to the world of grown-ups.

Despite not understanding her words, I see happiness in her voice and warmth in her gestures.

"I have no idea what you're saying because unfortunately I can't speak Dutch, but you are a very friendly little girl. Do you know any English?" She flashes a cheeky grin and holds out a razor fish shell before firing more Dutch at me.

"She wants to give this to you as a present," her mother translates for me. "She found it on the beach today."

"Thank you very much," I say to the girl before turning back to her mother. "How do I say thank you in Dutch?"

"Dank u!"

"Ah, that's simple! Dank u."

She and her sisters laugh together. I spend the majority of the journey talking to the kids in sign language, rather than with the parents who speak perfect English. My spirits are buoyed. I have been on the road for three short nights, but there have already been so many great, great people. In a 'normal' three days, I would meet no one new and even if I decide to go home now, my life is enriched.

But I will not go home now. I do not even know where home is anymore. Onwards and forwards, to Brugge, to Gent, to Maastricht, to the perpetual sunlight of Scandinavia.

The total distance from Den Haag to Maastricht, via Brugge and Gent, is less than three hundred miles. I hitchhike rides with ease, everyone friendly.

In Gent, my appetite for old European cities is whetted once more. Waterways, cobbles, castles and turrets, medieval architecture, and a pedestrianised city centre. I drink it all in. The world is so much more pleasant when it's beautiful and unspoilt by the interference of tranquility shattering motor vehicles.

Tranquility over, I return to the world of motorised transport once more.

Thumb out, smile. Wave occasionally. Make eye contact. I focus hard on these four things. By following this simple set of instructions, I pretend not to be as awkward as I feel.

More strangers, more cars, another sofa. Brugge, another town, as beautiful as Gent in all the same ways, yet inexplicably different. The rain pours down for the two days I am in Belgium. I walk the streets when the skies relent and take pictures of people with umbrellas when they open again.

Without my feet touching the ground, I am in Maastricht, Holland. Five nights on the road, five new towns, thirteen rides from strangers, everything logged in my notebooks. None of these numbers matter, but the organised part of my brain, the part that found beauty in the perfection of mathematics, that part likes lists of things.

I will always make lists of things.

On a big cobbled square, I stand at the door of another stranger. The tingling in my toes will not rise up above my ankles this time.

Knock, knock.

"Sandra, hi. I'm Jamie. A pleasure to meet you and thank you for having me." I recognise the dark hair from her profile picture. She is a couple of years younger than I and we shake hands, the easiest greeting of all.

"Hello. Did you make it here OK?" More perfect English.

"It was fine thanks. The most difficult time was when I was hiding from the rain under a motorway bridge. Only one car was passing every five minutes and I had already been waiting for over half an hour when an elderly couple stopped to pick me up. They told me they were both in their seventies and that they had never picked up a stranger in their lives, but they saw me in the rain and decided that they would help me out. They thought I was younger than I am and that is part of the reason why they stopped. A couple of days ago, I was picked up by a family with four young girls, but before I started, I had thought only truckers would give me rides. So yes, I got here OK thank you!"

We walk into a small living room. Another sofa, another home for a couple of days.

"I'm going to a talent show tonight if you want to come," Sandra tells me. "It's at the university, not far from here."

Say yes more. "I'd love to."

We walk to the shops and begin to fill up a small basket.

"I'd like to cook you dinner," I decide out loud.

"No, you don't have to do that."

"You're helping me out here. And besides, how about I get the food tonight and I get to choose it too? I haven't cooked anything all week and it's just a small token of my gratitude."

It seems a fair deal to both of us. After dinner we are walking. Cobbles and medieval architecture, trees lining the streets and quiet. I like the town.

"How far to the university?"

"About ten minutes walk. You'll see a little bit of the town on the way, but I'll show you the sights later."

"Only show me the bits that you like, I don't mind if I miss the main attractions. Anyway, what will be happening at this talent show? Is it lots of singing?"

"It's kind of hard to define, but you'll see when you get there. How about you, what talent would you perform?"

"I have no talent to perform!" I laugh.

"Everyone has talents. You can't not."

"The first and last time I was in a talent show was a contest when I was nine years old. My friend persuaded me to go up on the stage and tell jokes with him. Out of four acts, we came fourth and his mum was the judge. That's how much talent I have." Even at nine years old, I was dying on stage. All those eyes looking up at me, the people trying to laugh to help us. We just weren't very funny. Even back then I had known that we weren't funny and wished that I could have disappeared between the cracks in the floorboards.

"Maybe telling jokes isn't your thing. What do you like doing?"

"Football, cricket, snowboarding, skiing, cycling, swimming. Squash and badminton too, maybe even tennis. In fact, I'll dabble in almost any sport that doesn't involve shoulder padding or getting punched in the face, but I'm not good enough at any to call them talents."

"Alright, what about hobbies or interests? There must be other things you like. Do you play instruments?"

"I like making things. Scribbles in my notebooks, shapes on paper, videos on the computer. I read, I explore, I walk. I love to learn. But there is a problem that means I will never be truly great at any one thing: I am interested in everything, but persistent in nothing. I want to play music, but I don't want to take the time to learn how. I want it all and I want it now."

Sandra laughs at my outburst. "It's better to have too many interests, rather than too few."

We take seats in the semi-filled meeting hall. Students mill around, chatting with each other and greeting friends. The room is bare with high ceilings, unadorned walls, and a staircase in the middle of the room.

"How long until it starts?"

"Fifteen minutes."

I sit awkwardly in a room of people where everybody knows somebody. Except me. Twiddling my thumbs in-between times, I talk to Sandra as much as possible.

A girl walks into the clear area at the front of the room and calls for attention. Around us, every haphazardly arranged seat is filled and people stand against the walls. There could be more or less than a hundred people at this event, I literally have no idea. Quiet trickles into the room until an unseen individual summons unopposed silence from the audience.

"Good evening ladies and gentleman," the girl begins, "tonight we have lots for you to see at our open mic night. If there is anyone who hasn't signed up yet and would like to take part, please come and speak to me during the show." With a pigeon mix of Queen's English and an unplaceable dialect, I have no idea where the girl is from.

"What is that accent?" I whisper to Sandra.

"She's Dutch, but there are Germans, French, Belgians, everyone all sounding the same. They try to speak in a perfect British accent because it is seen as fashionable right now." I feel my eyebrows raise at this new information.

A young couple come to the stage as the first act. They are ordinary looking, in that there is nothing about either the boy or girl that noticeably stands out. I could have passed them a hundred times on the street and I would never have known. Without an introduction, the boy plucks at the strings of his guitar. Immediately I recognise the peaceful sound of Hallelujah floating around me.

The girl starts singing, her voice taking me by surprise. It is higher and more perfect than I could have hoped for. Around me, the whole room falls under her spell. Respectful silence flows and I hear nothing but the gentle strumming of the guitar, accompanied by the tranquility of the girl's voice.

And then it's over.

They leave the performance area to a shower of applause and delighted cheers.

"They were fantastic," I whisper to Sandra, "so tranquil yet powerful. It must take huge guts to come up on stage in front of everybody and perform. You're putting yourself out there for the whole world to see." That notion makes me feel dizzy. To make it even harder, the audience aren't simply strangers that they'll never see again, these are their classmates and friends that they will continue to see every day. Even if I did have a talent, I couldn't do it.

I think back to high school when I was involuntarily elected to a position whereby I was obliged to perform speaking duties in front of hundreds of people. On the rare occasions that I spoke, I would watch the clock at the back of the hall and wish that I could disappear. I didn't dare look at anyone in the audience. There was one day on which four of us were given a fifteen minute slot to fill. I stayed on the stage for about thirty seconds, then walked off and left someone else to cover for me. Funnily enough, that speech was about talents and I didn't have much to say about it, even back then. When I was supposed to come back on, I hid behind the curtains, protected by the shadows. An awkward silence was so much better than me dying on the stage in front of everybody.

A bearded man walks onto the stage. Quiet falls around us as he begins talking very quickly.

The world, society, machines, sadness, greyness, opportunity. I hear English words, but I can't seem to put them together. I think he is talking about the future.

The bearded man bows and walks from the stage. Bewildered applause follows him.

Act after act, ukelele after poetry, story after memory, the room is filled by people sharing what they love: their passion. I feel connected to each and every single performer, each and every member of the audience, every single person around me that I will never even speak to. I am privileged to be part of something so sacred, to be part of anything at all.

I don't want it to end.

A tiny Turkish girl walks to the stage. Pushing her long, dark curls away from her face, she holds a bottle of water, but no instrument. An unseen friend introduces her.

"Filiz would like to sing a Turkish love song."

She is so tiny.

Cautiously, carefully, clumsily, she moves as a child, placing her water bottle on the floor.

She looks down at her feet. I'm nervous for her.

Breaking the quiet, she sings.

She sounds the way that a rainbow feels after the storm has passed.

I am overwhelmed.

The room hangs on every intelligible word, a silence more profound than during any other performance of the night. People don't dare breathe. Even time itself holds its breath.

As the last notes echo around the room, the small Turkish girl stoops to pick up her water bottle and skips back to the safety net of her friends at the back of the hall. The whole room explodes in a disjointed chaos of delight, cheering, clapping, whooping. It takes several minutes to die down.

The last act of the night is called to the stage. A tall girl with long dreadlocks tells everyone that she is going to sing about Africa, her native continent. She laughs long and loud across the hall, her personality touching everyone in the room. I can almost taste the warmth and good nature emanating from her. As she plays, some people clap along, others click. Everybody in the room thinks as one. This is the crescendo. Electricity flows from body to body, through words they sing, from the way they clap their hands.

That glorious laughter warms the room once more.

One more song. This is it. She starts strumming. I know that song, it's 'Home' by Edward Sharpe and the Magnetic Zeros. Of all the songs in all of the world, she has picked one of the most perfect, a song that I love.

Swinging her dreadlocks as she dances and using the guitar as a drum, the girl carries the song, humming when she doesn't know the words. Everybody is clapping, everybody is moving, and I'm singing at the top of my voice. I'm actually singing and nobody is looking at me because they are all singing too.

My words tumble out through smiles.

I, a talentless individual, who knows almost nobody in the room, feel part of something amazing.

This is passion. This is how the world should be.

This is a perfect moment.

3. Yes and No

There is a knock at the door of the living room.

"You said you like playing football, right?"

"Yes, I do."

"Today there's a five-a-side tournament with some of the university students. There should be a few teams playing, do you want to join?"

"I haven't really got the right clothes, but as long as no one else minds, I'd love to play." I look at my pack, trying to remember what I have that resembles sportswear. The closest I can get is a t-shirt, baggy cargo pants, and Primark plimsols.

"Don't worry about it too much, it's a friendly event that I used to organise. Boys and girls will be playing and it's a nice day out."

Walking onto the sports fields, I'm filled with the nervous excitement that I find always comes before playing competitive football. There are about a hundred people on the pitches, some kicking balls around, some clearly intent on relaxing and not paying too much attention to the football being played. When we reach a group of Sandra's friends, she introduces me to my team and heads off in the opposite direction.

"Hi, I'm Will. You said your name is Jamie, right?" I tell him that it is and guess correctly that he is British. "Most of our team are British and our team name is British Smokers, partly because we all smoke and partly to kill all expectation: most of us have never played football before. You're on our team because you're British... and because we don't have enough players."

I feel my heart sink a little. I don't hate not winning, but to say I don't mind losing would be untrue. After growing up with four brothers, even eating breakfast was a competition. It wasn't about who won, but having a good battle, and my team's introduction does not fill me with confidence.

And there it is again, that little boy beneath the surface. The one who joined a football team, but used to call off training or stand out matches because he was too nervous to get on the field. Not only did I feign sickness when I got nervous before a game, sometimes I was so nervous that I actually became sick. I think back to my school report when I was eight years old, great grades for everything except sport. I made a resolution on that day to not embarrass myself and to become better at physical pursuits. I started playing sports not because I enjoyed them, I played because I didn't want to embarrass myself. Within five years, I captained my high school team and when I received my final high school report at age sixteen, sport, or physical education, was the highest of all my grades and my favourite subject. Rather ironic considering that was the year that I sat my first serious exams.

"Never mind Will. I'm sure it'll all be good fun." Yes of course it will be fun, I love being humiliated in front of hundreds of strangers. "Why are you over here anyway?"

"Same reason as all the other Brits, cheaper tuition. Since the Conservatives put tuition up to nine thousand pounds a year, more and more people are beginning to study abroad." I heard something about this, but can't remember the details so nod and agree. After meeting the rest of the team, I immediately forget all of their names. The general consensus is that we're aiming to score at least one goal in our seven matches or maybe even salvage a draw by not letting the opposition score a goal. What fun.

As the whistle blows, my toes are tingling once more. Got to do something good, got to avoid embarrassing myself horrendously. I am the worst dressed on this pitch, almost everybody is wearing proper sports clothing.

Got the ball, pass the ball. Damn, gave the ball to the other team. Chase back, chase back. I slide in and the referee blows for a free kick.

"No sliding!"

Curse five-a-side rules.

I stand in the way of the free-kick and it duly connects with my buttocks as I turn and jump, then races away to the other side of the pitch.

Run, run, run, I want the ball, give me the ball, I'll get the ball. Nope, change of plan. Run away, forwards, still want the ball, still want the ball, what's his name?

"Yes, yes, YES!" Buggar, the ball is actually coming my way. Got to run, got to be faster than the defender, got to be stronger, got to hit it, got to… goal! We have exceeded our expectations in the first two minutes.

And so it continues. After six games, we've won everything and all we have to do is draw our final game to be champions. Except that they have a national youth team player playing for them. As I try to mark him all game, I'm hugely aware that he has fancy yellow shoes, a nice outfit, and looks very comfortable with what he is doing. I look a little out of place.

As soon as it begins, it's over. 1-1.

British Smokers are the champions.

None of this matters because it was a one-off football competition that will be forgotten tomorrow. But right now, I feel so damn good.

"That was brilliant," I gush to Sandra as we walk home, "thanks so much for bringing me along." The exercise, the endorphins, more great people, happy shadows of the passion from the talent show the night before. All of these little things add up to a feeling of happiness.

"How about sushi?" Sandra suggests as we get back to her flat. I have always detested sushi, but here I am, trying to say yes more.

"Sure. As long as it doesn't have any seafood, I'm vegetarian."

After purchasing a small box of inevitably overpriced seaweed and overcooked rice, I pick at several different pieces, covering some of them in wasabi, others in soy. I endeavour to work through multiple pieces, but neither coating seems to make the salty seaweed any less disgusting. I swallow several mouthfuls with water, trying my best not to taste it.

"We had a lot of stuff like this in Korea when I lived there. This seaweed stuff."

"Do you like it?"

"It's one of my least favourite foods in the world."

When I lived in Canada during my university studies, I once went for coffee and sushi because I thought they sounded stylish. Unable to bear either of them, I ended up buying a sandwich and fizzy drink shortly afterwards.

Even the smell of the sushi restaurant makes me nauseous and I ask to leave. As the sushi once again leaves me hungry and disappointed, I resolve to eat only food that I like. We dump the remains of our meal in a public bin and head to an overpacked bar to see the eagerly anticipated Holland-Germany game in the group stages of the European Championships. Holland, tipped as a tournament favourite, lost their first game and have to win this one. A sea of orange fills the bar in support of the national team and I am witness to a different sort of passion from what we saw last night. The room is electric with anticipation.

As Germany score the opening goal, the buzz dies. Fifteen minutes later, a second. Late in the game, Holland pull a single goal back, but as the final whistle blows, their fate is all but sealed. They will be eliminated from the championships. Walking through the town, it feels as if someone important has died. Dutch fans berate themselves and their disappointing football team.

"That wasn't so fun to watch," I say to Sandra, stating the obvious.

"It was terrible. Look how disappointed everyone is, we had all expected to win that game."

"What they feel now is the same feeling that I feel when I'm playing. It doesn't matter if I'm playing in a friendly tournament like today or in a more important game. Winning brings smiles to my face and losing floods me with disappointment."

"What about when England play?"

"I support them, I'll go out of my way to watch them in the big competitions, and when they win, I'll cheer and shout and I'm happy. If they lose however, it doesn't bother me too much. I'm more of a player than a watcher. I see something interesting and I want to be part of it. Living life on the sidelines is never as much fun."

I grab hold of my stomach and squeeze it, trying to cancel out the pain. It hurts so much that I feel dizzy. I need to get up, but I'm afraid that if I do, my stomach will explode or I'll throw up.

Have I been shot through my belly button? Or stabbed?

I hear Sandra moving around outside the door.

"Sandra…?" I mumble.

"Yes?" She puts her head in through the doorway.

"I don't feel good. Can I get some water please?"

She disappears briefly and comes back with a glass of cold water, then sits with me as I drink it.

"Thank you so much."

I'm so grateful not to be alone.

Another cramping of the stomach and another wave of nausea. I get up and make my way to the bathroom as quickly as possible. So much for the sushi, that clearly went down well.

After every trace of nutrition is ejected from my body, I return to my sleeping bag.

"I feel terrible, I think it's food poisoning. Don't you feel it?"

"I'm fine." Sandra and I have eaten exactly the same food since I arrived two nights earlier. I have no idea what it is that's hammering my insides, but I don't like it very much.

"Do you mind if I stay here a bit longer?"

"Don't rush yourself. If you need to stay another night, that's not a problem. I'm not here tomorrow though, so hopefully you'll be better by then."

Knowing that I won't have to hitchhike today, relief washes over me. I don't think I could, even if I tried.

"Thanks so much, you're really kind." She brings me another glass of water.

"I'm going to the shops in about half an hour, would you like anything?"

"How about an injection to knock me out? Wake me when you're going, please."

"Jamie…"

I open my eyes. Oh no, I'm awake, I feel… surprisingly good. I get up and walk around the room. My head spins a little, but I think I'm feeling better.

"I think I'll come to the shop with you."

As we walk out the front door, the sunlight slaps me in the face like a punching bag. Ouch.

I take a step, but my leg locks. Stupid knee, I slap it with my hand and it springs forward. Then the other leg locks. I slap that too and stumble a few steps.

"Are you alright?" Sandra sounds worried. Alarmingly, I only have a tiny tunnel of sight and my peripheral vision is blurred beyond recognition. I have to turn my head towards her so that I can see her.

"Yur, nots aaaah, problem no."

"What?!"

"K. K. All is K K." What the hell am I saying? I slump to the floor. "Jussa min…"

My head hurts.

I close my eyes and press my fingertips into my temples. If I sit, just for a minute, I'll be fine.

Slumped to my knees, I breathe slowly.

A minute passes, then two or five.

I open my eyes and struggle to my feet.

"Can I hold onto you please?"

At least I can talk now. I still can't see much and my legs feel weak, but Sandra lets me hold her as we walk the hundred metres to the nearest shop. Every few steps my legs lock and I stumble, holding onto her for support. I seem to have reverted to a time before I could walk, see, or speak properly, but my mind is working absolutely normally and can't process why there is a lack of communication between itself and my body parts.

Sandra walks into the shop and I sit on the floor at the doorway. An orange juice vendor is nearby. I buy a cup of freshly squeezed orange juice. This is exactly what I need.

Greedily, I gulp at it.

Overcome by a sensation like I have never known before, my throat is warmed, then it catches on fire. A thousand tiny needles in my skin, fire ants feeding on my flesh, acid crumbling my throat. I close my eyes and grimace, trying not to call out. My tongue, my gums, even my teeth feel like they are bleeding. What the hell is wrong with this drink?

I hold it at arm's length and inspect the contents inside the plastic cup when the pain recedes. It looks like normal orange juice.

I smell it. It smells like normal orange juice.

I taste it again, a tiny sip. It burns like hellfire.

Sandra comes out of the shop and asks me what I'm pulling faces at. I hold out my orange juice and ask her if it's normal. She sips it and says it tastes fine. "Keep it." It looks so good, but it's full of taste demons that attack my body. I hold onto Sandra once more as we stumble back to her apartment, then slump back into my sleeping bag.

I just need a few minutes.

I awake mid-evening and pull on some clothes before battling my way to the bathroom. A thin film of sweat covers my body.

"Have I slept all day?" I ask Sandra when I finally make it to the kitchen.

"Yeah. I went out for about five hours and you hadn't moved when I got back. I thought it was best to leave you."

I pull up a seat and drink some water. I'll be alright tomorrow, I can leave then. It's time to chase the sun. A shockwave is immediately sent through my body as a warning to do no such thing. I log on to the internet and find two pieces of salvation. Bill, a friend from university, is in Paris and has invited me to stay with him. Secondly, a girl in Maastricht has offered me her spare bedroom for tomorrow night. I'm going to be fine, I don't have to go anywhere.

'Bill, I think I have food poisoning, but if you will still be around in two days, send me your address and I will find you.'

'Natsumi, yes please, I'd love to stay tomorrow night. How do I find you?'

I crawl back to bed and wait for the demons to leave me.

Morning, again. I missed the whole of yesterday, but I'm feeling better. Not perfect, but considerably better. I think I might be able to walk without my legs locking up. I try a lap around the room to make sure and when I make it back to where I've been sleeping, I give myself a little round of applause. I can walk again. And I can see. Hell, I bet I can even talk too.

I pack up my bag, check messages on the internet, and find two replies both welcoming me, one in Paris, one in Maastricht.

Sandra is already in the kitchen when I walk in. "Last night," I begin, "I had a dream about what I should do. In addition to never eating sushi ever again, I should have the words yes and no, one on each, inscribed upon the back of my hands for all time. It would serve as a reminder that while I should always say yes to things, I can say no too. Yes to hitchhiking, no to sushi, yes to football, no to coffee."

I hug Sandra goodbye, grateful for her kindness and grateful to have found another friend on the road of strangers. Then I walk out another door in search of a new stranger's home.

As it's still mid-morning, I idle down to the river and lie beside it to read. Natsumi works during the day so I have the whole day to myself. I put my backpack under my head so that when I fall asleep, no one can take it without me noticing. Within an hour, I feel the nausea in my head rattling around and drift into unconsciousness.

I awake. Noon. Sleep again.

Awake. Two-thirty. Sleep once more.

Awake. Four-thirty. Close enough. Time to get up.

Despite spending most of the day sleeping beside the river on a footpath where many people must have walked, no one has disturbed me. Even my book, fallen from my chest, lies as I must have dropped it.

"Hi, so nice to meet you Jamie." Natsumi greets me warmly in an American accent.

"Hi, thanks so much. Are you American?"

"No, Japanese of course. But I've lived in Holland since university." She is all smiles and I feel she is someone that I will like. "Let's get some food and some beer."

Natsumi picks up two packs of beer and a whole lot of food from the supermarket. As delicious as it looks, I have no idea if I can consume any of it. I still feel somewhat fragile, but the smell of food cooking after two days of consuming very little are overly tempting and persuade me that I am completely better. Surely now I can eat and drink as much as I please.

I tell Natsumi about my possible food poisoning as the aromas grow stronger.

"I know what would help you, acupuncture."

"Acupuncture? Needles in my skin?"

"Yes," she smiles.

"I'm on a run of saying yes to as much as I can, but right now I'm also thinking that it's important to say no sometimes. I don't know how I feel about large needles being inserted into me."

"These are tiny, you'll hardly even feel them." She disappears momentarily and reappears carrying a couple of small plastic bags which appear to contain very small drawing pins.

"These are the acupuncture needles?" I'm amazed at how tiny they are. She grins, already knowing I can't refuse. "Brilliant. Needle me up!"

I lie on my front as she inserts two needles into my back. I barely feel anything.

"I've taped them on. Just keep them there for the next couple of days."

"Wait a minute, you want me to keep these needles in my skin for the next couple of days?" I don't think I can do that.

"You won't even notice."

I nod dubiously and take another swig of beer.

When I go to bed, I'll quietly take them out without saying anything.

The spiders have returned when I awake, the spiders inside my brain and my stomach, that poke, poke, prod. I will tattoo yes and no onto my hands so that I never forget.

Beer and delicious food may not have been a great idea.

"So, are you hitchhiking today?" Natsumi asks. My stomach does a backflip.

"I think I'm going to take a bus. It's only two hundred and fifty miles to Paris, but I would prefer to throw up in a bus toilet rather than in someone's car." The image of needing to eject bodily fluids and being trapped in a clean car on the motorway sounds horrific.

Natsumi, who is on the way to Brussels for work, comes to the train station with me and together we take a train to Liège, a Belgian town a few minutes ride away. It still amuses me how easy it is to pop from one country to another in this very small part of Europe.

In Liège, we find out that the buses are full and get back on the train, riding to Brussels which takes over an hour.

In Brussels, I am greeted by one of the most unattractive bus stations that I have ever seen, filth and sadness everywhere. Mattresses are laid against every wall and filled with homeless families, many with young children. This is a completely different side to the Brussels that I knew a few days before. This is the part that everyone forgot about or pushed under the carpet so that they didn't have to think about.

Out of sight, out of mind.

The people look so unhappy.

I walk between the groups of rubbish and piles of people in order to reach the ticket office. The palpable desperation of those around me is disconcerting.

A two hour wait for the next bus. I hug Natsumi goodbye, another friend.

Getting off the bus in the east of Paris, I am met by a bus station even more tragic than the bus station in Brussels. A man reaches out to me for money, but I walk past him. He needs so much more than money right now, but I can't even bring myself to give him that. The whole place is so devoid of positive human emotion that it feels hostile. I am not comfortable with this at all. The only consolation that I have is that the spiders have ceased their prodding and I now feel that I can retain all of my bodily fluids.

More desperate souls call out to me. I slip my headphones on to drown out their sorrow.

Please leave me alone.

Through the bus station and down to the metro turnstiles I hurry. Surely the metro station will be nicer.

On the platform, I am hugely disappointed to find that the Parisian metro system is the most disgusting that I have ever seen in my life. Dirty and eerie, I am nervous of what lurks in the shadows.

I board the train, hoping to escape the hostility.

Listen to my music, ignore everyone else.

Why is this place so unfriendly?

Further down the carriage to my right, I hear a man shouting. Don't look. He shouts again, once more overshadowing the volume of my headphones. Maybe I should turn it up.

More movement to my right.

No, please no, the man is coming this way. He shouts at various passengers as he passes.

Then he reaches me.

He stops.

Buggaring brilliant.

Bending to my eye level, he puts his face to my face. Our eyes, mere inches apart, I hold my breath. I want neither to inhale his fumes nor give him any sign that I am anything other than a wax work.

I hold my gaze as if he isn't there. He cocks his head to the side. We're so close, our noses are almost touching. Should I head-butt him? Is that an appropriate thing to do in this situation? No, that would be silly. I don't even know how to head-butt someone and what would I do after? Offer him a tissue and apologise or run screaming as he gnaws on my leg? No, I will just sit here and pretend that we aren't eskimo kissing.

Please go away man.

I can't hold my breath for much longer.

He moves his face away, stands up, and continues down the train, resuming his shouting.

Welcome to Paris, the city of love!

I get off the train and Bill is there to meet me in a car he has borrowed. Seeing a friendly face after my experiences in the public transportation systems of both Brussels and Paris, relief washes over me. In this leafy Parisian suburb, the world feels peaceful once more.

Because of delays and having to travel halfway across Belgium, it's nearly midnight. It took me over twelve hours to traverse a mere two hundred and fifty miles and cost a ridiculous sum of money that I daren't even add up. Next time, even if I feel ill, I will hitchhike. Possibly with a bucket.

"Bill, great to see you," I gush. As chance would have it, we've met every few years in different parts of the world and catch up quickly. "Do you remember that time on Zanzibar when we both had our wallets stolen and lived on the beach for a few days? Having my wallet stolen was one of the best things that ever happened to me."

"It was? Well not for me."

"It just meant a few days of sleeping on the beach. Do you remember the nights we slept in that beach bar and the security guard tried to kick us out? We pretended to be too drunk to get up, even though we didn't have the money to drink. I read books and swam in the sea every day, then squatted at night. It helped me realise that you don't need money to live, although money does make things easier, particularly when dealing with people. It was unfortunate that we both lost our wallets at the same time though." Bill soon found work in a dive shop and I went to live with him until I left the island, but before that happened, he had to return to the mainland to change his flights. "Tell your story again," I plead, "I forget the details of how you lost your wallet, but I love it."

"Lost? Your wallet was 'lost' during a bus ride in Kenya. Mine was taken outright."

"I know," I grin. "Tell me anyway."

"Fine… I went back to the mainland to change my flights…"

"Because obviously they don't have phones or internet in Africa."

"… but the flight office was closed. This friendly guy had taken me to the office and he knew where we could find another office that was open, so I went with him. We got on a bus and rode to a different part of Dar, looking for this office while he made a phone call. When we get there, his friend turns up in a car. That was pretty nice of him, to get his friend to help me out by driving me to the office. It turned out it was another friend's birthday, so we go to pick up this friend. At this point, it's me and three Tanzanian guys in the car, all friendly, all helping me out. What they forgot, is that one friend wanted to get some Jack Daniels for the other friend's birthday. We swing the car around and go to pick up a fourth guy. Except that this guy doesn't have any Jack Daniels."

"How very curious."

"He gets in the car and we drive somewhere that doesn't look very much like a place where I can change my flights. Then they ask if I know what the mafia is. I do know what the mafia is, so I tell them that I know what the mafia is. Then they tell me that they are the mafia, at which point I express my disappointment. They take the seven hundred pounds of Tanzanian money that I had withdrawn to pay for my rent and then tell me that it isn't enough, so drive me to an ATM. I take out another seven hundred pounds which is the most I can take out and I give it to them. All the while this is going on, they're asking me about why I'm in Tanzania and if I'm having a nice holiday, what I do back in England, and how I ended up building a school. When they're done robbing me…"

"This is my favourite bit."

"… they give me directions back to the city centre and tell me which bus to take. I point out that I can't take a bus because they just took all my money. They apologise for this, give me back enough money for a bus, a hotel for the night, a meal, and a boat back to Zanzibar, then wish me a nice stay in their country. Then they drive off."

"Brilliant. That is the best mugging I have ever heard about. It makes me smile every time I think of it." Bill carries on driving. "Nothing will beat that story."

Bill and I got to know each other during our stay in Uganda, but first met by chance at a kayaking competition near Newcastle then in a Spanish class at university. It's one of those curious multi-country relationships that happen with people who like to move around a lot. "Do you remember the first night in Uganda?"

"I remember. The two of us sat up all night, looking over the Nile and watching the storm until that guy came to offer us some chicken."

"Chicken? What would we want chicken for?" I feign surprise and confusion, then open my hands revealing a magical secret. "Oh, THAT is chicken." In Uganda, the word chicken is apparently used as a code name for weed. Seeing two lone foreigners awake late at night, the Ugandan guy thought he'd found somewhere to offload his bag of chicken.

"We're nearly there," Bill tells me as we enter a small village.

I'm content, I'm happy, I'm safe. Even though I've only been on the road for a few days, I have spent the last few years living in different countries for various jobs and it is rare that I am granted the familiar comfort of meeting old friends.

Bill pulls up outside a gate which begins to open automatically. Two stone pillars guard the entrance to a grand house, visible only when the gate has fully retreated.

"This house is breathtaking, what are you doing here?"

"Gardening. It's my girlfriend's parents' house. I borrowed this car from them to pick you up."

Bill pulls forward and drives straight into the side of one of the stone pillars. A huge clunk is followed by a painful grinding noise.

Bill's face is a mixture of surprise and disbelief as the car stops abruptly.

I'm laughing so hard that I can't even open my eyes. Happy tears stream down my face.

4. Bright, Flashy Lights

Naked Couch Surfing and gay pride seem to be the main focuses as I look over the online profile of the only person to have invited me to stay with them in Paris. He is forty years old and according to the message he sent me, quite friendly. An extrovert maybe? Finding nothing of serious alarm, I tell him that I'd love to stay. 'Thank you and see you tonight.'

I go for breakfast.

Bill is flying back to the UK today, so I am going into Paris, a city I have never visited despite being in France more times than I can count on my fingers and toes put together. As a kid, I experienced wonderful holidays playing on the beach, walking through the forests, and smuggling grape vines back to England. These things could never have happened in an urban environment.

I check my emails one last time before heading into the city.

"Bill, look at this," I call. He comes over as I read the message out loud. "See you later Jamie. I hope you don't mind sharing a bed with me. It's no problem, but I sleep naked. Sebastian. Hmm… what do you think?"

"I wouldn't."

"Fair. Thank you so much for your kind offer Sebastian, but my plans have changed very quickly. I will not be in Paris tonight. Maybe next time. Jamie."

"Where will you sleep?"

"I'm not sure, but I think I would rather sleep outside than at the home of a stranger who invites me into his bed, naked."

Bill drops me off on Champs-Élysées, one of the most famous streets in all the world, and I am surrounded by unfamiliar bodies once again. For less than a single day, I had the comfort of an old friend.

I look up, see the Arc de Triomphe at the far end of the street, and carry on walking. I don't really feel like sightseeing right now.

I walk and I walk, then I walk some more. I don't know where I'm heading, but it feels like I'm heading towards something. When I have multiple options, I walk in the direction where I see most people. A sign post offers me the choice of heading towards two attractions if I turn left, five if I turn right. I turn right. What treasures will I find? Paris is supposedly one of the most beautiful cities in all of the world, but last night's bus station has done little to inspire me. I see busy tarmac with too many cars and busy sidewalks with too many people, all criss-crossing the spider-web of the Parisian streets. A boulangerie here, a patisserie there. At least I know I'm in France.

From my reading forays into pop-psychology, I learnt that in Japan, around twenty tourists a year are diagnosed with 'Paris Syndrome.' This new age psychological disorder is characterised by hallucinations, feelings of persecution, and anxiety while visiting Paris or shortly after returning to Japan. While the validity of this syndrome is highly debatable and the symptoms are most probably due to the stress of being in a foreign country, some psychologists have theorised that Paris Syndrome is caused by 'an individual's inability to accept the disparity between the ideology of Paris portrayed in Japanese culture and the reality when they see it for themselves.' Translated into normal speak, Japanese tourists imagine Paris to be wonderful, find out it isn't all that great, then have a breakdown.

Thus far, I am fairly disappointed myself. However, as far as I am aware, I am not seeing things that aren't there and I don't feel persecuted, so I can safely say I haven't developed a Paris-flavoured mind disorder.

I feel... nothing much at all.

In every direction I look, I can see hundreds, maybe thousands of people rushing by. Nobody stopping to say hello. Nobody taking the time to interact with each other. Everybody is so busy with their own little lives that they don't have the time for anybody else. I wonder what it would take to get noticed. I look around for somebody doing something noticeable in the hope of seeing if anybody else has noticed. There's a man on a skateboard, but people pay him no heed.

I walk over a bridge and see a large square that seems more densely populated than the other streets that I've been walking.

A man is feeding a small flock of birds from his hands. About five or ten people are paying him a moderate level of attention. I watch him for several minutes, fascinated, reminded of a Disney character, maybe Belle, who calls the birds and they come to her. Outside our small circle, everyone else has something better to do.

This is not enough to be noticed.

One part of the square seems to be more heavily populated than any other, so I walk over to see what people are attracted to.

There is a large, white religious building of some sort, rather gothic, that has been intricately carved. Beneath three gigantic, arched doorways, I walk to a sign and read more about it.

'Notre-Dame de Paris.'

Oh, Notre-Dame. With more than thirteen million visitors a year it is one of the most visited attractions in the world. Apparently it receives over twice as many visitors as the Eiffel Tower. I look up and study it in detail.

Yes, very pretty I suppose.

Lots of people.

Walking away, I find a sign pointing in the direction of Centre Pompidou. The name rings a bell and I walk down the street until I find it. It is one of the most bizarre structures I have ever seen. Large and rectangular, it is a network of criss-crossing coloured pipes, some offering structural support while others are half transparent and have people walking through them. Certain pipes seem to have no purpose whatsoever and it is almost as if the building has been constructed out of giant scaffolding, then left in a semi-complete state.

Inside I find that this seemingly unfinished building houses a centre for music and acoustic research, a library, and the largest museum of modern art in the whole of Europe. I suppose it is rather big.

On an escalator, I ride up the inside of one of the pipes, the perspex roof offering a view of the surrounding buildings. Then I ride another escalator. Up and up until I reach the fifth floor, the highest I can go. Standing by an open window, Paris is a stage beneath me, the city stretching out for miles, rooftop after rooftop. This must be the best view in the whole of the city. Grand churches and nameless castle like buildings and for the very first time, I see the Eiffel Tower, one of the most iconic sights in the world.

Yet I am completely alone.

So many people, so close, rushing by at a million miles an hour, completely uninterested in one another. Lives running in parallel, almost touching, yet light years apart. We are separated by invisible, unbreakable walls. I take my finger and in the dirt of the window beside me, I write my name. How many other people have ever stood in front of this magnificent scene and looked over this city feeling completely alone, surrounded by so many people?

Cities are the loneliest places in the world when you do not know anybody. I want to write all of my feelings on the window, but I don't have the energy.

Yet I must share something more than my name. I press my finger into the dirt of the window once more.

Words elude me.

I wait.

To be alone… When together… We as one… I have it.

'The greatest comfort in life, is knowing that we are all alone together.'

Something isn't right. A comma maybe?

'The greatest comfort in life, is knowing that we are all alone, together.'

Yes, that captures the feeling. Did I just think of that or did I read it somewhere? It doesn't matter.

Riding back down the escalators, the city disappears from view. I walk back the way I came, over the same bridge, into a flower market. What beautiful flowers,

I have rarely seen such delights.

Onwards I go, past Notre-Dame.

So many people.

What would you do to be noticed?

Another bridge, a quiet street, a bookshop with Shakespeare's head adorning the signage.

Inside the bookshop, there is quiet. Never before have I seen such a wondrous collection of words. From floor to ceiling, every space is filled. Chairs for reading, higgledy-piggledy shelves that don't quite run straight, and books squeezed into every unavailable space, this is the bookshop that time forgot. I want to run my fingers across the spines and touch them, every single one, but they are piled so high that I would need a ladder to do so. This is a time warp, the old world, a bookshop from the land of dragons and magicians.

Upstairs, more delights. A whole room of books that are not for sale and that cannot be removed from the bookshop. A reading room. I didn't know that such things still existed in the modern business world where we want it all and we want it now and we want everything optimised for space efficiency.

This is not good business. This is how a book shop should be.

There is a large and golden picture frame, filled with handwritten messages, pictures, cuttings, everything that people must have had on them. Nostalgic, alone, I want to leave something. I pull last night's metro ticket from my pocket and scribble a message for someone who will never read it, then push the corner under the frame. It sits there for every and no one to see.

I am done with Paris. I need see nor do no more.

My last action here, will be to sleep.

The only place I know where I can find a park to sleep in, is at the foot of the Eiffel Tower. It's set amidst lush and expansive gardens, filled with jungles of foliage.

Minutes later, I walk out of a metro station and along a river. The Eiffel Tower is right here according to this tourist map, yet I cannot see it anywhere. I walk some more.

In thick crowds armed with cameras, I am the only one with a large backpack and people bump into me as they rush past.

We touch, but the invisible barrier remains unbroken.

Where is this tower? According to the map, I am practically standing under it.

An apparition, it appears. I am shocked. I have idly stood in the shadow of the Petronas Twin Towers, once the tallest buildings in the world, but this takes my breath away. I never expected it to be so... big. Maybe it's that my expectations have been exceeded or maybe that my feelings towards Paris are so low that anything impressive seems monumental, but I cannot believe how incredible this structure looks above me. I walk around and around, looking up. What a curious creation.

Despite previously knowing that the Eiffel Tower was set amidst lush and expansive gardens that are filled with jungles of foliage, I realise that I do not or did not know that at all. Instead, there is a long, thin garden which consists primarily of grass lawns and tree lined paths. The occasional bush spattering is too sparse to provide cover for a tent.

I walk through the grassy areas as revellers drink beer and throw inanimate objects amongst themselves. Everyone is happy to be here. A North African man approaches me and offers me a small gold trinket for only one euro. It's a model of the Eiffel Tower. For two euros I can have one that flashes.

I shake my head and carry on. The trinket tout follows me for a few seconds before realising that I have no interest in his wares, however persistent he may be.

Another man approaches and offers a similar array of delights. Once more I shake my head, then continue through the gardens until I find a space relatively clear of people. I put my pack down as a pillow and lie upon the grass, listening to my music and reading as I wait for night to fall.

Sensing movement from the corner of my eye, I look up to see a wave of the trinket touts sprinting through the park. Either their sales are illegal or they are. Presumably figures of authority must have descended upon the park from the other side, but why is it that these men had to run? That was not a normal run: those men were running a desperate run, a run not to be caught because whatever was chasing them implied serious consequences. Did these men dream of leaving their homelands for this life? Did they dream of crossing the sea and the land to live in a place where they sold junk to tourists for little money, only to be chased through the park like mangy dogs? Oftentimes, dreams are larger than reality permits them to be.

Did I dream of hitchhiking in the rain and not having anywhere to sleep or a friend to talk to?

Every hour or so, the touts are chased through the park until step by step, they creep back to their original positions and continue their tiresome trade. As night closes in, I expect people to disappear, but they don't. On this June evening, it's almost ten o'clock before the sun finally sets and after that, the light lingers.

A lone girl comes and sits close to me. She could have sat anywhere else, but she sat right there, right here, so close. Shall I say hi? No, that would be silly. What would I say to her? Hello stranger, you're alone, I'm lonely, let's pretend we're friends and talk about something. Except that I don't even know if she speaks English. I'll just sit here and read my book and listen to my music and not do anything and hope that someone else does. Yes, what a wonderful idea. Wonderful things always happen when you sit around, doing nothing. I'm pretty sure that's how Steve Jobs created Apple. He just sat there, doing nothing, and it made itself.

Sigh.

The Eiffel Tower lights up in a dramatic display of lights, catching me by surprise and disrupting my thought pattern. It's quite a show. Flashy and shiny with different lighting sequences, I can't decide if it's horrendously tacky or almost acceptable.

By midnight, I'm tired of the light display, tired of reading, tired of the people. I'm tired all over and I want to sleep.

I take my headphones off as I get to my feet. Did someone say something? I look at the girl sitting close to me.

"Excuse me?"

"Are you backpacking?"

"Something like that." I move my pack over to where she's sitting and take a seat next to her. The invisible wall between us is broken by her three simple words: are you backpacking? Those three words are all it took to forge a human connection.

"What are you doing with your backpack in the park at this time?"

"I was just waiting for everyone to go home, then I was going to find somewhere to sleep. What are you doing in the park at this time?"

"I'm staying in an apartment close by with some family friends. I just wanted to come out and read for a bit. Don't you have somewhere to stay?"

"Yes, right here." I can't see her face in the dark, but she seems only mildly perturbed.

One of the trinket touts approaches us and offers us a bottle of wine. "Lovely boyfriend-girlfriend, wine?"

"No thank you."

"Beer?"

"No thank you."

"Wine or beer?"

"Really, no."

"Just one wine?"

"I don't want any wine or any beer. I want to sit here, that's all."

The man leaves.

It seems that the touts don't disappear after dark, they simply change their merchandise.

"What are you doing in Paris? That's a North American accent, right?"

"Yeah, right. I've been studying photography in Germany for the past semester. Now it's summer, I'm inter-railing around a bit before I go home."

Even in the dark, she must sense my eyes pop at the word photography. "I always wished I had spent time focusing on something creative."

"Why didn't you?"

"I was told that if I wanted a good job and a good life and to be a respectable human being, I had to study an 'academic subject.' So I studied mathematics because it made sense. Four years later, I had a Masters in it. I don't hate maths and sometimes I think how incredibly beautiful it can be, but it doesn't continually excite me in the way that making things does. It doesn't even matter what you make, but making something feels so worthwhile. And no one can ever tell you it's completely perfect or imperfect because there is no such thing. At sixth form I was signed up for photography, but on the first day of the course, I changed to mathematics because I was told that it was a better career choice. So many people tell you so many things that you should do. When I was thirteen years old, I dropped art even though it was my favourite subject because I was told by my teachers that studying art doesn't get you a job. And here I am, hitchhiking with no job and no desire for one." I wonder where I'd be now if I chose what I wanted to do, rather than what I thought I should do.

"You're hitchhiking?!" the girl exclaims in surprise.

From hitchhiking to photography, we talk in the darkness as the hours roll by. I pull out my camera, ask for every button and function to be explained, and learn more in one conversation about photography than I had ever known before. Sometime between three and four, we agree it is time to go to sleep.

"What is your name by the way?" I ask. At this point, after several hours of pleasant conversation, a name would be preferable to saying 'hey, you, girl.'

"I'm Jenna. And you?"

"Jamie. A real pleasure to meet you." I mean it.

Together we walk through the park, Jenna towards where she is staying, me scouting out bushes for camping. When our paths diverge, we stop to say goodbye. I don't even know what Jenna looks like as our every exchange has occurred in the darkness, but something tells me that we could be friends for much longer than one moonlit conversation. I should ask her to come hitchhiking with me. What a brilliant idea. Except that I won't because that sounds weird. Or does it? Actually, I won't ever see this person again. I'm not lonely anymore and I'm on top of the world, so I can do what I want and it doesn't matter.

"Good luck with your hitchhiking," she says as a parting comment.

"Thanks... You know, if you're interested in trying it, you are welcome to come with me tomorrow. I've been on my own until now, but company might be nice." Did I just say that out loud?

I think I did.

"Sure." I tap Jenna's phone number into my phone and turn it off again to save battery. I keep it off most of the time in case I need it for emergencies.

"I'll message you in the morning, we can meet for breakfast."

"Sure."

Jenna walks out of the park, I further into it.

Sure? What does sure mean? Sure I'll come hitchhiking with you tomorrow because that's what I do. Or sure, I'll just say sure so that you'll go away and here's a fake number and on top of that, Jenna isn't my real name after all. I try to think back to our conversation. We talked about photography, about hitchhiking, about all sorts of things. But only a little bit about us. She gave me the impression that she comes from a conservative background, so it is unlikely that she'll want to travel with strangers with only another stranger for company. Either way, tonight was pleasant.

I walk a full lap of the park without finding anywhere suitable to pitch my tent and concede that the grounds of the Eiffel Tower are not at all conducive to guerrilla camping. Half hiding my tent between a large collection of foliage and a low cut hedge seems like the best option from a very limited selection of alternatives.

On the outer edge, the foliage covers one half of my tent so that anyone outside the park can't see me. A person inside the park however, will blatantly see the top of my tent above the miniature hedge. I hope they don't have any form of security visiting the park overnight. Is it an offence to camp under the Eiffel Tower?

I look at the magnificent structure, perhaps only one hundred metres away from me. This must be the best room with a view in all of Paris and it costs absolutely nothing. Even if Paris wasn't my favourite, this is an experience I will never forget: camping under, well almost under, the Eiffel Tower.

Snuggled up in my tent, I feel content. I close my eyes for only the second time in my less than one hundred and eighty-three centimetre home.

Pitter-patter, pitter-patter, the rain ripples against the thin walls. I hadn't even noticed it was cloudy.

A gentle wind presses down upon my tent, causing it to lean to one side and further reducing the space inside. I roll away a few centimetres and find myself at the other side of the tent.

Titter-tatter, titter-tatter, the rain becomes heavier.

The wind pushes harder.

A distant rumbling permeates the park. A threat. I check the zip of my tent is done up. It is.

Is this tent waterproof?

The rain falls harder still and together with the wind, attempts to flatten my abode. I reach an arm out of my sleeping bag and push back against the wall. I can hardly believe the tent is still standing, I didn't even peg it properly. It's one of those tunnel tents with just two rods: a long curved rod at the head, by the door, and a short rod for the feet. Structurally, it isn't particularly strong.

A flash.

How did the storm move so fast?

This time the distant rumbling is a loud growl, close at hand. Imminent danger.

The wind relents and I put my arm back inside my sleeping bag. I can't hold the tent off me all night. As soon as I let go, the wind pushes my tent over once more and I pull my sleeping bag over my head.

Is sleeping next to one of the world's seemingly most perfect lightning conductors genius or idiocy right now? Will it take all the charge or will it simply bring the lightning closer to me? I think back to GCSE physics. Lightning always chooses the easiest path. Am I the…

Flash, crash, boom!

Hold tight.

Flash! A bomb in the sky.

Nothing I can do now. I have to ride the storm out.

Flash, the world of darkness is on fire. The skies roar, an angry monster hunting for blood, demanding destruction.

The scent of an untamed river fills my nostrils, the smell of danger. A torrent of crushing liquid, a vicious waterfall.

I wrap my arms around myself and curl into the foetal position.

"What am I doing here?" I whisper. "Why am I doing this to myself?"

The roar of the sky is so continuous that I cannot tell where one explosion ends and another begins. Each boom doubles my heart rate until I feel no more than the whir of a hummingbird inside my chest. The noise…

Lights! Bright, flashy lights. My tent is a disco.

My body is shaking, but I am neither cold nor wet. Pounding hard from the inside, my heart threatens to rip through my tent as the storm drums outside. Ominous drumming, the march to the gallows.

"WHY?" I scream. "WHY ARE YOU HERE?" Nobody will hear me over the skies. Nobody would be foolish enough to be outside in this seemingly tropical storm. I didn't think this happened in Europe.

Myself or the storm, who am I talking to?

I could be at home with a nice job, warm behind glass windows, safe inside a secure fence. I could be with the people I cared about, in comfort. But I am in a tent that is beaten flat by the wind and the rain, my heart racing with the storm, alone. The most raw and explosive display of nature I can ever remember in Europe and there is no one else to hold on to. It's just us storm, you and me.

"The storm and I."

However brave or foolish a man is, nature brings them crashing to their knees. At its mercy, you are no longer a big man. Your freedom is taken from you and you have no control. You are humbled.

I am humbled.

I clench my hands into fists and I squeeze my face tight.

"I WILL NOT BE MOVED STORM. YOU CANNOT DEFEAT ME."

Fearful adrenaline pumps anger through my soul. Why would this storm take me on now?

I will not allow this.

But I want to go home.

There is nowhere to run and there is nowhere to hide. I am a rabbit in the headlights.

I cannot out-roar this storm, this is nature.

I am nothing but a boy.

I must… enjoy the show.

Taking a deep breath, I search inside myself for something, anything to cling onto. A shred of courage maybe? There is none, but my hands are tied, the tent is my prison.

Relying on nothing but my desire to survive, I bring my head out from inside my sleeping bag and open my eyes.

This is it…

I open the zip…

Put my head into the rain.

In every flash, I see the world outside the tent.

Illuminated.

Under lightning, the Eiffel Tower is the centre of the universe, the source of all power.

The air tastes of fire.

Is this the most incredible sight I have ever seen?

I want to run out in the rain, under the light of the skies, but the cold stops me. I have so few clothes. Could I dance under the Eiffel Tower without them?

No. I am not totally delirious, but I feel wicked madness ripping through my body.

The storm warms my heart and washes my face clean.

I snuggle back into my sleeping bag, thunder and lightning raging around me, and close my eyes.

CRACKWHIP fizzle boom, pitter-patter, pitter-patter.

"Hush," I whisper, "I'm sleeping."

I am not alone anymore, the storm will keep me company throughout the night.

Lights! Such bright, flashy lights. They are so very beautiful.

5. Luxury

The world is steaming and I have slept with the storm.

Water drips from every leaf, the paths are full of puddles, and I am nothing but a tiny individual who spent the night beside the Eiffel Tower. I could run a marathon right now.

I pull out my phone and text Jenna.

'Breakfast at 10?' It's half-past nine.

A few metres away, a litter picker is collecting the remnants of the revellers' parties from the night before. He looks at me momentarily as if to say, 'Where the hell did you come from?' then carries on with his job. I am not interesting enough to hold his attention for any longer.

I pack my tent away, full of water, and know that I will have to get it out to dry later in the day. My phone bleeps. A message from Jenna.

'Yes. Meet you where we parted last night.' Perfect.

I walk another lap of the park below the Eiffel Tower. Under the shadow of grey cloud and without the mysteries of night, the tower has far less impression on me than when I first saw it yesterday. It is simply a tower. So many millions of people have been here before and looked up at it.

In daylight, I see Jenna's face for the first time. Immediately I am drawn to her brilliant blue eyes.

Always the eyes.

Whomever I meet, the eyes are the first thing I see. No other part of the body reveals so much truth about a person. Only by looking someone in the eyes, can you venture into their soul.

Then I see her smile. Set between brown hair and those brilliant blue eyes, her smile emanates friendliness and fills the whole of her face. Not everyone can smile with the whole of their face, but for Jenna, it seems effortless.

And perfect white teeth. How long I've been jealous of the American dental system. As a Englishman, dental care finishes at brushing two to three times a day.

We take a seat in a small cafe near the park. "Were you OK last night? The weather was pretty bad."

"It was quite beautiful watching it from under the Eiffel Tower." In the light of day, I don't feel the need to share how I lay in the foetal position with my arms wrapped around my legs for the majority of the light display, until finally accepting that there was nothing I could do but try to enjoy the ride.

At night, the world is full of possibility and terrors. In the day, it is real and it is simple: there are no monsters or parties, only commitments and responsibilities.

While Jenna seemed interested in hitchhiking last night, we are no longer talking in the darkness where anything is possible. We are in full daylight and this is real life. Most people say things at night that they do not truly mean, only to take them back the next day. I realise that Jenna has agreed only to meeting me for breakfast and not to hitchhiking.

"I would have loved to capture the storm on my camera last night, but I don't think I could have done it justice. Some things are better in real life."

"Light is elusive. A photo might take a little part of the light, but there are secrets hidden from cameras that only a real person can see. You could never capture the taste of the air or the electricity upon your skin during a storm."

Should I mention hitchhiking? Probably not. Just keep talking, asking questions.

"I have ten siblings," Jenna tells me.

"You have ten siblings? Wow! I thought I had a lot with four brothers. Are your siblings scattered across the world like you?"

"Actually, they are all married and living back in my home town. I'm the only one who hasn't done that yet."

"Because you are the youngest?" I probably should mention hitchhiking.

"My youngest sibling is only nineteen. At twenty-four, I'm somewhere between the middle and the youngest. I come from a kind of conservative background, we're part of The Church of Jesus Christ of Latter-Day Saints."

"Absolutely no idea what that means, but how about it then, are you coming hitchhiking?"

I feign indifference. I don't need company, but I found someone who I think could be a good friend if we spent more time together. With no job, no commitments, there is nothing else to get in the way of this. On paper, we are completely different people, but here we both sit with a shared desire of seeing the world. It might be true that you only need one common desire with someone to forge a good friendship.

As long as that desire is strong enough.

Jenna turns the decision over in her mind. I see hesitation as she debates between doing something that she wants to do, just for the hell of it. Or doing what every rational nerve in her body is telling her to do and what all of her friends, family, and people she's never even met would advise her to do. Accepting an invitation to go hitchhiking with a guy you've just met, a guy who spent the previous night sleeping in a park during a huge thunderstorm, is not an advisable life choice.

"I mentioned this to a friend last night and they said that I definitely shouldn't go. I also spoke to the people I'm staying with and they didn't recommend it. But I looked you up online and your stories seem real and I think you seem like a nice guy…"

"So…?"

"So sure, I'll come." I clap my hands in delight. "I only have a few days though as I am flying back to the US next week."

"Fantastic! It'll be a great experience before you leave. Where do you want to go?"

"What are the options?" I spread my arms wide and look to the sky.

"The world is before us," I say in a deep voice. I intended on sounding dramatic, but my voice comes across as creepy so I stop the strange voice before she changes her mind. "Wherever you want to go. Where would you go from here if you could go anywhere? That's normally a hypothetical question, but right now it's real."

"Italy?!" she suggests tentatively.

"Italy it is!" My search for perpetual sunlight can wait. Commitment free, I can go to Italy and then return north to Scandinavia afterwards.

I walk back to the apartment Jenna has been staying in and we look at a map of Italy on the internet. I ask her where she wants to go and she tells me about a town she has heard of called La Spezia. By the most direct route, it's over six hundred miles away.

"Let's aim for that and adjust as we see fit."

While Jenna packs her bags, I go back to the park and stop to buy some lunch on the way. A delicious goat cheese baguette, the thought makes my mouth water. Mostly I have been eating plain bread while on the road. On a bench, I read my book and wait. After a couple of hours, I wonder if Jenna has changed her mind. It would be understandable after all. Maybe she just got caught up in the moment of excitement and has had time to think things through.

I hope she sends me a text to let me know, it's past midday already.

A skinny man approaches the bench I'm sitting on. His legs are bowed, his gait queer and lurching. He could be Moroccan, but it's hard to tell. At a guess, I'd say he is older than me, but time has clearly not been kind to him. He is weary and tired, wearing a wet jumper and sports shorts.

The man tugs at my jumper. I look at him and raise my eyebrows. What do you want?

He moans and mumbles a few words that I can't understand.

"What do you want?"

He speaks at length, possibly in French, but I can only catch the odd word.

For once, I don't think it's my appalling level of French that is the problem. Most of what he says is slurred or in an accent that is too thick for me to understand. Did he just say 'froid,' the French word for cold?

He tugs at my jumper again. He wants me to understand, angry that I don't.

I think he wants my jumper, but I have only one and I do not want to give it to him. I shake my head. His eyes demand that I give him my jumper. I point at his jumper and he shakes his head.

I shrug my shoulders, he pulls a euro from his pocket. Swap a jumper for a euro? I shake my head.

"I don't want any money, I just want my jumper." He has no idea what I'm saying.

He pulls a second euro from his pocket and offers it to me. I get to my feet and make a double handed stop sign as he tries to pull out more money.

"I do not want to sell my jumper. Even if someone offered me one hundred euros right now, I would not want to sell it."

I take out the goat cheese baguette from my backpack and offer him this instead. He looks at it dubiously before accepting it, then walks off to eat it on another bench.

Delicious sandwich devoured, he returns to tug at my jumper some more. I shoulder my backpack and walk away from him, his gaze of disappointment and malice burning into my back.

In a small shop, I buy a bag of pasta. Yes, plain pasta will be the perfect replacement for a goat cheese baguette.

Jenna finally returns with all of her belongings and we catch the metro to the edge of Paris to find a quiet residential area where we can begin our hitching. I'm relieved that she didn't change her mind. Putting my thumb out for the first time with Jenna beside me, I have every toe crossed that whoever picks us up is friendly, for both her sake and because I told her it would be fine.

"Wave, thumb, smile, anything to catch people's attention. We want to look mildly eccentric, but not all out crazy."

Immediately, Jenna is waving and smiling at passing cars with more confidence than I have ever shown. I don't think this is going to be so hard for us to catch a ride right now.

"While I was waiting for you," I tell Jenna, "a man came to ask me for my jumper." I've been twirling this thought around in my head for some time and it needs some air. "He looked as if he was in a bad way, but I said no to giving him my jumper. I gave him my lunch, but I had always thought that if someone was in need, I would help them out. It reminds me of an old psychology experiment by Stanley Milgram, do you know it?"

"I don't think so. What was it?"

"To outline it very briefly, he tested subjects' responses to authority by making them believe that they were passing increasingly large voltages through the bodies of other study participants. They would ask questions to the other participants and when the given answer was incorrect or no answer was supplied, the voltage was increased. With minor prompting, around sixty or seventy per cent of subjects continued to administer a fatal level of electric shock. While this was done at the time of Nazi war trials and demonstrated the power of human compliancy in the face of authority, the thing that I found most interesting was that all people believe that they would terminate the experiment early. I believe that I would, but I have never been in that situation. Clearly the majority of study participants thought the same, but when it came down to it, they continued to administer increasingly large shocks. Does me not giving the man my jumper prove that I am in that sixty-to-seventy per cent of people?"

"I think you might be thinking about this too deeply."

"Maybe, but we all have a perception of ourselves and sometimes we start to realise that our perceptions aren't correct. I'm not claiming to be a moral angel, but I at least like to think I wouldn't do bad things without reason."

"You seemed genuine enough to persuade me to come hitchhiking with you."

A fair point, but not enough to put my mind at rest.

A black car stops and it is time for Jenna's first experience of hitchhiking. Please be friendly, please be lovely.

A tank of a man is driving. In the back seat is his daughter.

"I used to be a professional judo fighter," the tank tells us, "but I'm too old and not fit enough anymore." I look at the man whose biceps are thicker than my legs. I cannot imagine a more intimidating physical figure: he is a wall of solid muscle. But most importantly, he is a wall of pleasant and friendly solid muscle and we are safe with him.

Late in the afternoon, we've made our way down through France, but have a very long way to go before we reach Italy. It's super hot and the skies are brilliantly clear, the perfect day for being outside. Except that no one has picked us up for nearly forty-five minutes. Forty-five minutes! Are we going to be here forever?

The first car that stops is being driven by a large Senegalese guy with more gold in his mouth than teeth. His fingers are decorated with bling and he leans across the leather seats to look out of the window at us. Something about the way he looks at us makes me itch, but it's been forty-five minutes and I want to continue our journey.

I get into the car as the large man gets out, walks around to my door, leans over me, and checks that my seat-belt is clipped in. Then he does the same for Jenna. No one has done my belt up since I was too young to physically be able to do so. As a child wary of everything, my seat belt has always been secured within seconds of entering a vehicle.

"I am a bodyguard from Lyon," the man tells us in French, "I came to Paris for a special mission." A six hundred mile journey for a special mission?

"That is very far." He leers at me, showing off his gold teeth once more.

We potter down the motorway at seventy kilometres an hour, being overtaken time after time by cars racing by at twice our speed. With a legal speed limit of one hundred and thirty kilometres an hour, we are moving so slowly that it's dangerous.

The driver looks at us time and time again, his itchy eyes irritating our skin. What is he looking at? What does he want from us?

I roll wicked after wickeder situation through my mind, every scary movie I've ever seen, leaping to life. I do not want this to happen, I do not want to be here.

"Thank you, we will stop here and eat," I explain in broken French when we pull in at a service station. He pulls away and I am grateful to be out of his car.

Yes and no, we always have a choice.

"I'm sorry," I say to Jenna, "I know he was going all of the way to Lyon, but he made me too uncomfortable. I couldn't wait to be out of his car."

"I felt the same, he was a strange guy."

"Good. If you're ever not comfortable with a situation we're in, please let me know and we'll get out of it. It's better to offend someone than to not feel safe."

Within minutes, we're in the car of a fashion designer who rarely drops below the speed limit. We race past the Senegalese bodyguard in the blink of an eye as he continues his trundle down the highway. Our new chauffeur rolls a joint in one hand, plays with an iPad in the other, and steers with his knee. Have we leapt from the tiger enclosure into the lion pit?

I'm tense in the back seat as cars and the world flash by either side of us. It begins to get dark and although there is no way we will make it to Italy this evening, we are moving as quickly as we could hope to move.

"Would you like some?" the driver offers, waving the joint around. It might help to calm my nerves. So too might a general anaesthetic or a severe blow to the head.

I wake up to find that we are being dropped at a quiet fuel station. This is not conducive to hitchhiking, but we've covered good distance with the fashion designer.

"We have two choices," I explain to Jenna. "We can carry on through the night or we can sleep here. I have a tent." I expect my suggestion of sleeping outside a service station to be met with protests, but we hadn't made plans for the evening, so even if we made it to Italy, we would still have nowhere else to stay.

"Here is fine."

"Really?!"

Jenna has transitioned from a regular person, to an all out hitchhiker and free-camper in a matter of hours. I am wildly impressed.

The two of us squeeze into the one hundred and seventy centimetre tent that is too small for me alone and rest our tired, pasta filled bodies.

Inside the service station, our early morning activity involves flicking through a map of Italy, studying the coast closely. I leave the destination up to Jenna. "Where looks good? I am happy to go wherever, but let's find somewhere small and hope for a beach."

"How about this?" Jenna points at a place on the map that is smaller and closer than La Spezia.

"Portofino?" I roll the word across my tongue. "Por-toe-fee-no. I like the name, we'll go there."

We arrive in Santa Margherita Ligure, six hundred miles from Paris and three from Portofino, late in the evening after being treated to several hours of Spanish opera, courtesy of a warm hearted gentleman who bought us lunch.

It's almost sunset.

We race down to the beach and dump our bags on the sand. The whole town is an array of pastel buildings built upon hills that could almost be classified as cliffs. Hundreds of yachts and pleasure cruisers adorn the marina. This is a postcard scene of Italy, a haven for wealthy tourists. Dressed in suits and long dresses, an elegant group of people watch us inquisitively as we jump into the water to rinse off several days of accumulated sweat. Nearby, others sip wide glassed cocktails on exquisite verandas. We splash around as the sun sinks below the water, the surface tingling and shimmering, the colours of fire.

"Do you miss the Eiffel Tower?" I shout as I break through the surface of the water, out of breath.

"No."

"Do you wish you were sitting at home on your comfy bed?"

"No."

"Do you want to be anywhere else but here, in the fading light and the sea?"

Why did I sleep under the Eiffel Tower in a thunderstorm? Why am I living out of a backpack and taking cold showers on the beach? Why don't I give it all up and go back to everything safe and comfortable that I always had?

For moments like this.

I have been on the road for only two weeks and my old job and life seem a world away. I don't ever want to go back.

With the sun departed, the moon performs for us as we sit and cook pasta on the beach. Never again will plain pasta taste so good.

Jenna pulls a surprise jar of pesto from her bag and we smother our previously flavourless food. Explosions upon my tongue, this must be the most delicious meal of all time.

Full of life and calm of mind, I feel like the moon dancing upon the water. I could skip across the crests all night, twirling with the foam, rising and falling with the waves.

Except that the moon doesn't sleep and I do.

After discovering that the whole town is dramatically inclined or covered with concrete, we set up the tent on the one piece of grass that we can find. In this exclusive town where the cheapest bed costs in excess of one hundred euros a night, we lay our heads for free.

On the way to Portofino the following morning, we are stopped by an English lady who informs us that the peninsular we are on is where Wayne Rooney got married. Apparently, Frank Lampard is staying nearby on this very day too. We thank her for the useless information and continue on our way.

Met by watercolour buildings, turquoise waters, a picturesque harbour set amongst high hills, and rich vegetation, I realise that I was wrong about Santa Margherita: Portofino is where the postcard images come from. This old fishing village of less than five hundred residents is the most upmarket resort I have ever seen.

We leap from rocks into clear water, climb hills to find a lighthouse, and even fall asleep between the luxury yachts, high on ice cream and life.

Waking up, I am grateful that no one has touched our cameras, unprotected next to our sleeping bodies. Most probably, passers-by thought it best to let the vagabonds be. At sea, a naked old man drives his tiny boat around and on the harbour, people walk peacefully, enjoying their annual few days of precious tranquility.

"This is luxury."

From Portofino, we head one hundred and fifty miles north to Lago Di Como, a famous Italian lake town. Surrounded by mountains and blue skies, we leap into the water once more. It's so hot that we air dry in minutes.

"Life tastes as good as ice cream."

Invited to the home of some exchange students, we use an inside shower and know exactly where we'll be sleeping when darkness falls for the first time in our joint mini adventure. In the morning, I walk Jenna to the train station and bid her farewell.

"Thank you for hitchhiking with me, I really enjoyed it." For a brief five days, our paths have coexisted through some glorious parts of the world. "If we ever find ourselves in the same part of the world, we must do it again. By then, I'll need a whole load more photography lessons."

With Jenna gone, I am alone, so I walk. Up and up and up. I walk only up, no idea what I will find when I get there, wherever there may be. An hour passes, then another and another. I am dripping with sweat and I take off my shirt in the quiet.

I haven't seen another living person for so long. Like a mirage, a town appears. Why is there a town on the top of this mountain?

The murmur of voices permeates the air around me and I am shaken back into the real world. People do still exist. Together we stand and look over the lake and the city below us. We are so very high. Behind us is a funicular. Everyone else has raced up in minutes, completely sweat free. Ignoring the easy route, I return to my trance and head back into the trees, descending muddy paths through the forest. The whole world is quiet once again and nobody else exists.

"Ciao!" My trance is broken as an Italian couple catch me by surprise. They are the only people I have met who walk the same path as I. We nod friendly nods to each other and continue in opposite directions.

I stumble upon an abandoned building between the foliage.

A time capsule, a memory of lost human habitation, an abandoned building is a fragile link to our past, a sign of our fast moving future. As much as society disregards it, it stands tall, saying hey you world, don't forget me, I am still here.

Halfway up a mountain, I had not expected to find a huge house with neither windows nor doors. I approach it gingerly, step by precious step, the very walls observing my approach. It lures me closer, draws me in, so inviting…

An ominous presence

I rush away with great haste. If Jenna was here, we'd look around it. Of course, it wouldn't be as much fun on my own, what will I see in an abandoned building anyway? I look over my shoulder as I hurry down the slope, oblivious to the mysteries held within those decrepit walls.

Back at lake level, I find out that I have been walking through the forest for six hours. Six hours of perfect calm.

Paul, the exchange student whose house I am staying at, invites me to a midsummer party and in contrast with the perfect calm, I find myself hopping around a maypole with strangers, singing a song about a little frog in Swedish. We are surrounded by trees and the foreign words have been printed phonetically, but even that is near impossible to read. The Swedes, lean and tall with fair hair, the boys almost as pretty as the girls, laugh as people from all over Europe tie their tongues in knots trying to pronounce words that have no meaning to them.

How is it that I am celebrating midsummer with Swedish people in Italy when my plan had been to spend midsummer in Sweden experiencing perpetual sunlight alone? I will head north soon, I will find the everlasting sun.

As with the way of giddy summer parties in which alcohol flows freely, I find myself surrounded by pretty girls.

I move from stranger to stranger, boy to girl and girl to boy, Italian to Indian and Austrian to Australian. There are so many people from all over the world, but I have no more than a few minutes of familiarity with each of them. Like trying to memorise a brand new set of Tarot cards in a foreign language, each unique and different, interacting with so many new people is mentally exhausting.

Three Turkish girls with long dark hair and dark eyes approach me. Are they all quite beautiful or am I drunk on summer? "We heard you hitchhiked here."

I am grateful for a conversation that doesn't begin with a name and where I'm from. Better to be pigeon holed by an unusual past-time than by nationality. Stories of Turkey and Italy span past the introductory few minutes and the four of us sit on the floor, content to cease mingling. A welcome respite.

"Getting lucky?" Paul whispers in my ear hours later. "You've been with these girls all night."

I shake my head. I am grateful for their company, but simple conversation for one night is quite enough. Paul winks at me, ignoring my words.

Temples and roads, religious rule and pizza, what were we talking about again? Have we been talking forever? I get up from my little circle, thank the girls for being the most interesting people I have met all night, and excuse myself from the party. It's late, I am content, and I am tired. Hazily, Paul and I stumble back to his house and I wonder aloud if I will ever see any of those people again. What were their names? Whose favourite animal was a rat? Do I need to remember?

Less strangers, more single serving friends, and the feel of warm honey on my brain. Yum.

6. My Precious

Mountains as far as the eye can see, ribboned roads twisting up steep inclines, and snow under my feet. The weather is perfect and I can see for miles. If my fingers weren't about to drop off, I would want to stay here forever. The wind rips into my face and I climb down from the fence I've been standing on, regretting only wearing a t-shirt, and run back to the van. My nipples attempt to cut holes in my clothing.

"This is a beautiful place, like something from a movie." I praise the Swiss Alps to the proud and bearded Swiss cellist who is showing off his homeland.

"The most beautiful in all the world."

He turns on the heating and we continue driving. In the back of his van, there is nothing but a mattress and a cello. It's a home on wheels, the sort of open plan van I wrote about in my dreamy notebooks when I was a teenager, but never got around to finding.

"I used to hitchhike a lot when I was your age. I did a lot of illegal train riding out in America too. Didn't know a word of English when I went out there and ended up staying for three years." More exciting tales. Every day I hear enough good stories to fill a book. Before I came on this journey, I had almost forgotten that we humans are one and the same. We all live through life, breathing and bleeding, hoping and wishing, dreaming and dying. We all have a story to tell.

After twisting through more epic displays of nature, the bearded cellist stops his van in a high mountain pass.

"I'm going to go walking in the mountains. You can get out here and walk somewhere too or you can carry on hitchhiking."

It's an open offer to do as I please, but not an invitation to walk with him. As beautiful as the mountains are, I have a backpack that is too heavy, beds waiting for me in Zurich and Germany, but most of all, a desire to reach Sweden before darkness returns. I thank the man and tell him I will continue on my way. I have over a thousand miles to traverse before I even reach the south of Sweden and many more to go after that.

"If you are still waiting when I'm done walking, I'll pick you up again. Unless I sleep in the mountains." Fair.

In the fresh air of the quiet mountain pass, the views are stunning. I pull my camera out to take a photo and while I'm in the process of balancing it on my improvised tripod more commonly used as a backpack, a car appears over the hill. I scrabble back to the roadside and throw out my thumb, leaving my belongings where they are.

The first car to pass and it has stopped for me! Cold mountain air and low volumes of traffic will bother me not.

I run back to my belongings, throw my camera into the backpack, and shuffle back to open the car door.

"No, no, NO!" the man screams in terror as I open the back door. I slam the door in surprise. Am I monster, is there a dinosaur following me, do I look like I've got an infectious flesh eating disease? The car then races forward a few metres and I realise that there is a second car behind. In my hurry to grab my belongings, I didn't notice that two cars had pulled up within seconds. One was taking a photo and one was offering me a ride, but foolishly the tourists stopped right next to me. I'm laughing as I throw my bag into the right car and the girl driving laughs along with me.

"Did you hear that man scream?"

"I think you terrified him."

"I'm a scary looking guy."

She looks at me, turning her head on the side, then bursts out laughing. "Even I'm not scared of you." I like this girl already.

Outside the car, visual delights continue. Lakes, snow, mountains, valleys. It's all so natural and so very large.

We are so very small.

"What are you doing in the mountains?"

I tell her that I am trying to get to Sweden. "What are you doing in the mountains?"

"I just came to set up a summer camp. Next week I have lots of city kids coming to play games and to learn about the outdoors. We'll be in the mountains for a whole week."

Taking kids away from computer games and into nature? I am even more impressed by this girl.

In Zurich, I get out of the car and pull my bag from the boot. The car is blocking the road and another vehicle honks aggressively. I rush to get hold of my belongings, many of them spilling into the boot in my fumble. I must have left my backpack undone. Throwing everything into my bag, I give the biggest smile I can and wave goodbye.

What a great person, I think I'll write something about her in my notebook.

My notebook…

It's gone.

I root through my bag, but it's not there. It must have fallen out in the car.

The notebook was full of every precious thought I have, memories of the past and ideas for the future. A hundred pages of myself in scribbles and sketches. I could not have lost something more valuable.

Please, no. Anything but my notebook.

I slump to the floor, my head in my hands, eyes closed. How could I not see it? Is it possible I left it in Como?

No, I remember using my notebook as a platform to stand my camera on in the mountain pass. Maybe it fell off there. It's an hour or two back to the mountains, but it's worth going back if I'll find it. But I don't think I will, it must be in that car.

I will find that car. I will post on every internet board, every everything to find it. One way or another, word will spread and someone will get my notebook back to me. What was that girl's name again? I don't think I even asked.

'Lost notebook, left in car somewhere in Swiss Alps. Female driver.' I need more details, but I have none.

Think harder, there must be a way. Could I find the summer camp and track down the girl this way? I know that the camp takes place in the mountains… but the Swiss Alps are pretty big. Unlikely solution, but not impossible.

There must be a better way.

I'm still on the floor with my eyes closed when another car stops to give me a ride.

"No thanks, I need to think for a minute," I say to the driver. I look up. "YOU!" I shout in delight, leaping to my feet. "You came back!"

"I found your notebook."

"You cannot know how much this means to me. This is everything important in my life, my most precious belonging in the world." I want to hug her, but she's inside the car so I simply perform an involuntary celebratory jig, my heart swelling with gratitude.

"I understand, I have one too. I got home before I found it, but it looked like you had some important stuff in there."

"I think you are my hero, my notebook hero. Thank you, so so so very much."

She drives off and I am beaming, inside and out.

What a great, great person.

That's twenty-four great people who have given me perfectly lovely lifts. Or twenty-three if I don't include the bodyguard.

Maybe my friends were wrong when they told me that I'd be mugged or attacked. Maybe the world isn't so bad. Maybe, just maybe, people, when given the chance, are perfectly wonderful after all.

7. Receiving

Knock, knock, anyone home? No one seems to be answering. OK, I'll send her a message.

'I am outside your house. No one is answering the door.'

Beep beep, that was quick.

'I'm with sheep on the mountain.'

I read the message aloud, hoping to clarify the meaning, but it doesn't help. I'm standing outside the house of a girl I have never met, trying to get inside, and she is playing shepherd. Is this what happens in Zurich?

"What are you doing in our garden?" I spin around to find a short and feisty red-headed girl eying me suspiciously.

"I was… just… I was meant to be staying here… but the girl who invited me… is on a mountain. With sheep." Surely that is too unusual to have been made up.

"Well don't stand around in the garden like a creep, come inside." She talks at me like I am an imbecile.

Inside, I find an assortment of cubby holes fashioned into beds, and belongings scattered up the stair-case. There must be at least fifty pairs of shoes. We ascend three floors to find the kitchen and the fiery girl walks into a bedroom without a word, closing the door behind her.

In a kitchen full of people, I feel like an idiot. Hi, you don't know who I am, but I've come to stay in your house. "Hi, I'm staying here tonight. I think." Five people introduce themselves to me within seconds. They are a motley selection of regular looking students and hippy wannabes.

"Would you like some food?" says a sixth guy, appearing in the doorway with a huge bowl of food which he puts on the table next to some drinks and a smouldering ashtray. "Or a joint?"

"I just need water for now please. How many people live here?" I can't help but feel that I am in some kind of squat.

"Uh, no idea. Maybe twelve. I sleep here mostly, but I don't have a room."

Quite a special place. I ask where I should sleep and after checking out a few occupied cubby-holes, we find a spare mattress in the basement. I am sharing the dark room with an English couple who seem even more baffled than I.

For two days, I have no idea who lives in the house or why there are so many people there. I get taken to mountains, an open-air concert, and watch a football game on a crowded bed. Then I walk out the door one morning, not saying goodbye to anyone because they all seem to be asleep, and continue on my way. I never even met the girl who invited me to stay in the first place.

What a curious place. No private possessions, no locked doors, no need for rules: a kind of commune. If only all the world operated like that.

After rushing through Germany at many hundreds of miles a day, I am standing outside in the dark. Just two hundred miles to Hamburg, then I have another comfy bed for the night at another cousin's house. I wish I had made it already, but Germany isn't the best country for hitchhiking. It isn't terrible either, but Germans seem to be very functional and busy people and hitchhiking just isn't proper. Most often, I find myself met with looks of bewilderment and derision, but rarely wait more than thirty minutes for a ride.

Here we go again, one more lift. I stand under a street light and wave at the passing cars.

A gigantic truck stops, but the cab is already occupied by three people. One of them leaps out and directs me towards his cargo. It appears to be a giant, windowless cabin made of plastic.

"You want me to go in there?" The man speaks no English, but my look explains all. I am not getting into the back of a lorry with people I cannot communicate with.

Opening the door of the cabin, I peek inside, careful not to stand too close. Like the witch in Hansel and Gretel, I don't want to be thrown into a fire pit against my will. Inside, a man sits at a table. He's old. Not bent over old, but lined with old age, his head shaved to counteract hair loss. His face seems so harmless that before I can think about it, I'm climbing into the cabin when moments before I had refused to do such a thing.

"Hamburg?" I shout to the guy who is about to close the door. He says something I don't understand, then plunges the room into near complete darkness. The only light comes from a small perspex window above the table. I sit down opposite the man with the harmless face.

"Hello. Do you speak English?"

He shrugs his shoulders.

"Are we going to Hamburg?"

Another shoulder shrug.

We sit in silence for a few minutes, racing along the autobahn, one of the only roads in the world that doesn't have a maximum speed limit.

Oh no. What have I done? I'm in the back of a lorry, late at night, with no idea where I'm going. Where is my get out of jail free card?

The man, sensing my agitation, offers me a bottle of apple juice. Is it poisoned? Will it send me to sleep and I'll wake up...

I'll just sip it.

I open the cap, sip the tiniest amount, and smile at the man.

He has a harmless face. I point at him. "Deutsch?"

No, he isn't German.

He begins gesturing with his hands, throwing in occasional words here and there in the hope I understand. Occasionally he draws a figure on the table with the tip of his finger. Slowly I start to get it.

"You are from... Kazakhstan. You live in... Russia... no, you lived in Russia? Yes. Now you live in Germany? Yes. You lived in Russia for... guns? For military service! You love Kazakhstan... but something is bad... the military is bad... and the money is bad. But Germany is good." He must have come here for a better life. "You don't know what I'm saying right now, but even though we are worlds apart, I think you, I, and the whole world are all looking for the same thing. We are all looking for a better life, a way to be happy."

He continues his gestures and I continue my attempted translation.

"You have a daughter... nine, no eight years old... and your father is driving... no, your wife... your father's wife? Ah, your wife's father, your father-in-law is driving the truck. Wow." Even without language, we understand each other.

The truck stops and after a few seconds, the door opens.

"Osnabrück!" the father-in-law proclaims. I have no idea where Osnabrück is. In fact, I've never heard of it. I climb out of the plastic cabin, nod to the man at the table, and investigate my surroundings. An empty garage, a quiet crossroads, and a little bit of greenery. It's after midnight and the area is poorly lit. I sit at the crossroads and wave half-heartedly at the occasional passing car. It doesn't seem that anyone will pick me up.

At the edge of a legitimate campsite, but on the illegitimate side of the fence, I set my tent up in the shadows. No one will disturb me here.

I disappear into my sleeping bag once more.

SCHOooow! An iron monster races past. Panicked, I leap into the roof of my tent.

Mechanical, powerful, and screaming in a deadly voice, I open my tent to see a train disappear into the distance. I thought I had been underneath it when it passed. Investigating the other side of the fence, I realise that I am sleeping less than five metres from train tracks. Well done again, me.

Haunted by the thought of trains derailing and crushing me in the night, I drag my tent behind the largest tree I can find without leaving the safety of the shadows. At least here, I hope that any passing trains will be deflected around me.

How strong is tree?

Every hour on the hour, all through the night, another train passes. Despite this, I am pleasantly surprised as I awake to find that no train derailed and flattened me during the dark hours. Now that daylight has appeared, I stretch my tired limbs and concede that I must continue north.

Scandinavia is so close, I can almost taste it.

At my cousin's house in Hamburg, I am introduced to her two children for the very first time. They are both lovely and I ask how old they are.

"Two and three, nearly four."

"That's a long time since I saw you last." A curse of travelling, is that you lose touch with people, even your family. "I'll try and not leave it five years until I see you next time."

I'm gone again.

Three hundred miles to Copenhagen where another bed awaits me. Got to go, got to make it, got to find that sun. I will make it today.

Take me people, this is what I've been waiting for.

"Thanks for the ride," I grin, getting into another vehicle. It's happening.

"It's not a problem," the man says meekly. His persona is smaller than his strong build: a shy man in a boxer's body with only a hint of a German accent. "Where do you want to go?"

"North, towards Denmark."

"And you are travelling alone?" I nod. "And you travel like this?" I nod again. "What about sleeping?"

"Sometimes I camp, sometimes people invite me into their homes. It changes each night depending upon where I am."

Excited, the man beams. "That's really wonderful." For the next hour, he asks me question after question, growing in confidence and becoming more animated as our conversation flows. He says little of himself, reeling off questions about me before I have time to ask anything of him.

"I would like to live like you someday." His statement is a true expression of desire, free from malignant envy.

"I am sure you can do it if you want to."

"I know, I'm just not ready yet." Many people tell me that I am lucky to have the freedom to do as I am doing, but this man does not. Instead, he compliments me on my decision to grasp this opportunity. When we come to a small exit, he asks if I have time to see something. I tell him that I do and he drives me to a small clearing in the forest where a delicate waterfall ribbons down a rock face. Song birds flit from branch to rock and back again.

"You see, most people don't even know that this is here. They are racing by in their fast cars with their fast lives and they cannot see the waterfall. Can you hear the road in the distance? It's so close, but those people are so far away. That is the world I live in every day, the world of fast cars and fast lives."

I thank him for showing me the peace of the waterfall and we continue. He then offers to buy me lunch.

"Thank you, but you don't need to do that."

"I'd like to." Again, I try to politely decline. "Let me ask you something then. This is related to what we were talking about earlier. Where do you live?"

"I… I don't live anywhere. I live right here."

"OK, so you're homeless."

"That's a twist of my words…"

"What is your job?"

"You know I don't have one."

"So you are unemployed. That makes you homeless and unemployed."

"By choice."

"Yes, by choice. And do I pity you? No, I envy you."

"You envy me?"

"You have chosen to do something unorthodox and unusual, something against all rules of society, all because you want to. I envy you for being brave enough to do that."

"Brave?" I chuckle. "I think you have me wrong here. I'm not brave to do this. In fact, I'm too scared to continue doing something that I feel would crush my soul. That's why I left my job and everything else behind."

"What do other people think of your decisions?"

"To do this? They think I'm crazy. I'm not crazy: I just don't see myself spending my days in an office. Every routine day where I experience nothing of pleasure, I feel myself dying inside. Having a stable life is wonderful if you enjoy it and it gives you pleasure, but I haven't found a stable life that offers me that yet."

"But now you are doing something that makes you happy?"

"I am. In five or twenty years time, I will still remember all of these days. It is important to live through days that are special enough to remember."

"I want to do this, but I am too scared of leaving my job in case things don't work out. I've worked so hard to get to where I am and I am afraid that if I quit, I might end up with no money and no way back." I wait for him to continue and he waits for me to respond.

I relent first. "I do not know your life, but if you want to quit, quit. I left all I had not just because I was looking for something else in life, but because I wasn't happy with what I was doing. You don't have to travel the world or move mountains to find happiness, you simply sustain it with a series of positive and pleasurable events, no matter how tiny. I think the real question right now, is what do you have to lose?"

"Not much."

"Someone wise once taught me this little exercise, would you like to try it?" He nods. "When you get home tonight, take a piece of paper and rip it into three. On one piece of paper, write the next ten years of your life assuming that you change nothing and continue on your current path. On the next piece of paper, write the next ten years of your life, assuming you make changes and things go badly. Finally, write the next ten years, assuming that you make changes and things go well. Then take the three pieces of paper and compare them. Which of those lives would be the worst to live? Then make sure you stay away from that one."

Both deep in thought, we drive in silence for a few minutes.

"Have you heard of the Kaballah?" the man asks, breaking the silence.

"It sounds familiar."

"In my limited understanding, it concerns teachings and ideas from Judaism. I'm not a religious man, but I read about this purely for interest. In the Kaballah, the first stage of giving and receiving involves the simple act of one person giving something to another. The second stage is the giving of a gift that benefits the receiver. The third stage is where the bestower of the gift receives pleasure from giving the gift. The fourth stage is where the receiver accepts a gift that they don't want, purely for the pleasure it brings to the giver. There are more stages, but they elude me. Basically, I would like to buy you lunch to say thank you, so please accept it, even if you do not want it because it would make me happy."

"I don't think I have ever heard such a persuasive argument for a free lunch!" His words make sense in a curious way. Since I've been on the road, I've already had so much given to me in the form of drinks, food, and whatever else drivers have with them. Often people stop at a garage and come back with a sandwich or cold drink, limitless gestures of kindness, despite me expecting nothing.

After lunch, we part ways and the gentle boxer tries to hand me some Danish currency from his dashboard.

"I can't accept this. If I was to perform on the streets and to wow audiences, I would accept money, but I am just wandering an idle path and seek no reward from others. My journey itself is my reward."

"I don't plan on ever going back to Denmark and it would make me happy to give this to you. Remember the Kaballah. Besides, it's only about five euros worth."

Reluctantly, I accept the notes and wish the man well. I cannot help but feel that I have just met someone very wise.

"I hope you find what you are looking for."

"I hope you do too."

I contemplate his words as he disappears. What he said about homes and jobs makes perfect sense. Everybody asks me the same questions when they meet me: where do I live and what do I do? When they ask me where I live, they will judge what type of person I am by associating everything they know about my homeland with how I must be as a person. Then they will find out how successful I am and what prestige I hold within society by assessing my occupation. Mostly when I tell people I have no home or job, they look at me with disdain, confusion, and sorrow because they assume that I want a job and a home, because that is what they want.

People can only offer you advice based upon what they want and don't want in life. They can only advise you what to do based upon what they would and wouldn't do.

I choose not to have a big TV and a fixed interest mortgage. I choose not to work hard all my life and to save for a comfortable retirement. I choose not to choose a career path. I will live in the moment, the here and now, blown whichever way the wind takes me. This is not my path forever, but for now.

I am not changing the world and I am not setting records. I am doing little more than following through on the whimsical ideas that race through my mind. The glorious highs and disastrous lows matter to no one but me. But none of it is permanent and none of it lasts forever.

Nothing lasts forever, not even the universe itself.

Thank you Mr. Gentle Boxer man, you know much more than I. You have given me so much more than a free lunch.

Next time someone asks me where I live and what I do, I will tell them that I am happily homeless and blissfully unemployed. For now. And I will mean it with all of my heart.

8. Transience

"Je suis un Musulman."

I look at my Algerian driver. What does that mean? Is he a muscle man? Maybe he works for a museum? A museum man. I wish I knew more French.

He makes some gestures and finally I get it. He is a Muslim!

He tells me of the magic of Allah and how his own voice fills with love when he sings the words of the Quran, then rhythmically chants well practised Arabic words.

I listen.

Explaining that these words are more special than normal words, he begins to sing in French. Can I hear the difference he asks, the magic in the words of the Quran? I apologise and tell him that I can't. Sometimes, we hear what we want to hear or an absence of it. Have I ever considered becoming a Muslim? What an unusual question to ask.

"No, but I have tried Ramadan," I attempt to translate into French. He looks at me with surprise then asks me to tell him more.

"At university, I couldn't sleep at six in the morning so I was walking in my student housing and found some people eating waffles in the common room. They invited me to eat with them and told me about Ramadan, suggesting I try it to gain a little appreciation of what they go through. For two days I didn't eat or drink during the long sunlight hours. There was a big celebration one evening with hundreds of people, nearly all Muslims, and they asked me to watch as they prayed. Unfortunately, I was in the middle of the room and when the call to prayer started, everyone dropped to their knees. The room was so full that it was impossible for me to move. There I was, standing in a sea of people who were on the floor in prayer. My rabbit brain said copy them, so I dropped to my knees and for the next few minutes, copied everything that the people around me were doing." Even telling the story flushes my cheeks with embarrassment. I bowed and straightened time and time again, wishing to be anywhere else but there at that moment in time. Fortunately, everyone around me had been amused, rather than offended.

Mildly comprehending, the Algerian man seems to look favourably upon my story. He drives me to his home and gives me a box of Algerian dates before taking me back to the highway and dropping me at a service station. A white van immediately pulls up and I can't believe my luck. This is my ride into Denmark, I'm almost at the border.

To my dismay, rather than offering me a ride, the van drops off another hitchhiker before speeding away.

A guy with long red hair walks towards me, flicking it away from his face with his fingertips as he approaches.

Oh no, he is going to steal my hitchhiking spot. I'll never get to Denmark like this, surely no one will pick up two guys.

"Hello," is all I can muster.

"Hello." It takes only one word for me to realise that he is Irish. "My name's Sam." I shake Sam's hand. He looks much younger than me and tells me that he is on his university holidays. That makes him about twenty.

As we are both heading into Denmark, we decide to continue together.

It would be rude not to.

We climb into a Bulgarian truck and Sam begins speaking fluently with the driver in Russian. Inside the cab there are two bunks behind the seats, so as Sam chats happily with the driver, I rest in one of the bunks. This is great, I don't have to do anything.

Bouncing along with the truck, I feel myself drifting into dream land, happy to be entering Scandinavia. I've never been to Denmark before…

"Get up!"

"What? Was I sleeping?"

"We're in Denmark." I shake myself awake, nod to the driver, and pass our backpacks down the ladder to Sam who climbs out before me.

"That was a pleasant ride."

"What, all five minutes of it that you were awake for?"

An excitable, techno loving German picks us up next. After a few minutes of English conversation, Sam breaks out in fluent German. This guy could be useful.

I watch the world outside the window, once again unaware of the topic of the conversation. We get out of the car at a small junction. The land is flat and the wind blows off the sea which we can see on the opposite side of the motorway. A few cars race by at high speed, but it seems unlikely that any of them would have time to stop in such a location. I suggest to Sam that we move to the small roundabout on the slip road. It looks pretty quiet, but at least cars will be able to stop.

After the best part of an hour, light is fading and only a handful of cars have passed. We look at the sea longingly, contemplating a late night swim and sleeping on the beach. Sam asks if I'm ready to give it up for the night.

"Three more cars. Let's give them our sad faces."

The first car approaches the round-about and races by without looking twice.

"One down, two to go."

It's ten minutes before another car comes. Presumably a mother and daughter, we put on the saddest, most hopeful faces we can muster.

"No chance," I laugh as they race by us and towards the motorway. Girls do not want to pick up strange men from the side of the road.

"One more car to go, then the beach."

A strange mechanical whirring approaches from behind. We look up the slip road to see the mother and daughter reversing back down towards us.

"Ha! It was the sad faces that did it!" We run up the hill and gratefully climb into the tiny car. It seems that many drivers pass hitchhikers, only to be stricken by guilt seconds later. At this point they are already in the flow of traffic and it is too late to turn around. Fortunately for us, the road is deserted so the car was able to come back. The girl tells us about being a Thai-boxer and drives us all the way to Copenhagen.

"Do you have somewhere to stay tonight?" I ask Sam.

"I have a sleeping bag." Sam has been sleeping outside with just his sleeping bag and no tent since he left the UK, but I tell him I'll ask my host if he can stay too. A text message a few minutes later confirms that she doesn't mind.

We sit down at the table in another stranger's home. Anna is a very reserved Danish girl who works long hours and offers us the freedom of her home.

"Would you like something to eat? I have some salad." Eying delicious bean-filled salads, we nod excitedly. Neither of us have had anything to eat for most of the day. Anna disappears into the kitchen and we soon smell fish frying.

"Sam, you're going to have to eat that if she brings it through. I'm vegetarian."

"So am I!"

"Damn. Go and tell her that we can't eat it."

"You go and tell her that we can't eat it." The smell of fish grows stronger.

"There is only one way to settle this: rock, paper, scissors."

"One, two, three…"

Sam's rock breaks my scissors. I scrunch my face up and flex my fingers in agitation. Someone I have never met before has invited me into her home and when I asked if I could bring a new friend, she said yes. She then prepared dinner for the two of us and now we're going to tell her that we won't eat it because it's not vegetarian. This is so awkward. Why do things have to be so awkward?

I walk into the kitchen and it gets worse. Two fish steaks are frying, one for Sam and one for me. Anna isn't even making any for herself.

"Anna…"

"Yes?" She has such an innocent and friendly face.

"Sam and I… are vegetarians… we don't eat fish." Anna flushes with as much embarrassment as I feel. I try to offer my best apologetic face, but take on the appearance of someone sucking on lemons.

"It's OK, I'll eat it for lunch tomorrow. I don't normally buy fish anyway, I just…" Her words trail away as she tries to brush off the incident with an unconvincing smile.

At the dinner table, Sam and I eat while Anna drinks water. "Why are you both vegetarian?"

I look at Sam who looks back at me. We met hours before and know almost nothing of each other, so take it in turns to speak. Sam explains his reasoning and I tell Anna that I haven't eaten meat since I was seven.

"I don't need it to survive, so I choose not to eat it for environmental and moral reasons. If I ever find myself in a survival situation, I would prefer to kill an animal myself than to buy it from the supermarket." Anna nods which is a friendlier response than I get from most people. I'm normally met with a proclamation of how delicious meat is or that we should save the trees and eat the vegetarians.

Anna goes to bed early, leaving Sam and I alone. We explore the city by night.

"Normally," Sam begins, "I don't buy food." Oh no, have I just met a kleptomaniac? Do I have to hide my camera from him and to watch him if we go near a shop?

"How do you eat?"

"I go dumpster diving."

"The same as skipping?"

"Yeah." He eats from bins! That is a million times better than stealing.

"I tried it once. A friend of mine was doing a research project on being thrifty and we went out in the town late one night to see what food we could find in the supermarket bins. There was so much waste. I looked up some figures online and found out that around half of food that is produced, never gets eaten because it isn't perfect or it gets discarded on its sell-by-date. It's such a waste when there are so many hungry people in the world. Do you do this back at home? And where is your home?" There I am, asking the same question I have been asked so many times over.

"I'm at university in the north of England and I go skipping every week. In fact, this year I only bought food about five times."

"And presumably you're studying languages?"

"How did you guess?!"

The city of Copenhagen is neither beautiful nor ugly. It's indistinct. I could be almost anywhere in Europe, but it's hard to tell. We walk through unmemorable streets until we find some shops and I decide that I would like to try skipping again.

"How about this one?" I say, pointing to a small convenience store. We investigate all around the shop, but find only large metal doors and presume that the bins must be inside. At the next three shops, it's the same situation. Outside a bigger shop, the bins are padlocked inside a large metal cage. This metal cage is also padlocked, but has no roof.

Sam curses the people who put padlocks on the bins, then explains that some supermarkets do it to stop people getting hold of discarded food. "They think that they are losing sales, but the people who go dumpster diving were never going to buy things in the first place. Actually, most of the people I know who dumpster dive, do it to reduce waste, not for financial reasons."

As a child who grew up in forests, climbing trees, a seven foot cage takes me all of two seconds to scale. I drop in through the open roof and try to open the bins. My heart is racing. What if somebody catches me here? Is it a crime to take rubbish?

The padlock is in the middle of the bin and allows me to lift the corner up by a few inches. I try and look in, but it's too dark and anything that is in the bin is too low for me to reach through the small gap. Frustrated, I climb out again and tell Sam I want to keep looking. The fear of being caught is coursing adrenaline through my veins.

The next bins are unlocked and exposed. As we approach them, someone leaps out from them and I jump into the air. The guy runs away, clearly thinking that we had come to stop him rooting around in the bins. How curious that I've bumped into a hitchhiker and a skipper all in one day. We take a couple of cartons of out of date milk and concede that most of the produce must have been taken already, but once again, my heart is racing.

Adrenaline is addictive. One more shop.

Once again, the bins are in an enclosure. This time it is wooden and taller than I can reach with my arms outstretched. I take a run-up and cling to the top. Pulling myself over, I drop to the floor inside. No one can see me. Adrenaline courses once more.

Inside the bins, I find multiple loaves of bread and pots of cream. I shout to Sam who catches them as I throw them over.

"We can't carry any more," he calls back. I scrabble back over and investigate our findings in the dim street-light. We have multiple loaves of delicious, dark looking bread that cost several pounds each. In total, our finds are financially equivalent to several days on the road.

"This is incredible. Delicious bread and for free." I am so happy at this new revelation.

"I normally find more than this," Sam says, disappointed.

"What's the legal status of this?"

"It varies from country to country, but I once got stopped by a policeman in

England. I asked him if he was really going to arrest me for looking around in a bin and he sheepishly conceded that I wasn't causing a problem and let me go."

We take our stash back to the apartment and offer it as breakfast the next morning. Anna needs never know where it came from.

In Copenhagen, there is a small community known as Freetown Christiania that Sam tells me about. We head there to investigate and I find my eyes being opened to a world that I never even knew existed. Christiania is a self-proclaimed autonomous neighbourhood often regarded as a large commune by civic authorities. Inside the small area, we are met by ramshackle buildings, some brick and some constructed from discarded materials, that host an eclectic mix of hippies and alternative individuals who have chosen to live outside the traditional conforms of society. Graffiti covers most surfaces and it seems that the whole place is an outdoor art exhibition proclaiming freedom from authorities. Sadly the area may soon succumb to government pressure and be forced to amalgamate with the rest of the city. Despite this, multiple stands sell nothing but marijuana and Sam and I stop at a small clothing rail to investigate what they have for sale.

Sam picks up a pair of white cotton trousers and holds them aloft.

"What do you think?"

"Hippy pants!"

We both invest in a pair of trousers and marvel at how comfortable they are. Mine are dark red with an elastic waist band and if I pull the elasticated ankles up to my knees, they remind me of pants that Aladdin might wear.

"Now we look like hitchhikers, right?!"

Back at Anna's house, we look up maps and roads into Sweden. There is an email from my mother who I have told that I will meet anywhere in Europe if she wants to spend her birthday abroad. She tells me that she'd like to go to Italy.

From Paris to Italy I went with Jenna and because of this, I had to traverse one thousand miles back up the continent in order to reach Scandinavia. But that's OK. I had a wonderful few days with Jenna in the prestigious Italian resort towns and if my mother wants to spend her birthday in Italy, I will go back there.

The people you visit places with are sometimes more important than the places themselves.

"Sam, I'm not coming to Sweden with you anymore. I'm going back to Italy."

Such is the transient nature of travel.

9. Struggles

Seven nights until I meet my mother and one of my brothers in Italy. We've settled on Desenzano Del Garda, a town on the supposedly beautiful Lake Garda that can be reached easily from Milano airport. It's over a thousand miles away. I send an email to my mother telling her that I will meet her there and find another from a friend, inviting me to visit him in his small French hometown, Vitry-le-François. I scribble his address down in my notebook and add the new town into my route on the computer. I am met with a one thousand, four hundred mile journey.

Can I traverse fourteen hundred miles in one week and still enjoy myself? Probably.

Sam and I start walking out to the highway. Neither of us have enough cash for a bus and are unwilling to withdraw any of our dwindling funds to save a short walk.

An hour later we part ways, he heading east to Sweden, me west in search of the southern road to France. The invariably broken promise of travellers, we agree to try and meet up somewhere in Eastern Europe in a few weeks.

Three hours on, I almost find the junction I have been looking for, but it is obstructed by roadworks and large fencing. I am so close to the road out of the city, but I am in need of a ride and there isn't anywhere for cars to stop. I've been walking since early morning and I have got nowhere.

In red hippy-pants, I climb the roadwork fencing with my backpack on and drop to the other side. It takes half an hour to traverse the tricky building work, only to find myself shuffling along a narrow walkway above a river and climbing more walls and fences. How does this happen? What a ridiculous situation I am in.

At the junction, I find traffic lights and signs indicating that I am in the right place. Sam gave me a marker pen and I write a big 'DEU' in one of my notebooks and hold it up for passing cars to see. Look at me people, I'm going to Germany, take me with you.

No one wants to take me.

Every time the lights turn red, I run along the stopped cars and wave my sign at them. Occasionally a driver shrugs apologetically, but mostly they pretend not to see me. Are people embarrassed to look at me? Is this what it feels like to busk on the streets and be shunned by passers-by? Next time I see a busker, I will at least look and offer a smile.

After an hour, I concede that I won't get a ride and climb back over the fences, over the river, and through the building site. I put my bag down next to a bus stop. Six hours ago, I left Anna's house and since then, nothing. This is not how things were supposed to be.

A flat-bed truck turns the corner sharply in front of me and his poorly strapped load tumbles into the road. I run out to pick up the fallen window frames as cars approach and help him to load them back onto his vehicle, flashing him my DEU sign. He looks at me blankly before taking off.

Back in the bus stop, I am waving at everyone. Help me out of this city!

A low car swerves into the bus stop at high speed and I jump back in surprise. An extremely attractive girl leans out the window and offers me a ride in an almost British accent. Streaked hair, a slightly upturned nose, and the hint of an Aussie surfer girl come elegant Scandinavian. After six hours of walking and waiting, I jump into the car before asking where she's going.

The wait forgotten, we happily chat away about the world and how great it is.

A car slams on its brakes ahead of us.

I point, my eyes popping out of my head.

The girl, looking at me and concentrating on our conversation, sees it incredibly late. She slams on her brakes and we skid across the road into the lane of oncoming traffic. A lapse in traffic means we don't hit another car.

"It's OK," I tell her, my heart pounding, hands clenched into tight fists. "We're OK."

The girl is physically shaking and she struggles to re-start the stalled car, speaking quickly under her breath in Danish.

"We're OK," I tell her again. "Look. We're safe." Inside I am shaking as much as her.

She gets the car going and we tentatively edge forward, keeping a large distance from other cars.

"We were so close to hitting that car," she says when the ability of speech returns to her.

"I must confess, I thought we were going to hit it. I'm not a big fan of cars at the best of times."

"Then why are you hitchhiking?"

"Free travel, a good way of meeting people, the unexpected. And aeroplanes freak me out even more." Do I believe myself yet?

We drive into the Roskilde Festival ground as the girl tells me that she is volunteering in exchange for free tickets. It will only take a few minutes to pick them up.

We are in a sparsely populated area surrounded by trees and fields, but tomorrow over one hundred thousand people will attend the four day event.

"Do you think they need any more staff?" I ask tentatively? This is too much of an opportunity to pass up.

I follow her into the staff area. If I work here, I would still have three more days to make it to Italy. I approach a group of people and ask if they need more volunteers. They tell me that they probably do, but I will have to wait for an hour until their boss arrives to confirm this. Should I stay and wait in the hope that they need more people or should I continue and visit my friend? I don't like to gamble and the element of doubt persuades me to continue on my path. Back in the car, I listen to stories of how amazing the festival is and begin to rue my decision, but it's done now.

Buoyed from the friendly conversation and not crashing, I am bouncing around on the side of the road as I try to get another lift.

An hour later, my spirits are dampened.

Stupid red hippy pants making me look silly, Danish people laughing and not picking me up, hundreds of miles from where I need to be. I change out of my hippy pants and back into my cargo shorts. Now I look more normal. A kind man offers me both cold Pepsi and a ride within minutes of my clothing change.

"Take these for the road," the man says, holding out four more cans.

Buzzing on sugar, I am back on top of the world. So what if I have only travelled a hundred miles in ten hours, so what if it is six o'clock and I am still seven hundred miles from my friend's house?

A Polish lorry pulls up.

I climb another ladder and take a comfy seat next to the driver. Hitchhiking with truckers always guarantees a comfy ride and more often than not, a long one.

The man speaks only Polish, but I show him roughly where I'm heading on his map of Europe. I can't remember exactly where the town is, but I know the general area.

In sign language, we communicate until I learn my first Polish word. "Pivo?" he asks, before handing me a cold beer. I nod enthusiastically.

When one beer is gone, he hands me another. The friendly trucker radios through to unknown voices every hour as we traverse around four hundred miles and enter the middle of the night. Stopping in a quiet truck park, I am loaded from one vehicle to another.

He found me another lift!

In the new truck, I find a husband and wife. The man speaks very good English and he laughs at me for claiming I had an eight hour conversation with his non-English speaking co-worker.

"What did you talk about?"

"It was more hand gestures and beer rather than talking," I concede.

As the night wears on, I am tired. The trucker says that I can sleep in the top bunk and before I know it, it's morning.

"This is Saarlouis." Looking at his GPS, I figure out that I'm only one hundred and thirty miles from my friend. I've travelled well over seven hundred miles while drinking beer and sleeping. This is what hitchhiking is about!

On a beautiful day, clear skies and scorching sun, I catch ride after ride. Only a few miles each, but everything is going great.

An English van pulls out of a fuel station, the first British vehicle I have seen since leaving the UK nearly a month ago.

"Hey, you! Englishman!" I shout obnoxiously, pointing at the license plate. I'm so excited and dizzy on sunshine and hitchhiking that all etiquette has gone out the window. Amazingly, the guy pulls over. I'm met by a large and loud, topless, but altogether pleasant northerner. I tell him where I'm going, but after looking at a map, I realise it isn't on his route.

"Not a problem mate, I'll take you there." Not wanting to put up too much resistance, I only ask once if he's sure that it isn't a problem, then gratefully accept the ride. This is so perfect.

Undulating green hills roll by the windows as we twist down country roads. Reaching the dot on the map I was aiming for, the Englishman turns around and goes back where he came from, leaving me to find my friend. Of all the places in the town that he could of dropped me, I find myself standing right outside my friend's house. What a perfect day.

I press the buzzer on the gate of the house.

Nothing.

I ring again.

Did he not get my email?

I press the buzzer over and over again.

"Allo?" says a sleepy voice at last. Despite speaking perfect English, Leon still has a very distinct French accent.

"Leon, it's Jamie!"

"Oh, really?" I hear the surprise in his voice. It was only a little over a day ago that I emailed him and told him I was in Denmark and he hasn't heard from me since.

With cold beers we jump into the swimming pool.

Delicious cheese, red wine, and fresh vegetables: my taste buds are on fire. And a real bed!

We awake the next day to be met by more glorious sunshine and take a picnic to a lake. With people I haven't met and armed with a wakeboard, we take to the water in a boat. I've waterskied loads of times and snowboarded even more, surely this will be easy. I leap into the water and as the boat pulls away, I realise that it isn't as easy as I first thought. I let go of the rope as I tumble back into the water.

Try again. Fail. And again. Fail. I look ridiculous, but I will do it.

Six times, seven, I fall back in. Why can I not get the hang of this?

"I'm spent," I shout, "bring the boat back around." I don't want to fail again. I like at least having a chance of winning at games and falling flat on my face is a very public way of losing. I must look ridiculously pathetic, I couldn't even get up once. It takes many minutes of kicking a football around to try and forget about the failure.

After three nights in the small town, I am handed a handwritten address to an apartment in Lyon. Supposedly Lyon is one of France's very pretty cities and the apartment is empty although Leon's brother normally lives there. If I can get to the apartment, the keys are hidden inside the postbox.

Bouncing on tip-toes, I can barely keep my happiness to myself.

Another goodbye to more good people, friends old and new, then back to the road.

Mid-morning, I'm hitchhiking on the motorway, not a place I want to be. I was dropped here by someone who thought it wasn't as dangerous as it seems. It is however, rather dangerous. I seem to be at some kind of major motorway junction and in every direction there are more roads to cross. My only hope is that someone gives me a ride before the police turn up. Hitchhiking is perfectly legal across Europe, except on motorways due to it being so perilous to hitchers and drivers alike.

A Moroccan lady tells me I am in a very bad place after slamming on her brakes to give me a ride, then laughs along to every story I tell terribly in French. I ask her if I can get out near Lyon and after four hours, we roll into Saint-Exupery airport. Despite being named after the author of one of my favourite books of all time, I do not want to be at the airport. Together we walk into the terminal. She has to catch a flight and I want to make it to the city.

Seventeen euros for a train to the city? I'd rather walk.

Affectionately, the girl plants a kiss on each of my cheeks.

What a nice gesture. I like that the French have a defined way of greeting and parting. It's one of those awkward moments in the UK when you never quite know whether to wave, shake hands, hug, or kiss, so invariably end up head-butting your acquaintance in the face before giggling uncontrollably until the embarrassment disappears and you can talk again. Greetings are minefields.

I am resigned to walking as I come out of the airport, fairly sure that no one will pick me up. People are often exasperated and in need of a break after a relaxing vacation. Without even having to signal, an elderly French man pulls over and drives me into the city.

Do journeys get any better than this?

At the door of the address I have written down, I know I am just metres away from the postbox containing the keys. All I have to do is get through this one door. I wait for a few minutes in case anyone goes in or out of the building. No one does.

I can wait a few more minutes.

Still no one.

I might have to press the buzzers. I definitely don't want to press the buzzers. That would involve speaking to a stranger that I can't see. In French!

Still no one.

I close my eyes, take a deep breath, then rub my fingers along the control panel, buzzing every single person in the apartment complex.

Please let me in, please don't speak to me.

Buzz! Yes.

I grab the keys from the postbox and start climbing the stairs. A rather disgruntled elderly lady shouts at me from her doorway. Presumably she buzzed me in and I am not the person that she was hoping to see.

"I forgot the key." I dangle the keychain in the air to show her that I now have it. No doubt this is nonsense to her as I am waving around the very object that I claim to have forgotten.

With the cheapest bottle of house wine that France has to offer, I read in a spacious apartment, alone indoors for the very first time in a month. My music plays softly in the background. For two days, I don't have to make conversation, I don't have to meet anyone, I don't have to do anything at all. It can be so tiring to constantly interact with so many people. And for the first time, I have a bed and the owner of the home is not there, so I do not have to think about how I act or what I do. This is just what I needed.

Leaving the apartment building the next day, I see that the disgruntled woman who buzzed me in has now become a very forlorn woman. She talks sullenly with an elderly man on the staircase. Was this the man she was waiting for? Is this why she shouted at me?

The city of Lyon must have been mixed up with Paris. Archaic buildings, twisted streets, rising hills, this is how I pictured the city of love to be. I climb to the highest point in the city and look down on the rooftops, then wander through historic structures. Today I do not feel lonely. I could walk through this city for days and days.

However, I do not have days. With one night before my family arrive, I hit the road. I have only three hundred and fifty miles to go and after my recent experiences, even the mountain range I have to pass will not slow me down.

After a city bus and several hours of walking, I still can't see a decent place to hitchhike. The sun is unrelenting and my t-shirt, soaked. I wish I brought more water. I enter the forbidden territory of the motorway and hope once again that I get a lift before the police find me.

I do.

But now I've been stuck at this péage for over an hour. Every passing vehicle has to stop to pay their toll at the booth before driving on. They can all see me. I wave fruitlessly.

A daring trucker swings across multiple lanes and I jump in. Slowly, slowly, I will make it.

The peace of the mountains. Why did the truck driver leave me here? Of all the places he could have left me, he has driven me off the highway and to a quiet road several kilometres away from passing traffic. With mountain streams, thick pine forests, and snow covered peaks in the distance, it's beautiful, but I do not have time for beautiful.

I need to hurry, but how can I hurry when it is out of my own hands?

This car is good, but that's another hour lost on waiting. At least they are driving quickly, I'll make time.

I chat with the girl in the passenger seat. Her skin-head boyfriend occasionally chimes in with the only words of English he knows, all offensive. When he tires of the conversation he can't understand, he cranks up the volume so that I can barely hear myself think. I am cut off mid-sentence, the girl shrugging apologetically.

We begin climbing the mountains, a favourite practice arena of tightly clothed cyclists on bicycles that weigh less than the average miniature poodle. As we are close to the invisible French-Italian border, two nations that love road cycling, there are an awful lot of cyclists. Or 'targets' as I am sure the driver sees them. He swerves dangerously close to each cyclist, spraying his windscreen wash at them, laughing maniacally as he does so. He has intentionally repositioned his wiper nozzles sideways for this very pursuit.

He is a very big man showing me how very big and manly he is. I can't even pretend to laugh as he looks back to see if I am amused.

We rejoin the motorway for a brief period, then leave it again and drive down into the valley. I'm fairly sure that the only way to cross the mountains is by passing through the large tunnel on the road we just left. I get dropped off on a quiet road, far from everything except a seemingly abandoned building. Is this another of his funny jokes?

That man was not a nice person.

High in the mountains, the air is cooler. This is a beautiful place, if only I had time to explore it.

At length, I return several miles and reach the motorway.

I do not care if the police come this time. I stand in the road, waving at every passing vehicle. It is evening and if I do not get a ride soon, my mother and brother will arrive in Desenzano Del Garda before I do and they are only staying for two nights.

You truck, take me!

Or you!

There is only one road, why will no one pick me up?

Look at my star jumps car, look at them. Shall I dance for you too?

A ride at last, a car pulls over. A twelve kilometre tunnel, bridges clinging to sheer cliff faces, more holes through solid rock. Man has carved into nature itself.

I am left in a deserted truck park, just off the highway. I climb a big metal tower and look into the distance. All I can see are trees and mountains, not a town in sight. The Italian motorway is surrounded by unassailable perspex fences that make it impossible for someone on foot to walk without being in the way of passing cars. Cars that are passing at immense speed.

I have failed. It is almost dusk and the lorry park may actually be abandoned rather than deserted. Except for me, there isn't a single person here. In a matter of hours my family will arrive in Italy and I will be over two hundred miles away in a lorry park. How depressing. How is it possible that such an unfortunate chain of events can happen in one single day? All I needed was one ride, one good ride, and I would have made it. They're flying all the way to Europe to meet me and I'm not going to be there. What a failure.

One hundred and fifty miles in twelve hours, that's twelve and a half miles an hour. A bicycle could do that!

I sit on the floor sulking, my body threatening to involuntarily curl into the foetal position.

I don't want this anymore. I want it to work.

A sign at the rear of the lorry park indicates that there is a town about thirty kilometres away. That's less than twenty miles. The average human being walks around three miles an hour. If I push hard, I can exceed that, even with my backpack. That's only six or seven hours of walking. That means that by the early hours of the morning, I can be at a town and I can find a way to reach the lakes. That is what I will do.

Five more minutes of moping first.

And five minutes more.

OK, five more. This is like the morning battle with the alarm clock.

I'll move when it is totally dark.

A lady, misreading the signs, turns off the motorway and into the lorry park. I watch as she twists down the entrance ramp and then spins around to drive straight back out the exit ramp.

I get up and I start running. I see her shocked face in the wing mirror. She thinks I am trying to rob her and accelerates away from me.

"Please!"

I stop running and my arms drop to my sides, defeated.

She slows down as she enters the exit ramp, then comes to a stop altogether.

I walk to the car, slower this time. When I get to the window, I clasp my hands together in pleading and offer her my 'please help me' face.

Look at my sad eyes, don't you want to help me? Did I just bow to her?

The woman tentatively opens the door.

I ask her if she speaks English. "A little." Is this my saviour, the woman who got lost on a straight road?

"I need to get to the city. My mother and brother are arriving in a few hours and I'm stuck here. Please can I come with you?" Every part of my being is begging and pleading. She looks at me nervously. I don't think she even knows why she stopped.

"OK."

"I'll just get my bags," I say, every movement and every word deliberate. I have to be careful because she looks as if she still might drive off at any moment. I have rarely seen someone so scared of me. I walk slowly back to my bags without closing the door, making it that little bit more difficult for her to leave. Fortunately, she doesn't.

"Thank you so much." I implore upon her that she has done the right thing.

She tells me that she has never, and would never, stop for a stranger on the side of the road. She stopped only because I looked desperate.

"I was. I am."

In darkness, still petrified of me, she drops me on the outskirts of Turin.

I will ride the train the rest of the way. That way nothing can go wrong.

"Excuse me, do you know where the train station is? No English, OK. Train? Tren? Gare?" No understanding, never mind. Try again. "Excuse me, do you…" No, you don't want to stop for me. That's OK. "Excuse me, do you know where the train station is? Do you understand? You are pointing out of the city, where I just came from. I don't think you understand."

This is hopeless.

Not having eaten all day, I enter a supermarket. My backpack is confiscated and held on the reception desk. Clearly I look like I am going to steal things.

Yum, more plain bread.

I munch on my bread as I walk towards what I presume is the centre of the city. There doesn't seem to be a single bus stop, but surely I'll find one soon.

After fifteen minutes, I find both a metro station and a bus stop. I feel like writing a couple of sentences about my awful day.

Oh no, not again.

My notepad was taken from me when I entered the supermarket in case I snuck a loaf of bread inside it. They never gave it back. The clock outside the metro station reads, '20h55.' For some reason, I remember looking at the supermarket's opening times. It closes in five minutes. It's almost impossible to get back to the store that quickly with this weight on my back.

I run across the street and throw my backpack onto someone's balcony. It contains my camera, my clothes, my everything in the world. But not my notebook. I must get my notebook.

I run and I run, my red hippy pants flapping wildly as I dodge people and objects on the street. My flip-flops flop and flip, hindering my progress. I take them off and run barefoot through the streets.

The supermarket is in sight, but the metal rollers are coming down over the front doors. In my mind, I picture a dramatic run and slide, just like the movies. In reality I reach the doors as they close and kick them, thump them. Open, please open.

A baffled security guard appears from around the corner, demanding to know why I am attacking his shop.

I wave frantically and point at the locked entrance.

"I need to get in, I forgot my notebook."

Despite not understanding the words, his face lights up in comprehension. He disappears around the corner and returns a minute later with my notepad.

"Grazie! Grazie! Grazie!" I repeat over and over.

I take off, running in the opposite direction. Time to reclaim all my other stuff. I'm out of breath after the sprints, but my backpack is untouched where I threw it. I climb onto the balcony to recollect it and then disappear again before the owners look out their window and spy a delinquent on their property. So many things have gone wrong today that by the law of averages, I am sure that nothing else can.

I walk into the metro station and wait for the train. It pulls into the station, but the doors do not open. Messages in both English and Italian inform myself and others that the train will not be leaving the station. The last train for the day has already gone.

I grab the front of my hair and tug at it with a closed fist. Why is this so difficult?

Trying to help, an old lady tries to take my backpack off me, but I refuse and she takes my notebook instead. Better keep her in sight.

I'm led to a bus stop where a flock of locals gabble at me in Italian.

A bus pulls up and I am herded onto it by the crowd. I grab my notebook back from the old woman before I lose it forever and a woman who was part of the round up, steps onto the bus and shouts down it in Italian.

"I speak English," says a teenager in response. I tell him that I want to get to the train station. He tells me not to pay and the bus driver doesn't seem to care, so I stand with him as he consults neighbouring passengers on directions. A heated debate ensues in which every single person seems to know a different way to reach the train station. These people are almost too helpful. What's not helpful is that the bus doesn't announce where it is and the stops are not labelled. This might be the most confusing bus network for foreigners that I have ever seen.

"You should get off here, then take the bus to Porta Nuova."

Porta Nuova, Porta Nuova. Don't forget, Porta Nuova.

I find the bus stop name on the timetable. It is on the 720 line.

The 720 bus turns up and as I try to board it, the old lady who had carried my notebook stops me from doing so. She must know what she's talking about. I let the bus pass, then look at the timetable again.

The 720 is definitely the only bus I can take. I point at Porta Nuova and for the next half an hour, she makes sorrowful, regretful moans as I wait for the same bus once more.

This time I get on without being restrained and thank the lady for her well intentioned hinderance.

Is the world conspiring against me today? Is this what people mean when they say that they are having a bad day, but nothing serious has happened? At least the driver seems uninterested in collecting a fare from me.

I count the twenty-four stops all the way to the train station. With no bus stop names, I have to rely on spotting every stop we pass and adding it to the tally.

Twenty-four stops down, I get off the bus. What a useless public transport system for people who don't know where they are going. At least I've found the train station.

And more brilliant news. I have to take two trains to reach the lakes, with a seven hour wait in Milano.

I lie down on the floor in Milano train station to try and sleep. There are about ten others doing the same.

Who is prodding me?

A man dressed similarly to a policeman is poking me with a stick. He says something in Italian and indicates that I can't sleep where I am. I get up, walk a few steps, and wait for him to disappear, then lie down again. The others around me do exactly the same.

I'm being prodded again. This is not a fun game.

Every half an hour or so for the rest of the night, the man comes, wakes us all up, makes us get to our feet, then disappears again. What a pointless exercise. I roll my eyes at a girl who is trying to sleep near me and she shrugs, acknowledging the pointlessness of his nightly circuits to wake us. Another silent connection.

This man is what I would call a paper-pusher: someone who does a pointless job without pleasure, simply for the purpose of doing what they have been told to do. I want to tell him that I have nowhere else to sleep, nor do the other people, and all we want to do is harmlessly rest for a few hours until our train. Even if I spoke Italian, I doubt he would listen. No doubt he would say that he is just doing his job.

Another cog in society's machine.

I arrive in Desenzano Del Garda a few hours after sunrise. What a perfect day, I can't wait to see my family. I walk from the train station on the top of the hill, all the way down to the lake. The streets are old authentic Italian streets carved from pastel colours, adorned with elaborate arches and intricate balconies. A castle perches slightly above the town to my left and delicious smelling bakeries tempt me on every corner. The restaurant lined marina is well kept and reminds me of the amazing scenes I saw in Portofino. Yes, this will definitely be a nice place to spend a birthday.

I put my bags in the hotel my mother has booked, feeling out of place surrounded by fresh linen in my dirty clothes. Returning to hot sunshine, I want to leap into the lake.

I walk around a lighthouse and investigate the vast array of yachts that are moored. Living on the water would be nice. No timetable, nothing except the sun and the open water. I have the sun and the open road. That's enough for now. In fact, it's more than enough.

And I actually made it. I had every hinderance I could think of in my short journey, but here I am. Pizza and the familiarity of family await.

Of course I made it. I would always make it.

Everything is going to be OK. Everything is always OK. Until it's not.

10. Trust

Two days of lake swimming, gorging on pizza, oven-hot sun, and birthday champagne on the beach: a taste of luxury by anyone's standards, let alone someone who has slept on the floors of strangers or in rainy parks for the past month. These precious few days were everything that I could have hoped for.

I hug both my mother and brother goodbye then wave their train away, standing forlorn as I look at the map of Europe they brought for me. Despite living outside of the UK for half a decade, it was the first time that my family have been able to visit me abroad due to my continual movement and living far from England. No, the second time. When I broke my back in a skiing accident, they immediately flew out to meet me in the hospital.

That day I fell was one of the worst of my life. Racing downhill through an icy glacier, I was ahead of several skiers, all more experienced than myself. Despite my job involving ski tours of the mountain, I had only been skiing for a couple of months and was pushing myself too far. We dropped from one piste, aiming for another, traversing the steep and rough decline between the two at great speed. Shooting across the lower piste and off the other side, the transition from steep drop to flat threw me off-balance and my weight was thrown backwards. I crossed the piste in a fraction of a second, so by the time I hit the descent on the far side, my balance was all wrong. I rotated backwards in the air and came to an abrupt stop, my lower back and bottom swallowing the impact.

First, I couldn't breathe. Then I writhed in pain. It was as if my whole back was spasming so tight that it might burst and explode. I gulped desperately short breaths, trying to keep from suffocating, my heart racing. Were my lungs punctured, had they collapsed entirely? Would this be it, suffocating on a mountain? I later learnt that I had fractured two vertebrae, T12 and L1, which I'm told is where the diaphragm is attached to the spine. Every time I tried to take a breath, my diaphragm sent ripping pains through my body by tugging at my damaged vertebrae.

I tried to get up and to continue because I didn't want to be injured, but everything was too painful. I collapsed at the top of a chairlift, begging for it to be a bad dream.

It could have been a minute, it could have been an hour, but I don't remember how long I lay in the snow before the paramedics turned up. I wanted the snow to swallow me up, to make me disappear and take the pain away.

The paramedics put me in a neck brace, strapped me to a body board, then transported me to hospital. Strapped inside a coffin shaped gondola, the paramedic asked me to flex my toes and fingers, checking for paralysis, an exercise I would be asked to repeat again with the doctor.

Down on the ground, my back was x-rayed from multiple angles. I already suspected that I had fractured vertebrae as I knew of someone who had experienced a similar accident several weeks before, but when the doctor confirmed my suspicions, hot tears rolled down my face. Unable to hide my distress, my boss took my hand to comfort me and I squeezed tight, as if doing so might save me. The whole world had opened beneath my feet and I was falling with no way to save myself. The hospital, the doctors, the people whose job it was to save me, even they couldn't help me. No sport for a year the doctor said. A body cast from the thighs to the lower back for three months: I wouldn't even be able to bend at the hip. Flying home on a private hospital jet. My soul was crushed.

A big needle took me to cloud nine and for several hours, I floated between the harsh real world and somewhere much better. The next morning, my parents walked through the door of my hospital room. There was nothing that they could do to help my physical situation, but I was so very happy to have them there with me. They told me that I would be OK and helped reassemble my broken soul.

I will always be grateful.

That was a few years ago. This time I am not hurt, but I am alone and I am happy for the days shared. I walk through the town for the final time, admiring the quirky twisted streets. It is as pretty as it has been, but there is something missing. People I care about?

Is this what I want to be doing? I think about where I grew up, about the jobs I could have, about living life on an even keel.

Yes. This is what I want to be doing. I want to see the world, I want to meet more people. I want to live a life that is memorable to myself.

Still full of delicious food and luxuries, I shake off my sadness. I am sad to see them go, but more than that, I am happy that they came. There is a whole world in front of me.

Italy is one of the most delicious countries in Europe, so I will cross it, all the way to Venice. Then maybe I'll meet up with Sam, the Irishman. We set a tentative date in Prague, just over a week away. Another thousand mile journey with a wealth of treasures to visit on the way.

But on the way to where? Now that my dream of perpetual sunlight is crushed, I don't have a focus. I'll get to Sam in Czech Republic, then make plans.

In Verona, I discover a historian's wet dream: a large amphitheatre and endless Roman architecture, this is how I imagine Rome should look. I have nowhere to go and nowhere to be, so in a large square, I sit against my backpack, admiring the impressive buildings. A well dressed, older man approaches me and asks if I speak English.

"Nothing else unfortunately."

"I am going into the amphitheatre now and they won't let me take this in." He shows me a mostly full bottle of wine. "Would you like it?" Everything my parents and teachers ever told me says don't trust strangers and definitely don't take candy from them.

"No thank you," I smile. What ulterior motives does he hide?

"OK, well have a nice day." He walks over to the bin and is about to drop it in when I realise that for the past few weeks, I have trusted only in strangers and nobody has screwed me over.

Yes and no. Have a little faith in the world.

"Actually, wait!" I call him back. "The wine would be great, thank you."

We talk for a few minutes. He is on holiday from Belgium with his family and there is an opera performance starting in a few minutes. He is incredibly friendly and emanates genuine warmth. I wish him a pleasant evening's entertainment and head back to the highway with my wine.

Is it safe to drink? Should I dump it?

I'll decide later.

I walk though the evening and into the darkness. No cars for a few hours, just me, human powered. It feels good to walk.

I swig the bottle of wine as I walk. It's good red wine and I savour the taste.

Leaving the last suburbs of the city, the roads are no longer good for walking. There is a large roundabout, fifty metres across with lots of vegetation. It's perfect for camping. I can hitch or I can sleep here for the night.

One more ride.

Drunk party goers shout to me from a high apartment as I am thumbing on the edge of the road. I wave to them and they all dance around, jumping in the night. One waves me over, but I don't want to party tonight. The solitude and thought of camping appeal far more than forced conversations with strangers.

A Sri Lankan man picks me up and we discuss cricket. Yes I like cricket, yes I know of this player, yes I like to bat, yes he is good.

He drives me to a train station.

"I don't want to take a train thank you, I'm hitchhiking."

"OK, I know where." He drives me to a bus station because buses are cheaper than trains.

"It's not merely a finance thing, I don't want to take a bus, I want to hitchhike."

"You cannot do it, hitchhiking is impossible."

"I have been hitchhiking for weeks now without a problem, it is possible."

"No, it's impossible."

"Please, can you just leave me on the main road?"

"I really don't advise this."

Eventually he relents and leaves me in a small town where I can find a hotel. It's utterly inappropriate for guerrilla camping and I have to search for a place to sleep. I would have been better sleeping on the roundabout with access to the motorway.

In a small orchard, many minutes walk from the main road, I set up my tent between the trees, battling the wind that blows over the nearby vineyard. In the dark, every swaying vine, every dancing tree, is a great monster.

This is a creepy place.

I can see the lights of a farmhouse a few hundred metres away, but apart from that, I am in darkness, shielded from the lights of the town by a large slope.

I brush my teeth in the wind, tentatively studying the swaying foliage.

Maybe this wasn't such a good idea after all.

Before I can change my mind, I leap into my tent. Just don't look.

If I close my eyes and don't look, I won't see the monsters.

I wake up swinging. Heart pounding, cold sweats, someone has slit my tent open with a knife and reaches through the cut with dark motives.

I clasp at thin air, attacking an untarnished canvas.

Where has the attacker gone?

I open the tent and look around. Nothing but the wind. It must have been a dream.

Shoes back on, I walk through the vines and trees. My eyes have adjusted to the darkness and I can see clearly, aided by dustings of the moon. There are no monsters outside my head, there is nothing but me. This is my orchard, my vineyard, my night.

The vines are protective strangers and the trees are friendly monsters watching over me, keeping me safe.

By morning, I remain uneaten. What a pleasant surprise.

I walk more, enjoying the sunshine. Is Italy always blessed with such glorious weather?

On the opposite side of the road, Gandalf. In body length white robes, sporting a long silver beard and carrying a wooden staff, I can hardly believe my eyes. Elaborate wooden necklaces swing around his chest as he calls a friendly greeting, catching me by surprise. What is Gandalf doing in Italy?!

I return his waves and smiles, happy to see another walker, even if he is travelling in the opposite direction.

Another connection, another person passing by. Why didn't I stop and say hello? I bet Gandalf has a whole world of fascinating stories to tell. Should I run back and catch him? No, onwards I go.

From the side of the road, I watch as a large dragonfly is struck by a passing car. How I happen to see it, I have no idea, but the poor creature's fragile body bounces off the fast moving windscreen and lands by my feet. A huge yellow and black body, bright green eyes, windowpane wings. Even close to death, nature's canvas is more beautiful than anything we can create. As a kid, I wanted to be a vet and save every animal in the world. Then a farmer shot my cat, shattering its back leg and tail. Somehow, the bullet also caused it to go blind. The next day the vet came and put my cat, my Wolfie, into eternal sleep. Never again did I want to be a vet because even they cannot save everything. I place the stunned dragonfly on a flower stem and leave it there, surely to die.

After passing me once already, a trucker in a large green lorry turns around and pulls up beside me. Clearly inquisitive, he asks what I am doing in a thick Italian accent and I tell him that I am hitchhiking.

Interested, he invites me into his cab and asks more questions of my journey. I explain to him that I'm hitchhiking and how I sleep outside or in the homes of strangers.

"You are vagabond!" he proclaims with delight. Despite the negative connotations associated with the word, I concede that by definition, I am currently a vagabond: I wander from place to place with neither home nor job. I am invited to the home of the trucker, but decide to continue on my way, thanking him for his generous offer. Despite driving a huge truck, he takes me far into the city of Padova before returning on his original path.

"Goodbye vagabond," he calls. I take his email address, scribbled onto the back of a tachograph. If I ever I come back this way, I might just take him up on his offer. I put the tachograph into a small pocket that is accumulating email addresses and business cards from many of the places I have passed. When I am bored, I flick through them and remember where each one came from.

Finding a park and sitting against a tree, I watch a rat race from bush to bush, always hiding from predators, always searching for food. Once upon a time, humans would have battled for survival, but now we are so far developed that survival is no longer an issue. We are the dominant species of our planet and for many of us, we chase leisure pursuits instead of those that keep us alive. Here I am, doing nothing for my survival, yet each day I survive. Each day I live and each day on the road, I remember. That ability to choose leisure over survival is the biggest luxury of all.

I am lucky not to be a rat. Or is a rat lucky to not have to choose what to do?

On a quiet street I find after leaving the park, I photograph a spray painted image of Snoopy waving a heart shaped balloon. It mimics Banksy, a UK street artist. For me, viewing it is both a leisure activity and a human connection with someone I don't know. It brings a smile to my face, knowing that someone left it here for the world to find, but would never see the pleasure it created.

"Hello, Jamie?"

"Hello? You must be Ania, right?"

Ania is a tall Polish girl who has invited me to stay with her. She recognised me photographing Snoopy as I am the only person carrying a backpack.

Back at her house, we talk about Padova and she tells me about the elegant streets before parading me around them. I am enthralled by another ancient Italian city that I had never even heard of only days before. Just thirty miles away is Venice and this is my last intended stop in Italy. I tell Ania that I am going to hitchhike to Venice for the day and she is excited at the prospect.

"I always wanted to try hitchhiking."

"Then come with me tomorrow. We'll go in the morning and come back in the evening." She hesitates.

"I want to, but I'm nervous."

"It's OK to be nervous. Being wary keeps you safe."

After sharing a couple of hitchhiking stories with her, Ania decides to come with me.

Venice is full of candy coloured buildings like so much of Italy, hand drawn streets, and post boxes that look like faces. It is prettier than I had hoped for. Like cattle, we march step-after-step through the city, a herd of tourists.

"Let's go this way," I say. We turn into a quiet side-street and walk along one of the innumerable canals. The city is a museum. What is that I can hear?

I hear quiet.

Never before have I heard quiet in a city. The island of Venice is largely pedestrianised, cured from the incessant drone of vehicles.

We get lost in the maze of streets, climbing over bridges, walking on cobbles, and enjoying everything around us.

"This might be one of the most perfect cities that I have ever seen."

We return to Padova at sunset. Sixty-five rides with strangers, shared between myself and three strangers, now friends. From Venice, I am only six hundred miles from Prague where I will meet Sam. So many numbers, so little meaning.

Leaving Padova, a friendly German-American gives me a short ride to a toll booth, but misses the stopping point and drives me down the motorway. Unfortunate. I get out of his car and jump the railings. The road is encased by industrial fencing on either side and traffic is moving away from where I want to go. I am trapped by a fast moving motorway with no escape.

But there must be an escape.

In one direction, more motorway, in the other, more motorway and the toll booth I must reach. But I must not walk in the path of passing vehicles. Even now, cars are racing by at alarming speed. I wish that he didn't leave me here.

I walk beside the railing until a large prickly bush blocks my path. It stretches the few short metres from the industrial fencing to the motorway railing. I could push through if I want to rip my clothing and skin to shreds. Do I need my eyes? I could walk the other way, the way without a prickly bush in the direction that definitely isn't where I want to go.

I will walk on the fencing. Awkwardly in my flip-flops, I climb onto the metal fencing and struggle with the weight of my backpack to walk along the thin strips of metal. I let the thorns tear at my shoulder, leaning against the prickly bush for support rather than falling before the speeding cars. The world seems so much sharper. Every noise, every sound. I feel a heightened sense of things as I know that a stumble could leave me in imminent danger. Taking on a fast moving car, head-first, is unlikely to end well.

A car beeps at me, offering neither wave nor ride, just an acknowledgement of my existence. Another car beeps, then another. Why are they all beeping at me?

I inch, step by precarious step, along the railing, looking only down. The wind of the cars buffets me as they pass.

The bush finishes and I am met by a drop of several metres. I climb down from the railing and shuffle along the narrow ledge of concrete until it meets the industrial fences again. Ahead I spy more bushes, bigger than the last.

There is no way I am walking on the railing again.

I have the choice of living in this tiny space for the rest of my life or trespassing in the unknown compound.

I throw my bag and flip-flops over the fence, then counteract the eight foot of anti-climb fencing by squeezing my toes into the holes and rolling over spikes. I drop to the floor. Nobody is around, nobody has seen me. If I had the right set of morals, I would make an excellent burglar.

Large white buildings and expensive cars surround me. What is this place?

I walk through the compound until I find the exit. A security guard appears from a small booth.

Is that a gun? It is a gun.

He throws an imposing question at me in Italian, but I shrug my shoulders and try to carry on walking, mumbling something about only speaking English.

Please let me go, security man.

He blocks my path.

"Do you speak English?" he asks.

"I do."

"What are you doing in here?" I explain how I was trying to get to Austria by hitchhiking, but I was dropped on the wrong road and I had to walk along the motorway, but it was too dangerous so I climbed the fence and I didn't want to create a problem, I really didn't, but I didn't want to get hit by a car either and I'm so very sorry.

His attitude changes immediately. He wishes me luck and shakes my hand, telling me to be careful about where I end up. Trespassing in a place like this could leave me in trouble.

I apologise and make myself scarce as I see another security guard approaching us from across the car park. He might not be so friendly.

At the toll booth, a group of Australians on Harley Davidsons pull up and offer me a ride on the condition that I have a helmet.

"Generally I don't have a helmet in my backpack. Thanks anyway."

I wave at passing cars until the toll booth security come and tell me that I can't stand where I am. I look up and down the motorway. Once again it is surrounded by high perspex fences and there is no way for me to leave the toll, other than in a car. Not their problem they say, but I have to leave.

I walk down the motorway a little and try to stand out of view of the motorway cameras. Two security vans turn up and invite me into their vehicles.

"Thank you, but I think I'll just wait for someone else to give me a ride."

They are very insistent. I take a seat in the back of the lead van, hoping they aren't going to fine me. I have no clue where they are taking me.

Dropped at a service station, I am issued with a verbal warning not to hitch on the motorway again. "And here is two water. Cold and nice."

"Thanks!"

One hour, one bottle of water gone. Two hours, so is the second. Three hours, I need to move. Four hours, I move again. Five hours, I'll just walk along this road. Six hours, finally a lift. Who would of thought that a nineteen year old girl would have been the only person brave enough to pick me up? To my dismay, the girl leaves me at a quiet fuel station after dark. Another glorious night in my spacious tent.

In Austria the following day, I marvel at the huge mountains as we descend from a high pass into rolling green hills and meadows. How could I have been so ignorant as to have assumed Austria to be an ugly country? This must be why people marvel over the scenery in The Sound of Music, a movie I have never seen.

"Do you want a beer?" my Italian driver asks. His long hair hides some of his face, but I guess that he must be about twenty.

"Sure." I open one for him and one for me. An hour later he asks if I have a driving license and I tell him that I do.

"Do you mind swapping for a bit?" We change seats and he opens another beer for himself and asks if I want one.

"Not for me thanks, I'm driving." Although when I get out of the car, he will be driving in my place.

He pulls at the ceiling light and reaches into the cavity it leaves.

"It was in here somewhere…" It takes him a couple of minutes of arm wriggling, but eventually he pulls out a small bag full of dried green plants.

I program my next stop into his GPS and follow it for several hours as he happily smokes and drinks in the passenger seat. When we reach our destination, he gets back into the driver's seat and continues on his hazy way.

I feel irked. What if he crashes? What if he hits someone else, someone completely innocent? Even if he didn't listen, I should have said something, at least tried to make a difference. How taunting hindsight can be.

Inside a hippy camper van, my teenage dreams are rekindled as I try to forget about my intoxicated ex-driver-passenger. A hammock, a book shelf, a full kitchen… one hell of a fuel bill, and a massive carbon footprint. When they invent cars that run on water, then I'll drive one.

"Of course you can still learn to play, as long as you don't want to play professionally," an Austrian pianist tells me later the same day. "If you have a desire to learn, you will learn, no matter your age."

I leave Austria and the pianist with a Czech trucker, writing a short description of every ride in my notebook: 'Hungarian Chef, You Drive I Smoke, The Pianist.'

"Erotica! Erotica!" Mr. Erotic screams in delight, laughing heartily as he points out every brothel and scantily clad billboard. His laugh is so warm and natural, that I can't help but laugh along with him. Apparently the Austrians like to pop over the border for cheap Czech delights.

As we pass smaller, more subtle buildings, he nods gravely and says the word erotica in a softer tone, shaking his head. What goes on behind those walls? It is a world I will never know.

Late at night, I am alone on the outskirts of Prague. I can see the glow of the city ahead of me. Just a few more miles to go. I have no Czech currency to pay for a bus, so I'll hitchhike. Or should I sleep? It might be safer to sleep, but Sam is waiting for me. I have the address of a bar where he will be.

Cloud hides the world from stars and moon alike. It is so dark, I can't even see the road beneath me.

A car approaches. No one will stop for me now. I wave when the headlights turn my way.

It stops.

A simple calculation tells me that this is not a good idea. The small hatchback has three men in it. Three versus one.

Yes and no. We always have a choice, but I have to make it to the city.

"Where are you going?" I ask, buying time.

"Into the city to party and meet girls." Plausible.

"Just to the city?"

"Yeah, we're going there now."

"Oh. And you have space for me?"

"Yeah, get in." I have no more questions to ask, no more time to buy. I get into the car driven by a guy whose accent is tinted American. Next to me in the back is a guy twice my size with a brutish face. Is this a terrible idea? We're already moving, it's too late. Yes and no are out the window. I really must get them imprinted upon my hands.

We drive for about ten seconds before the car is spun around in the middle of the road.

"I forgot, we were meant to pick up my friend too."

Oh no, oh no, this is it. This is exactly what happened to Bill in Tanzania when he was kidnapped and driven to the ATM. People pretend to help you out, then they outnumber you, drive you far away, and tell you that they are the mafia. Shortly after, you find yourself relieved of your possessions.

I take my camera and notebook from my bag, then move my backpack to the middle seat, forming a barrier between myself and the brute. When they stop the car, I'll get out and I'll run, taking nothing else but what I have in my hands.

Everything is going to be OK… Everything is always going to be OK… Until it's not. This is not.

We weave at speed through dark streets, moving further away from the city until we reach an isolated apartment complex. Uninspiring, it is drab and monotonous, dirty grey walls from ground to roof surround small, functional windows. I get out of the car quicker than anyone else.

I wait.

They get out the car one by one and light up cigarettes.

"What are you doing in Prague?" the driver asks me.

"Meeting a friend." Why haven't you done something to me yet?

Their fourth friend turns up dressed in a shirt and jeans, announcing it is time to go hunting for girls.

Do I get back in the car or do I stay here, wherever here is?

Trust in people. Make a choice.

I choose to believe.

I get back into the car. We leave the apartment complex in a different direction. I am in the middle seat now, there is no escape. More dark roads, further isolation.

Then lights.

And more lights.

This is Prague!

I am driven to the bar where I gratefully rush in to meet Sam. The four guys come in with me, fail miserably with girls, then head off to easier hunting grounds.

"Those were strange guys," Sam says to me after they leave.

"I know. I expected them to do something bad to me, but they didn't. It seems that time after time, we expect the worst, only to find the best in people. I blame the news, that's why I never watch it. I have always thought that if we have news, there should be three different channels: the good news, the bad news, and the news about things that simply happened. Why is it that we only listen to the bad news? That's what makes us all afraid. We don't hear the stories of people doing amazing things or regular things. Instead, we hear the stories that concern the deepest, darkest dregs of humanity, the sludge from the basement floor."

In the light and safety of the bar, I am not afraid.

In light and safety, we have never been afraid.

11. Vodka

On one side, Sam is pressed against me. On the other, the wall of the tent. My legs are bent up and my mouth is dry.

I struggle to my knees in my 'too small for me but now holds two fully grown men' tent and crawl out the front flap. We are inside a bush. Quite a feat to set up a tent inside a bush. Outside the bush, I see feet passing and full daylight. Last night's empty bottle of vodka lies upon the floor.

I walk into the sunshine and look around. We are in a busy park with almost no vegetation except for our one bush. From a couple of metres away, the tent is invisible. Hidden in plain sight, it is a truly brilliant hiding place.

Sam stumbles out of the tent behind me.

"It's three o'clock," he mumbles.

"Wow. I guess this is what I get when I agree to travel with an Irishman."

The night before, we climbed a security fence and entered a small park. There we sat on the river, floating idly in a pedalo while eating our dinner. Behind us drunken revellers passed, oblivious of our presence as we watched the city shimmering upon the surface of the water. Over cobbled streets, we moved beneath tall turrets and orange rooftops in a bohemian city famed across the world for its beauty. No matter where you go, everybody knows the name of Prague, even if they don't know which country it is in.

At Charles Bridge, a five hundred metre bridge that supports several hundred bustling tourists and trinket sellers during daylight hours, we walked in complete silence. The whole place was transformed, as if from a dream. As we crossed each arch, only our footsteps could be heard in the darkness. No artists, no musicians, no camera phones. Nothing but cobbles, an Irishman, and an Englishman.

The magic of the night, when free from terrors, is something that should last forever.

Prolonging our night, we sat with a bottle of Czech liquor, drinking and talking beyond dawn. Then we woke up in a bush.

"How was Scandinavia?" I ask Sam as we pack up the tent. I had imagined he would still be there. No doubt I asked him last night, but the answers are wallowing at the bottom of the empty liquor bottle.

"Great place, but terrible for hitchhiking. Everybody is too scared to pick you up: every ride I got was from a foreigner."

Tent packed, bush left, we walk through the streets idly. It's Sam's first visit to the city. With every step, I become less comfortable. I know these streets, I have walked them before. Many years ago in a different life, I loved the metro and the way the wind blows down the tunnels. I loved the winding streets and the beauty. I loved how you could climb the towers and look across the city, seeing nothing but orange rooftops and the castle which looks back down upon you.

That was then and everywhere east of here is a blank canvas. I want only to explore this new world.

"I think I'm ready to leave."

"Now?"

"I came here once before. It doesn't feel right to be here again."

Sam lets it slide and we sit down to look at the map my mother gave me, debating where to go. Refusing to read guidebooks and choosing novels from different regions of the world, I know nothing of anything that lies across the magic, uncrossed line ahead of me. Sam has spent time in this part of the world and points out some places.

"I'd like to go to the Baltic states to practise the languages." Sam circles his finger around the northern most states on mainland Europe.

"I don't even dare to ask how many languages you speak. However, that works for me. I have never been to Latvia, Lithuania, or Estonia and I know nothing about them. I might even make it up to Scandinavia this way instead."

"Ooo, that is a good idea. We could take the ferry from Tallinn to Helsinki. I would love to go to Finland again, I just love their language and their cute little voices."

"Agreed then. We'll aim for Finland, via Poland, Latvia, Lithuania, then Estonia."

"Lithuania comes before Latvia."

"In all honesty, I didn't even know which countries were counted as Baltic states until you just pointed them out."

Sam and I plan a rough route from places he knows, then find an internet cafe to send a few messages ahead of time in the hope of arranging the occasional bed. Our intended route is over twelve hundred miles and involves several stops in each country that we'll pass through.

I check my emails and find a third reason to return to Italy. The owners of a Tuscan farm that tout themselves as being organic, gay-friendly, and in touch with nature have invited me to volunteer with them. I had almost forgotten about the volunteer network I had joined on the day I first met Sam. He had told me all about WorkAway, an online organisation that allows willing travellers to contact hosts wanting help with their projects across the world. In exchange for a prearranged amount of volunteering per day, 'WorkAwayers' are given lodging and sometimes food. I had sent a couple of messages asking people if I could stay with them and this Italian farm was one of the hosts I had chosen to contact.

While the previously mentioned reasons are all strong attributes for some people, what drew me was the apparent tranquility of the place, the rustic lack of connectivity, but mostly, the fact that they keep bees and goats. If I go to this farm, I will learn about beekeeping and looking after goats.

"Sam, look at this." I show him the posting and the message they sent me, inviting me to stay for a month and asking when I can arrive.

"Looks interesting, are you going to do it?"

"I have always dreamt of keeping bees and goats one day. I still do and I don't think I can turn down this opportunity to learn first hand." Sam looks a little put out. I already bailed once on our joint plans for Scandinavia. "But after the Baltic region of course."

Sam asks when I'll return to Italy and I try to work it out, looking at our planned route and thinking about the return journey before realising I have no idea where I will be at what time. Eventually I settle on telling them a tentative two to three weeks, but offer no clue as to how long I can stay with them.

If you think everything is going to be OK, it probably will.

In the north of Czech Republic the following day, we stand aloft a hilltop castle, looking out over the world. In every direction, we can see for miles and mountains. Other ancient castles stand on different peaks and in days gone by, they would have signalled to one another when an attacker was drawing near.

"Imagine standing here," I begin, "hundreds of years ago and seeing the signal of an approaching enemy. Imagine knowing that in a few short hours, you could be dead. Those men must have stood on the battlements, bored out of their minds, praying that nothing happened because when it did, it only meant bad news."

"That's a happy thought," Sam mocks.

"I like to imagine it, knowing that I am only here to walk and to look. Tomorrow, we will be in Poland doing who knows what and we don't even know what tonight brings. What I do know is that we aren't bound to these battlements or living in fear. We have nothing to hold us back. That feels, for lack of a better word, really good."

As we cross into Poland, we are in a mini-van of Polish workers. They get dropped off one by one until there is just Sam, myself, and one older passenger. When we are let out of the van, the older man runs into a store and comes back with a bag of beers. He leads us into a park and there we sit, quietly drinking breakfast beers behind a tree, talking about nothing at all with our lack of common language. It seems Polish is one of the few languages we have encountered that

Sam doesn't speak. I appreciate the respite from being mocked for my lack of language abilities, but my pronunciation of Polish towns is still incorrect enough to raise a smile.

All that we can ascertain from the conversation is that drinking in public is a big offence in Poland. This must be why we are sitting behind a tree, in the furthest part of the park from the road. We leave the park, thank the man for the early morning beers, and cook brunch in a bus stop.

A young guy on a bicycle approaches us and in good English, invites us to drink beer in the park with him. We politely decline, but thank him for the offer.

"It turns out the rumours are true," I muse to Sam, "the Polish do like to drink."

"Almost as much as the British Isles!" Rumours in the UK say that in the east of Europe, alcohol consumption is incredibly high. However, after looking up statistical data from the World Health Organisation in anticipation of our proposed route, we both know that the UK and Ireland have higher consumptions of alcohol per capita than Poland and all but around fifteen countries in the world, of which most are in fact, located somewhere around eastern Europe.

Ride after ride, we cruise through Poland waiting only minutes. I am overwhelmed by how friendly every Polish person is and immediately feel affection towards a whole nation and its people. Not a motorway in sight, we hitchhike on every road, don't feel like hiding when we see police, and for the very first time, see multiple other hitchhikers.

"Is this the best country in the world for hitchhiking?" We agree that it probably is.

In Wrocław we are met with five shot glasses, one for every person staying in the one bedroom apartment.

"I am Mateusz. This is Polish vodka. We drink." And we do. What an introduction!

"I like Poland," I concede to Sam as the second shot is poured. We're told that we can sleep anywhere we find a space and amidst the pizza boxes and empty bottles, we find somewhere that we are happy to call home.

"Let's wander through the streets before we forget."

"Forget the streets or forget to wander?"

"Both, but not the first, let's do the second. Which one was that again?"

Pretty lights, so many tricky cobbles, and vodka... vodka everywhere! Like a wise old man, the city has become beautiful with age, but I am regressing to a caveman with every further tipple.

"One more, no more. That's the rule. We drink one more, then we go home."

I definitely don't want another.

"Again, one more, no more."

This really is the last one.

"One more?"

Oh no.

The bar is getting hazy.

And the music is so loud.

And I'm lying on a sofa.

And the bar has gone.

Where has the bar gone? Where have the people gone?

I am back in the apartment. It's daytime.

Giant speakers boom teenage pop songs at such a volume that passers by must be able to hear them on the ground. We are ten floors up.

Just dance.

Everybody is dancing and it feels so damn amazing.

The chorus chimes in and everybody sings as loud as they can...

"CALL ME MAYBE."

Are we really singing this? Yes, we definitely are. We all are. And I'm loving it. I love these people, I love that nobody judges, I love everything.

Glorious Poland, you are so much fun.

"Whose round is it?" Sam asks. For the benefit of meeting more fun people, we decide that we will carry one bottle of liquor at all times. Just in case.

"I think you bought the last." I buy a bottle of vodka, slip it into my backpack, then get a second. Just in case. "What I can't decide is are we drunk on copious amounts of vodka, the glorious people of Poland, or life itself? I feel it might just be a little bit of all three."

This is the hippy life I imagined: care-free, easy rides, warm people. Both of us wearing our hippy pants. Poland has it all.

12. A Secret Smile

'I'm the girl with the pink bicycle,' reads the text.

"Sam, look for a girl with a pink bicycle. She should be somewhere close."

We are on Kraków's market square, a huge medieval town square surrounded by historic townhouses, palaces, and churches. In the centre is a large hall sporting many arches and a tall parapet covered in carvings. The square is buzzing with activity, but our eyes are drawn by the architecture.

In the far corner of the square, there is a large basilica, a church. We gravitate towards it.

"Do you see any bicycles?" I ask.

"Not yet."

It's another scorching hot day and I feel the warmth of the sunshine beating down on my face. I wish my backpack wasn't so heavy.

"There, by the fountain. A pink bicycle."

We stop in front of the dark haired girl who is fiddling with her phone. She looks up to see two scruffy hitchhikers carrying backpacks. We are both wearing our loose fitting hippy pants, mine red and Sam's white, beneath sweat soaked t-shirts. My hair has grown so long that I sweep it across my forehead and hold it there using sweat from the summer sun. Without doing so, my hair would hang below my eyes, yet Sam's red hair is more than twice as long, resting upon his shoulders. We look like a couple of dirty hippies.

"Jamie, Sam?"

"Hi Emilia, thank you so much for having us at short notice." For half a moment, I am taken aback. Dark eyes, long dark hair swept across her face. Then I blink and it's gone. There are pretty girls all over the world, I see them every day.

Emilia, in little pink shorts, jumps up from her seat by the fountain and we shake hands. Leading with her bike, she guides us across the bustling market place, pointing out buildings as we go. The cloth hall, St. Mary's Basilica, names I forget as quickly as I hear them. I fall behind, enthralled by my surroundings as Emilia chats with Sam.

As an individual who longs for country rather than city, to enjoy urban areas in such a way is somewhat alien to me. This is one of the prettiest towns I have ever seen and blissful peace from mechanical whirrs, there isn't a car to be seen or heard around the square. A few tourist horses and golf buggies buzz and trot between the crowds of people, but the centre is pedestrianised.

Across the square and down another pedestrianised street, we reach a small park full of trees. Emilia says something about the park circling the whole of Kraków, but she is still talking with Sam and I catch only glimpses of their conversation. Exiting the narrow park, the buildings are tall and dark, wise old kings sitting upon their thrones. Each of them must be able to tell a thousand stories. Each of them must have watched hundreds of lives pass them by, but there they stand, regardless of what goes on around them. Most of these buildings must have lived through two world wars, but they hide the signs. Just one hour outside the city, we passed Auschwitz, the concentration camp responsible for ending over a million human lives. How awful it is to say a million. A million doesn't mean anything because I don't know who they were, what made them feel alive, what they dreamt about at night. What flavour ice cream would they have chosen? I cannot imagine what a million anything looks like, let alone one million lives being taken. Do the buildings know those horrors?

We stop at a crossroads on the first road we've met since walking from the central square. People outnumber cars, trams cross in various directions. A large electronic billboard advertises something in Polish, looking curiously out of place amongst the old buildings. Along the tram lines we walk, this part of the city humming a different tune to the centre. A passing car, the rattle of the tram tracks. Nowhere does music blast out and none of the sounds are overwhelming. This is a peaceful city.

We stop outside a large wooden door set in a stone building.

"This is it," Emilia announces. She pulls the door, much larger than her, and we enter a wide hallway with high ceilings. I imagine that the building dates back to Soviet times, but there is beauty in its rustic simplicity. Sam and I follow Emilia up the stone staircase and into a regular sized door. The room inside is dark and narrow. We can see almost nothing.

Shoes off, I shuffle down the narrow entranceway. The room opens into a square space with high ceilings once again. Very few places in the UK are so grand. There are five rooms leading off the central room, each allowing natural light from their windows. Three are clearly bedrooms, one a bathroom, and the other, which I can't see into, is presumably the kitchen.

"You will both stay here in my room, my flatmate is away so I'm taking her room." Emilia leads us into a huge rectangular bedroom, as large as my whole studio apartment in South Korea, but with ceilings twice as high. Large wooden windows at the far end of the room fill it with natural light and about the room, keepsakes and photos show that this is very much a home.

A young guy walks into the room, skinny and smiling. "Hello, I'm Tomasz, I live in that room." He points out of the door to the room opposite. My eyes follow his finger as if I might see something new by looking at his room. We stand and chat with him for a few minutes as Emilia moves a few things around, flitting in and out.

"We are going to meet some friends in an hour if you want to come?"

"Of course. Do you mind if I just take a shower?"

I slip out of my hippy pants and wash away the sweat, feeling clean and refreshed. It's a nice day outside, but the evening will be cold. I pull on my one pair of jeans and my one shirt over a t-shirt, then lie on the sofa to read while Sam washes. This must be the most 'normal' I've looked since I was on the road. When Sam is done in the shower, I get up and catch my reflection in the mirror. I no longer look like a hitchhiker at all.

Whatever that means.

We board a tram without buying a ticket and illegally ride it across the city. Like a field mouse scanning for hawks, my eyes roam the crowds for ticket inspectors while Sam, Emilia, and Tomasz talk casually. It would be so embarrassing to get caught. Once again, my senses are heightened.

Exiting the tram without incident, calm returns to my body.

With friends of Emilia and Tomasz, we take low orange seats around a large, round table in a woody bar. The walls are red and everything about the bar suggests quality. Ten of us in all, with nearly as many nationalities. On my left is Sam, across the table, Emilia and Tomasz, too far away to talk to.

An American guy introduces himself to me. What was his name again? We chat idly for a few minutes. Is he studying here or just visiting? I can't remember. A seat opens up across the table and he swaps with someone. Hello new person. You do this and you do that. I hitchhike. That's nice. Another switch. This is like speed dating. Hello, have we met before?

In the background, music plays softly as the bar begins to empty. I've nursed my first drink for well over an hour, but it's empty and I lean back to catch the waiter's attention. One more beer please. The girl next to me excuses herself and leaves for the toilet. Sam is talking to my left and for a moment, I am stranded on an island, the guy with nobody to talk to. Should I sit here awkwardly or feel grateful for the respite?

A small kick to my chest, Emilia slips into the seat next to me. What was that?

"So Jamie, why are you hitchhiking?" Her smile, so natural, lights up her dark eyes. Almost crooked, it holds a secret, teasing, alluring. I sip my new drink before speaking. All the while, those eyes, that smile, fixated upon me. Or is it I upon them?

"I wanted to see more of the world and to meet more people. Hitchhiking seemed like a good way to do it. Low cost, lots of people, and you get taken places that you never even knew existed." It's the same stock answer that I've said over and over again.

"But aren't you scared?"

"There is nothing to be afraid of: everyone I've met has been lovely. Besides, it's all about balance. You balance out the good with the bad and the chance of something bad happening is small. The chance of something good happening is very high. You weigh up the low possibility of something bad happening against the high possibility of something good happening, then you see which one is more powerful."

"Simple maths right?" Is she mocking me already? I think she is.

"Or you can take a big knife to protect yourself." Touché.

"Personally, I think a gun would be better. Or one of those electric shock things that the police carry. You could hide it in your pocket."

"A taser? Yeah, sure. I thought about getting one of those so that I could shock the drivers and steal their cars. Then I wouldn't have any problems at all."

"That's perfect, I think that I must try it sometime. Maybe we can steal cars together." Her accent lilts, a delicate Eastern European twang. Like a young knight drawn to a dragon's lair, every word excites and lures me. It's English, but prettier.

Another hint of a smile, so brief, I could have missed it if I blinked. It's a secret smile, only for me, a smile that the rest of the world doesn't even know about. Emilia, what a pretty name. How beguiling the flick of her dark hair is, how…

Stop! This is ridiculous.

"How strong is this beer?" I change subject. Am I drunk already?

"About five per cent I think. It's just normal beer." After one beer, it's not alcohol going to my head.

"I wasn't sure if Polish people liked to sneak some vodka into it. We've had an awful lot since we arrived."

"Of course, we normally drink it with breakfast."

"And you give it to the kids as well right?"

"We wouldn't want them to be left out."

Around us people whirl constantly, moving from seat to seat. Except that I don't want to play anymore. I want to stay exactly as I am and I want to talk to Emilia. I want those dark eyes, that dark hair that sweeps over her face, that secret smile, all to myself.

She mocks me when I say something stupid, jokes with me when I'm being ridiculous, and pleases me only when it pleases her. I like this girl who doesn't ask the normal questions, who doesn't act politely for the sake of acting politely, who thinks for herself because she is an independent person.

"I'm reading this Swedish book…" I begin another story.

"Swedish, which one?" She's excited by the mention of Sweden. Around us, the bar empties further.

"It's called Let The Right One In. It's a vampire story where…"

"I know it."

"You do?"

"Yes, I love to read Swedish books."

"In Polish?"

"In Swedish. I study Swedish as one of my degrees and I lived in Sweden as part of my Erasmus."

"Oh, wow. How good is your Swedish?"

"Better than my English. In fact, English is only my third or fourth language." She says it matter of fact, neither inviting praise nor boasting. It's almost an apology for her near perfect English because of the fact that it isn't completely perfect. In reality, she speaks the language better than many natives I know and for the past year, all of my friends in South Korea were English teachers.

Two degrees, four languages, she's smart as well as funny, attractive, and independent. I must tip-toe gently away from the dragon's lair.

A staff member tells us the bar is closing. I finish my second beer and we all leave the table. The spell is not yet broken.

Outside, we say goodbye and everybody heads off in different directions. My attention was so fixated on Emilia that I can barely remember which people I spoke to.

"I'd like to see some more of the city," I announce. "No bars, no special tourist attractions, just whatever you think is the best part of the city." I believe that I just set a challenge.

Tomasz concedes that he has to work the next day as he has just graduated and has a new job. We wish him goodnight and he disappears on a night tram, leaving just Sam, Emilia, and myself. Emilia accepts the challenge willingly. Guiding us through quiet streets, she familiarises us with unknown corners of the city. Just like our walk from the main square earlier in the day, I let Sam and Emilia do most of the talking as I idly roam with my eyes. Yet this time, I am listening to the words of the conversation, her soft lilt tickling my ears like the gentle touch of a familiar hand. Her smile in the darkness, like rich cloying honey.

So inviting.

"This is my favourite place in the whole of the city." We are on a curved street with high buildings on either side. Below us are cobbles and I can see little in the darkness. In the deserted street, only our footsteps break the silence. We walk slowly, as if on sacred ground.

I point at a window, elaborately decorated, my eyes adjusting to the dark. Shapes begin to appear and Emilia points out an intricate chapel. Little soft things, so lovely in the night, so easy to miss in the day.

"If I ever get married, this is where I want it to be. On this street, in this chapel. This is the most beautiful place in the whole city. I felt like that even when I was a little girl."

I imagine what the young Emilia must have looked like, dancing down the street, her long dark hair flowing behind her. I look at her now and see her as full of wonder as that little girl was so many years ago.

Even in the darkness, I feel her eyes burning with life. They have the zest that dies when people grow up. Human beings reach the real world of proper jobs and they stop dancing, they put on their suits, they act like grown-ups. I want those eyes to burn forever and beyond.

"Thank you for showing us this special place." To hundreds of others who pass each day, it is no more than a street like any other, but right now, it is all of the world and more.

The three of us walk back to the apartment, Emilia showing us different parts of her city as we go. The side attractions. I walk slowly, not wanting the night to end.

Through the large wooden door into the high entrance hall. Up the stone stairs to the small wooden door that leads to the narrow entranceway and into the small hall. We take our shoes off quietly and move into the kitchen. It's much smaller than the bedrooms with only a wooden table and four chairs. Emilia sits in the corner of the room, Sam and I on the other side.

"You know what I have in my bag?" Sam grins at me devilishly.

There are times when alcohol fuels conversation, but today conversation is fuelling the alcohol. With a bottle of vodka and a packet of cards, we drink a shot to start our games. On a normal day, vodka tastes like hairspray, but as the cards are dealt, it flows sweet and delicious.

I lose. Another shot for me.

Sam loses. One for him.

Emilia loses. One for her.

Back and forth the games go, each one getting longer, none of us wanting to drink too much.

My head is dizzy. Life, vodka, the girl, I no longer know what the cause is.

That secret smile, I catch it again. Another kick in my chest.

A flick of the hair, burning eyes.

The cards become less important. Words flow easily, but with decreasing precision.

Am I talking to Emilia too much? I think I am, yet her attention seems as fixated on me as much as mine is on her. I am powerless to stop this. Or do I not want to?

In the bathroom I splash my face with cold water, looking at myself in the mirror, staring deep into my eyes, into my soul. My reflection stares straight back. Can it see into me?

A shirt, tanned skin, hair almost styled, I don't look like the same person I have been for the past couple of months.

Another splash of water. I'm still here.

I walk back to the kitchen. The murmur of our voices fills the room, a constant chattering. Outside, the world is sleeping, preparing for another day. What would I be doing right now if I was in England or South Korea, or one of my previous homes? Those places seem a million miles away.

"I have a game," Emilia suggests. The cards forgotten, I am happy for a change of focus.

"I hope it's a good one."

"It's called the country game. We each take a piece of paper and divide it into six columns. One for countries, one for capital cities, one for animals, one for movies, one for singers, and one for brands. For each randomly picked letter, we must fill in each column with one thing that begins with that letter. First one to finish says stop and that's game over. Got it?" We both nod. I think I have it. "OK, let's go. E…"

E, how easy. OK, country… Eritrea. I like that. City, Edinburgh. Animal, eel. Movie, Eternal Sunshine of the Spotless Mind. What a brilliant movie name. Good movie too. Another sip of vodka, yuk, why did I do that? Two more. A singer, Eminem. And the easiest one, a brand. A brand… a brand beginning with E. There must be hundreds or thousands. I look around the room for a clue. Why is this one so difficult? E, e, e. Eeyore, eyelids, everglades, is that an air freshener? Could try and pretend, but that's not fair. Elephant, ear, Exxon. That will do.

"Stop," says Emilia before I have time to review my answers.

After several rounds we total up the scores. Emilia is the winner.

"Not bad for people who don't speak English."

"I speak English," retorts Sam.

"Irish, like English, but different." I can't tell if he is amused or annoyed.

Another round, another shot.

The game is soon forgotten.

"I have just thought of something brilliant, I must write it down." I rush out to my bag and pull out my notebook. What was that great idea again? If I just sit here, it will come back to me. I sit on the bed, biting the end of my pen. The idea is inside my head, I just can't remember where. The harder I think, the more distant it becomes.

"Are you coming back?" Emilia is at the doorway of the bedroom. I must have been not thinking for quite some time.

"Yes, I am. This is my notebook. For ideas."

"Can I see?" She sits on the bed beside me.

She is so close, I can almost taste her.

I flick through the notebook, never stopping on a page long enough for her to read more than a word or two.

"It's kind of… my thing." There must be one page I could share with her. Most of it is nonsense, pages full of words, illegible to all but I. I find a hand-drawn map of Europe. "How about this?"

"What is it?"

"It's Europe. It's where I want to go." There is a line up to Sweden and a second to Finland. Both of us reach out at the same time, resting our fingers upon the page.

Our hands are touching and our bodies are so close and I'm not looking at the map anymore and nor is she, but she's looking at me and I'm looking at her and there's that smile, that secret smile, that soft face behind her hair and I watch as her eyes close, but I feel my eyes close too and our lips are so close, I can feel her breathing and they touch, our lips touch, actually touch, I have walked into the dragon's lair. A kiss.

Fizzy jelly beans run across my skin, warming me outside and in. She has such soft lips.

Just as I looked at myself in the mirror, I look at Emilia and she looks right back at me. I feel completely comfortable in her gaze, as if I have known her for so much longer than the hours we have been talking. She bites her bottom lip, nervously, seductively. The corner of my mouth half raises, an almost smile.

Her secret smile, my secret smile, shared. Is this really happening or will I awake in the morning to find it was a wonderfully disappointing dream?

Our fingers intertwine and time stops or races or maybe it does backflips.

Sam is alone in the kitchen. One more minute. One more minute. One more minute.

Sam is alone in the kitchen and looking irritated when we return.

"More vodka?" I ask. That should help.

All I can think about is the girl across the table from me. She moves with such fluidity, every action intentional, her hair flicking across her face, her eyes burning bright.

More cold water on my face.

Is it nearly morning?

Another game. I don't care about the game.

Sam goes to bed.

Another stolen kiss, a secret smile.

This is not what I expected.

13. Pain

I am on fire.

I am a broken shell.

I am the balloon that has just been trampled, deflated, and stomped under foot.

I am in a lot of pain.

Clench my teeth and let it pass. It eases. What is that pain? I cannot even tell what hurts. Somewhere between my stomach and my groin, another rip, another stab.

Breathe deeply and let it pass.

Breathe.

Wait.

Breathe.

Wait.

The embers of the fire burn, but I can open my eyes.

It's bright. Where am… ah!

Close to me, Emilia is still sleeping in shorts and a t-shirt. I am wearing the same.

She looks as soft as she looked last night, the smile upon her lips even in slumber.

This is where I should be right now. How could it be that I haven't known this girl for years?

Emilia begins to open her eyes as I shuffle around.

Does she feel the same? Or did she just drink too much? I don't think we drank too much.

Her face lights up.

She feels the same.

"Good morning." I kiss her.

"Good morning."

I see Sam moving around outside the room through the open door. I should probably get up, but I am so comfortable here. Two more minutes.

One more minute.

OK, get up.

In the kitchen, Sam stares at me as I walk in, his face like thunder.

"Morning," I mumble.

Maybe he didn't hear me. Maybe I didn't hear him. I'll just carry on and get some water.

I wince as the fire ignites once more. What is that pain?

At the table, we sit in silence.

What an interesting street I can see out of this window, I think I'll keep staring into the distance. Is Sam still looking at me? I could look at him, but probably best not to. Just keep doing nothing.

Water empty, refill glass, sit down, look out window.

Water empty, go to bathroom, avoid kitchen.

I change out of the shorts I slept in, sporting jeans instead.

Now what? I definitely don't want to go back into the kitchen. Maybe a walk would be a good idea.

"Does anyone want to go for a walk around the city?" I call across the apartment. Tomasz is at work and Emilia has to translate a Swedish book into Polish. The question is only for Sam, but I pose it to everyone.

"I have to work for a few hours," Emilia calls back, telling me what I already know. No response from Sam. I can wait.

Although I don't really know what to do right now. "Sam? Want to go for a walk?"

"Alright."

Down the stone stairs, out the giant wooden door, and into the street we go. Another beautiful day of blue skies and a new addition, an unidentified pain that stabs harder every few seconds as I walk.

We walk in silence, one street, then another. Nothing to say. Probably should say something.

"Nice day. Very blue. Good weather in Poland." Brilliant, what a conversation starter. When in doubt, always go for weather observations, something everyone can agree on. Yes it is nice, yes it is blue, yes the weather is good in Poland. Yes I can't think of anything interesting to say so I simply put out words.

Another blade to the stomach. I wince.

I want to lie down on the floor and curl up in a ball, wrap up the pain, throw it away. Bang, bang, bang on my head.

"I'll just fucking come out and fucking say it then!" Sam explodes to my right. I don't think this is about the weather. "Last night was fucking out of order." Definitely not about the weather. "You guys are like fucking children, all over each other, giggling and touching, it makes me sick. I would have thought better of you after all the time we've spent together, at least give me the decency. And her. I haven't got much respect for her. She meets some guy and suddenly, oh wow, I'm in love. It's pathetic, both of you. This morning I was going to just pack my bags and go without saying anything, but I thought I'd at least give you the decency of explaining yourself." Sam is bright red, a spitting, raging, fuming bull. He brushes his long red hair out of his face every few seconds, only for it to fall back again.

All I can think about is the knife in my stomach.

"I don't feel so good."

"You don't feel so good? That's all you can say, that you don't feel so good? I don't feel so good either. Maybe you shouldn't have drunk so much vodka or been awake all night and then maybe you'd feel OK. Do you really have nothing to say for yourself?"

"I don't really know what you want me to say."

Sam's normally calm demeanour has been transformed into a beast off the leash, hungry for blood. "Well how about sorry for a fucking start, that might be a good fucking idea."

Is Sam the dragon?

I mull over the idea of apologising in my head. "Sorry for what?"

"Where do I start? Sorry for ignoring me, sorry for acting like a teenager, sorry for sitting on my bed so that I couldn't go to bed, and sorry for sneaking off together like children to get your notebook. That was such a pathetic excuse, I'm not fucking stupid."

"I do not believe you are stupid. I am sorry… let me think… I am sorry that I upset you. And I am sorry for sitting on your bed. I am not sorry about Emilia."

"You talk to this girl for ten fucking hours and you think you two are meant to be together? I thought I knew you. I meant what I said, you don't know how close I was to just walking out that door this morning and leaving without you. I don't even know if I want to travel with you anymore."

"Sam, if you want to go separate ways, we can go separate ways. That's fine. However, I never said we were meant to be together, but ten hours isn't a tiny period of time. If that was someone you knew at work who you only interacted with for ten minutes a day, that is the same as knowing someone for several months. I think I like her." The words, unexpected, almost catch in my throat. But they are true. I like this girl enough to say it aloud. Maybe it would be easier if Sam and I went separate ways right now.

"I think it's really immature." Sam continues speaking for another couple of minutes, venting and losing steam until he returns to the Sam I have known for the past couple of weeks. Concentrating on the pain, I miss most of his words.

"Can we sit down here for a bit?"

There is a large brick wall and high above it, a castle overlooks the city. We lean against the wall and my body is immediately grateful for the respite.

"What's wrong?"

"My stomach or my groin, or something just hurts really badly. It's a shooting pain that is worse with every step I take. Sitting down makes it less intense."

"That doesn't sound good. Is this caused by Emilia?" he smirks, dark thoughts.

"We can joke about this now? No, it isn't caused by Emilia. You saw the door was open and we were both clothed. I just slept in the room, that was all."

"Because you like her?"

"Because I like her."

"So what's this pain?"

"I have no idea, but it isn't very pleasant. You know, you were really angry and I don't think I have ever seen you angry before. You always seemed very nonchalant and noncommittal, then suddenly this morning it was as if someone had awoken the monster in you."

"I don't get angry very often, but when I do, I get really angry. It takes a lot to piss me off that badly though. I can't remember the last time it happened."

"Well I'm happy to be the source of intense emotions although it is somewhat more peaceful when you're not cursing at me and snarling. Although I do suppose it's better that you spoke out loud rather than internalising what was pissing you off. You might have imploded if not."

"I prefer to speak out."

"Agreed. The only thing worse than telling someone that you're pissed off with them, is being pissed off with them and not telling them. When I think you're a dick, I'll tell you too, although I think the word fuck sounds considerably better in an Irish accent. You can keep that word. And I don't think I would be able to sustain anger for quite so many minutes, that was impressive. I don't suppose you want to stay here for an extra night though?"

"Are you kidding me? No I don't want to stay another night. Tonight is more than enough."

"Fair, but you can't blame me for asking. So tomorrow we'll continue to Finland?"

"We will." The answer I expected, but I can't help feeling a little disappointed that I won't have more time with Emilia.

Feeling that I am now only being prodded rather than stabbed, we walk new roads through the city, as impressed as when we first came into it. How had I never thought of visiting this place?

We enter an ornate church to find more secrets: tall stained glass windows, elaborate sculptures, respectful silence.

"How about exploring the park?"

"Sure. Emilia said it's a series of gardens that are about four kilometres long and circle the city centre."

We stroll leisurely with others doing exactly the same as us, walking with no purpose other than walking. Some people sit on benches, others on the grass. Surrounded by trees on a strip of green no wider than thirty metres, we pass ponds and fully blooming flower beds. It's as if we aren't in the centre of a city at all.

Ahead of us, there is quite a commotion. People are gathered around two individuals, watching their performance. Are they wearing togas? Or grain sacks? It's hard to tell, but the two young guys holding everybody's attention seem to be attired in long white, shapeless dresses. The bizarre clothing hangs down to their ankles, sitting just above their bare feet and is decorated with handwritten messages.

One of the guys is juggling. Then they are both juggling. Now they juggle together, shouting, whooping. All the balls drop to the floor.

"We are from Slovakia," proclaims the guy in a headband, "and we are hitchhiking to the north of Poland without money. So please, if you like what we are doing, give us a coin, a note, anything to support our journey."

I've already taken a seat to watch them. I don't even remember sitting down.

The other performer pulls out a ukelele and begins strumming it, singing a medley of famous songs. The four chord song!

"This is our final act," they announce, strapping a slack line between two trees, two metres from the ground. The slack line, an unorthodox tightrope, is wide like the ribbons used to hold materials down on lorries. They tighten it with a crank, but it shivers softly in midair. If they fall, they will impale themselves upon the spiked fencing below them.

The boy with the headband climbs the tree and gets onto the slack line. Behind us, two police officers are taking the details of three youths drinking in the park. Apparently drinking laws are enforced here. "Shh," gestures the headband-toga wearer. "We don't have a license for this." The police are metres away from him, but their vision is obscured by a tree. He begins to juggle and walks the line, two metres above the ground. Around me I sense people watching tentatively. Are they hoping he doesn't get arrested or that he doesn't impale himself upon the spikes? Oftentimes people like watching other people fail, but this is not one of those times.

Inch by inch, he makes his way across to the other tree, then drops all the balls and leaps to the floor. Ta-da! Applause breaks out around us and quickly they disassemble their apparatus.

Some people walk away, but many more come forward to drop a few coins into the hat.

"I might say hello," I tell Sam. I wait for him to come forward with an idea, but he simply agrees with my sentiment. What would I say to them? No, probably nothing and besides, look how busy they are. I think I will just leave.

We walk away from the crowd and back around the park.

"No! I will say hello."

I march back up to the two performers, drop a few coins into the hat, and stand awkwardly as they talk to someone else.

"I really like what you guys are doing here. How has travelling without money been going?"

"Really great so far except for the police. We've been in trouble a few times, but we've learnt to try and get permits where possible. We're actually on our way to a juggling festival up north and thought of this idea last minute. What are you guys doing here though, you aren't Polish?"

We tell them that we too are hitchhiking and that is what made their show even more appealing to us. They pull out a video camera and ask us a few questions on film. I shift from foot to foot, unsure where to look with a lens pointed in my face. My name is Jamie, I'm from England, and I look ridiculous.

Wishing them well, we continue our stroll through the park.

Sam and I chat happily as we walk. The pains of the morning are far away as we return to the apartment and cook dinner, playing vodka free games with Tomasz and Emilia. Every moment alone with her is a stolen moment, something precious. We have only a few hours left together. It has been so long since I found someone so intriguing, so easy to be with: someone whose eyes I could look into with ease.

By morning, a weight sits upon my head. Not alcohol, not sickness, just sadness. We have known each other for two days, interacted for many hours, but now our paths depart. Two intense days signifying more time than typical relationships are given in many months. I don't want it to end, not yet.

I'm nervous as we pack our bags, my hands fidgeting as I tie my laces. I tell Sam I will catch up with him as he goes out the door.

"Emila," I begin. We are alone in her room. She looks at me, her eyes wide, a neutral expression on her pretty face. "I am going north in a few minutes, to the L countries, whichever way around they are, to Estonia and then to Finland. But I am coming back past here. I am going to Italy, to volunteer on a farm and to learn about bees. I could stop, I could not rush by. I could spend some more time with you. If you want me to of course. I mean, I could just not, I could go straight past. It's just an idea." Surely she will laugh me down. She will say how silly I am, maybe even pity me and say I'm cute, then hug me goodbye.

I hold my breath for an unbearable half second of silence.

That smile, the secret one. The one that lured me in unexpectedly. Her face lights up as she kisses me. "I would like that a lot." Her lilting accent, every blemish, perfection.

Fireworks upon my brain, a carnival inside my forehead.

I skip out the door and catch up with Sam.

"I'm coming back!" Sam isn't impressed.

I'm going north to Finland, to all sorts of places I know nothing about. I am alone, but I am with people. I have plans, but nothing is set in stone. I am free in the world, free to go anywhere, but with every step away from Kraków, I feel that I am a little further away from where I want to be today. The smile, that lilting accent, the eyes that look back at me without embarrassment. They have me.

I am caught in a trap. A delicious honey trap that offers me everything I need in the world. Yet still I walk away.

14. Survival Instincts

"Sam, did you know that Lithuania has the highest rate of suicide in the whole world except for Greenland? Except that Greenland doesn't really count because it isn't a country." Sam looks at me, perplexed. We are sitting in the cab of a lorry, heading towards the Polish, Lithuanian border, a few hundred miles from Kraków.

"How the fuck do you know stuff like that? You can't even remember where Lithuania is on a map."

"I like lists. Plus, when I was a mock English teacher in Korea, the kids were so overworked that they bordered on depression. I looked up the suicide rates and found that Korea had the second highest suicide rate in the world, just behind Lithuania. Excessive amounts of work, academies every evening after school, and testing almost every month contribute to the Korean suicide rate, but I have always wondered why Lithuania has such a high occurrence of choosing to end one's life early. The greatest pleasure for most of my kids in Korea was the opportunity to play video games for a few hours a week. As a kid, I used to play video games excessively because they were an escape from reality and allowed me to be something more in the world, but what is the problem in Lithuania? I know nothing of this country."

"Do you think you can learn some of the language too?"

I roll back into the bunk bed of the lorry, uninterested in talking about languages again. Yes I'm useless, no I don't want to talk about it. I curl up in a ball until we are dropped on the side of the road once more.

"One hundred!" I shout in delight. I have just counted off one hundred cars without a ride and it is Sam's turn to signal. He pulls himself out of slumber and stumbles to the side of the road. After more than a week of hitchhiking with an Irishman, I am fast becoming exhausted by our night time activities. Despite neither of us suffering typical hangovers, we get up in the mornings, function normally when engaging in new activities, but suffer heavy eyelids every time we stand on the side of the road. Is this what it would feel like to be an alcoholic? Drink heavily, feel OK, then have to take an afternoon nap?

I lie down on the side of the road and close my eyes, thinking about the past week. We didn't even drink for more than half the days, but still I'm tired.

"Get up, it's your turn."

"Already?" I feel that a hundred cars must have passed in a matter of seconds.

A car pulls over and I shout at Sam to get up. That's five in a row for me and I am grateful for the extra few minutes rest that I am permitted as we wait.

"Tell him to go away," I whisper as we stand beside a motorway bridge somewhere east of Warsaw in the evening. We've been waiting for over an hour and a new hitchhiker is approaching us. His backpack looks even fuller than mine although his tiny frame accentuates it. "You probably speak his language and there is no way we will get a ride with three guys."

"Where are you going?" he calls in English.

"Towards Lithuania. You?"

"Lithuania too. I'm flying to Georgia from there to go climbing."

I ask if I can feel his backpack and he tells me that it is full of climbing equipment, weighing over forty kilograms. I can barely stand with it on my back.

We fruitlessly wave at passing cars as both the night and storm clouds settle in overhead.

"Let's find some cover and look for food."

Far from a town, we hide our backpacks in some bushes and investigate the one supermarket that we can find. All of the bins are in a locked compound that can't be easily accessed without climbing a fence. Inside the fence we see workers scurrying to and fro. As the rain starts, we run for cover, pulling our backpacks from the bushes to sit under a canopy, watching the world being watered a few metres away. This is not the summer hitchhiking dream I had in mind.

Sam suggests we check a lone dumpster near the petrol station. I have little to no hope of finding anything in it and protest against walking into the rain unnecessarily. Aside from wild apples we foraged, we haven't eaten since being gifted breakfast pastries and raspberries early in the morning. Our hunger draws us half-heartedly into the rain.

"Goldmine!" In my delight, I am unsure if it is I or someone else who yells it. The bin is filled with full packets of cream cheese and hundreds of desserts. Yoghurts, creme caramel, even a wheel of camembert. How could people waste such delicious food? We grab as many armfuls as we can manage, then run back to the shelter of the canopy to arrange our finds in a great pyramid. There is enough food to last several days and that is just the tip of the iceberg. The bin has so many more treasures to find. Sam runs back into the rain to fetch more. What is this other guy's name? We talk until Sam returns, further adding to our stockpile.

The Slovakian guy, or was it Slovenian, pulls out a large metal cooking pot and begins heating it over my camping stove as we devour desserts. We fill the pot with pasta and when it's boiled, add three full packets of cream cheese: one each. The pasta is swimming in deliciousness. With temporary utensils, we sit around the large bowl, feasting on cream cheese and carbohydrates. After not eating for most of the day, we devour the pot as if we might never eat again, the rain dissipating with our hunger. Then it stops completely.

The awning that covers us is located on the edge of a car park, populated by sleeping lorries. The world is dark and no people are in sight. In a forest, we would be alone with nature, but here, there are signs of people close at hand.

"Look at that," I say to Sam and our nameless friend.

A red car drives slowly around the car park. Inside, neon blue lights illuminate the two inhabitants who watch us with lingering eyes. A little strange, but the car disappears behind the lorries.

We carry on eating and the car appears again, this time crawling even slower across the car park while taking a great interest in us. Oh no, here we go. I can see it now: 'three foreigners attacked in a car park.' What were the three foreigners doing in the car park in the first place? Imbeciles.

The car returns for a third lap, each circuit taking a full minute as they circle the group of lorries, studying us at slow speed, then repeating the process.

"I'm not comfortable with this, I want to leave," I declare, getting to my feet.

"It's fine." Sam dismisses it and the Slovakian, Slovenian guy does the same.

"I am moving, pack up everything, let's go, let's go, we're going!"

A fourth lap. A fifth. Is this the sixth? We finish throwing our widely spread belongings into our backpacks as the car begins its seventh lap of the car park. A second car joins it, crawling around the car park in an equally menacing fashion. I take a good look at the people inside the cars. Two guys in each, all four with shaved heads. Why do people with shaved heads look so much more intimidating? Maybe it's because they drive around car parks late at night with lingering eyes.

The cars almost stop before crawling out of sight once more. We have at least thirty seconds before they return.

"Go, go, go!"

The three of us run across the car park as fast as we can, aiming for the cover of the parked lorries. We sneak into the shadows as the cars return for another lap. Behind us, both cars accelerate. Are they looking for us?

Look, nothing. Go.

Stop, wait, look… go.

We dodge from shadow to shadow until reaching the safety of the garage forecourt. Under lights and cameras, no one will touch us. The two cars come out of the lorry park and stop for a few seconds. They are definitely looking at us, but they can't touch us now, surely they can't. We are under lights, there are cameras and other people. The cameras will protect us.

Accelerating hard, both cars wheel-spin out of the garage and into the night.

Please don't come back.

The three of us pull out the food once more and continue eating under the light of the garage. Five desserts each, a block of camembert, it doesn't matter. We're hungry, alive, and all of this food was being wasted.

"Sorry for making us move guys, but I feel better that we did." In a previous life, I might have sat and waited for something bad to happen with my fingers crossed.

"Next time, we have these," the climber announces. He pulls two great ice axes from his bag. Designed expressly for the purpose of smashing into solid ice, the ice axes are the perfect weapon. I could not think of a better head splitting tool.

"You had those all along?! Why didn't you say something?" If anyone was threatening to attack me, I don't think I could have wielded a more intimidating implement, aside from a gun. "Next time, we'll just sit with our ice axes and no one will cause us any problems."

Yes, of course I will. I will stand there with my giant ice axes, battling off the whole world like the Spartan warriors. I'm clearly such an intimidating figure. I remind myself why I don't carry a knife for protection: don't wield something that you don't know how to wield. If I was trying to defend myself with a knife, I have no doubt that I would hold it at arm's length and like a rattlesnake, it would be as dangerous to me as to the other person. Yes, better to keep relying on my instincts and sneaking through the shadows.

When we can eat no more, we fill our backpacks with as much as we can carry, then return the excess food to the bin where it came from. Outside the forecourt, the rain begins to fall again.

The three of us rush back to the bridge on the motorway where we first met and take cover under it as the rain becomes heavier. The two roads under the bridge are separated by a large concrete column and beside the road, concrete slopes steeply upwards before forming a flat shelf, one metre wide. It's dark, but street lights nearby provide enough glow for us to see what we're doing. The warnings of friends and teachers ring loud in my ears: 'You'll end up sleeping under a bridge.' Is this as low as I can go?

At the top of the slope, we put our bags down on the flat platform. It's high enough that we are out of the streetlight's direct beam and anyone passing below would struggle to see us. An unplanned roll would pose quite a painful, albeit brief journey to the road.

"This is a good place to sleep." Sam is very jovial. We are under a bridge and it is raining. We are going to sleep under a bridge. "I'm glad this bridge is here, it keeps us nice and dry."

If my mother could see me now, how proud she would be. Her son, a graduate of mathematics, sleeping under a bridge, eating from a bin, running from unknown skinheads.

The three of us get our sleeping bags out and spread ourselves across the narrow ledge. I close my eyes and the pitter-patter of rain becomes rhythmic. The passing cars are almost unnoticeable and the street lights form a bubble of safe shadows around us. Beaten back by the rain, the night is free from mosquitos and the concrete I lay upon is far comfier than I had expected.

The world moves into night, people slowly passing by as we lay undetected beneath the motorway. Cars pass at speed overheard. None of them know that they pass over our resting bodies.

Maybe sleeping under a bridge isn't so bad after all.

JAMIE BOWLBY-WHITING

15. Choice

Oh my god, we're going to collide head on and it'll all be over, the end, bye-bye, no going back. Why the hell is this happening? It shouldn't be happening, I don't want it to be happening, I can't stop it happening.

The lorry we're overtaking aggressively pushes us towards the verge of the road and we slow down on the gravel. Ahead of us, cars approach at high speed.

We have a matter of seconds before impact.

After everything, this is all it comes down to, one simple decision, one mistake. I want to scream and shout and dance and sing, carve pictures into the trees and care for bees, walk through forests and swim to islands, sail the seven seas that I can't even name.

I am not ready yet.

"Look," is all I can muster, pointing meekly ahead. Sam is already looking, his eyes popping out of his head.

What makes me saddest of all is that the mistake is not my own, that I don't have a choice in what is about to happen.

Whatever will be will be.

At the last possible minute, the lorry relents trying to run us off the road and we swing wide on the gravelly verge. Without slowing down and moving in the opposite direction, a car passes between us and the lorry.

My death was much less dramatic than I expected, with considerably less flashbacks. It would have simply happened and then all would have been over and I would know no more. The world would not stop spinning, people would not stop living their lives, and by midnight, another day would have passed. Just another day, the day on which I died.

"Normal, normal," the driver assures us, laughing jovially. Normal or not, I far prefer when traffic passes in two directions, not three. Least of all when I am a passenger in the most precarious position, not quite on the road. I want to shout it out and tell him that it isn't OK. Instead, I reinsert my eyeballs into their sockets and sit with my hands in my lap, my heart racing. Sam and I exchange a glance that speaks a thousand words. It says that was pretty close to us dying, let's never let that happen again. We both start giggling uncontrollably like schoolgirls. What is the evolutionary benefit of finding hilarity shortly after a near death experience? It's

124

not funny, but we can't stop laughing.

I'm grateful to get into a new car piloted by a pleasant young woman and her father. Surely this won't involve three lanes of alternating traffic. We stop to drink cold drinks with them in a roadside cafe, more gifts of the road.

Accept kindness, never expect.

"Can I join you guys?" asks another hitchhiker. We look begrudgingly out the window at the small hatchback. The boot is full and we already have our backpacks on our laps. Reluctantly we concede that if he doesn't have a ride by the time we leave, he can join us.

He doesn't have a ride.

The three of us squeeze into the smaller than aeroplane seats and bury ourselves under our baggage. For the rest of the journey we will be talking backpacks.

An hour later, I gratefully stretch my legs, allowing my blood to circulate as we split into two groups once more. We're all heading in the same direction, but the other hitchhiker is in a hurry and it seems likely that we'll get a quicker ride by splitting up. Sam and I walk down the road, looking at the map to hypothesise where we are. "I think it's about three hundred miles to Vilnius. Maybe four hundred. Or less." We have absolutely no idea. Keep following the road and eventually you'll get where you're going.

An old white car, driven by a man with leathery skin, skids to a stop beside us. "Get in," shouts a voice. I recognise that voice.

It's him, hitchhiker number three is sitting in the passenger seat. We bundle into the back seats of the car and a quick glance at Sam acknowledges that we are both thinking the same thing: it was a good idea to let hitchhiker number three ride with us despite the cramped conditions.

The driver lacks comprehension in German, French, Lithuanian, Latvian, and who knows whatever other languages Sam and hitchhiker number three throw at him. Finally they get a response in Russian.

"He's from Kazakhstan and is driving to Kaunas to buy a car." That's a drive of several thousand miles. He must have literally been driving for days.

"Can you tell him that is a long drive?" I ask Sam.

The driver nods enthusiastically.

Using Sam as an interpreter, I converse with the driver until Sam tires of the game and refuses to translate anymore.

"Just one more question?"

"No."

I watch hundreds of miles roll past the window until we finally reach Lithuania, one of the seemingly most depressed countries in the world if suicide rates are anything to go by. A Kazakh, an Englishman, an Irishman, and a man of unknown origins enter the most depressed country in the world. It sounds like the beginning of a bad joke.

All the world has been rolled flat and painted green. It is neither ugly nor pretty. More than anything else, it's rather boring and I could be on any flat part of farmland in the world without knowing the difference. There is nothing to distinguish where we are, but while uninspiring, this can't be the cause of so much sadness.

We thank the Kazakh man for driving us several hundred miles and get called over by a guy smoking a joint. He barely looks old enough to drive, but offers to take us towards Vilnius, our intended destination. Delicately I touch on the subject of the high suicide rate, desiring to know a real person's opinion of the problem.

"I didn't know about the suicide rate, but people here are depressed man. It's all about money. Look at me for example, I'm twenty-two years old and I'm a saxophonist. I have a daughter and a wife at home, but I don't play the saxophone because nobody has money to pay for music. We're so poor in this country that we do all we can do to survive. Instead of playing music, I work a terrible job so that my family can get by. You don't want to be here too long, it'll get you down." It's a story of warning rather than a sob story.

"Sorry to hear that, but if it's so bad here in Lithuania, why don't you go somewhere else?"

"No, I've thought about that, but I can't leave. Lithuania is my home so I just have to live here, I just have to get by. This is my place now actually." He points at a large, dreary apartment block, even more uninspiring than the flat landscape we passed through. "I'd love to offer you guys a ride into the city, but you know, gas is expensive. You can find a bus or something just down the road." Embarrassed, I thank him for already being so kind.

We climb four floors to the home of Darius, a teenager who invited us to stay in the apartment he shares with his mother and grandmother. Sam gets into the shower.

"You guys need to be careful in this place, walking around alone like that. Man, this city is twisted. I've been stabbed four times, but none of them got me properly. That's why I'm still here. Look, I'm still here, they can't kill me." I sit nodding, wishing that Sam wasn't in the shower. Darius takes off his shirt and shows me the apparent stab wounds. There are definitely marks of some sort, but I have no desire to question their validity. "If you want to stab someone properly, you do it like this." Darius unsheathes a leather handled knife, amply long enough to go through an arm or reach a vital organ, then waves it alarmingly close to my face. Holding it blade down, he swings it emphatically, showing me how to inflict real damage by indicating where on my body he would strike.

I don't like the demonstration, I don't want to know how to stab someone, I want Sam to come back from the shower. In fact, I shouldn't even be here, I should be hundreds of miles away with Emilia, getting to know her more, sharing that secret smile. Even sleeping under a bridge again would be preferable to this.

"How about we go out for a beer, see a bit of the city?" I suggest.

"I'll show you some of the city, but no beer, it's too expensive here."

"I'll buy you a beer." I'll sing and dance for you if you put the knife down.

Darius changes his clothes and puts a harness across his body to which his knife holder clips. He is now carrying a concealed weapon that is potentially lethal and taking me into a city that he describes as twisted. This is not OK.

"I don't think you need that." Take off the knife you lunatic. "I am sure we will be fine having a quiet walk." I am not walking with you if you take the knife.

"You don't know this place."

"Please."

"It's not safe."

"I can't get arrested with someone carrying a dangerous weapon." Eventually Darius concedes. When he leaves the room and Sam has returned, I whisper, "Sam, he's got a huge knife and he just told me about stabbing people and being stabbed and now he wants to take his knife out with us, but I said no. I think we should leave."

"We don't have anywhere to go."

"Good point. Tomorrow let's leave. I'll tell Darius that we have to go in the morning."

We walk through a dark park, along a busy road, across the main square, and into winding alleys, all without being threatened or stabbed. Pretty towers spring from various buildings, but all in all, I find the city as nondescript as the landscape. At a quiet bar, we sip beer outside, learning more about Lithuania and its apparent flaws.

Without the knife, Darius isn't so bad after all, he's just a young guy trying to impress. He has his flaws and his positives, just like everybody else in the world. And Lithuania isn't so bad after all. The sadness, the suicide, the problems, all of them seem to be finance related according to the people we talk to. Money, or lack-thereof, drains happiness from so much of the world. What would it have been like to live in a world hundreds of years ago, a world where everybody simply survived and didn't have to know how poor they were compared to everyone else in the world? That sounds like the kind of world I would like to live in. Money should never be important enough to cause sadness. Yet happiness cannot be bought. No, this must be more complicated than a financial issue.

"People drink a lot here too," Darius tells us. "Especially the poor people. They make their own alcohol and it only makes their problems worse." No doubt a cocktail of misery and alcohol can only end badly.

Without knives in our backs, we sit at the breakfast table and munch greedily on the mountains of pancakes that Darius' grandmother has laid out for us. She chats happily with Sam in Russian, layering pancake upon pancake tower. We smother them in runny jam and sour yoghurt, foods typical to Lithuania that I haven't seen before.

"I think you should tell her to stop making them," I whisper to Sam. "They're good, but I am about to burst."

"I already have, but I think it makes her happy to have someone to cook for."

Unable to eat any more, I finally give up and the pancake marathon comes to an end. A mound of untouched pancakes remains upon the table. Is this the stage of giving that the German waterfall man told me about? I definitely didn't want to eat those last few pancakes, but I ate them to try and make someone else feel happy. Now I feel thoroughly miserable and sick.

"That poor lady," Sam explains as we head back to the road once more, "is trapped in that apartment. She is too unwell to get down the stairs and day after day, she sits at home doing nothing at all, not talking to anyone except Darius and his mother who have both heard all of her stories. She was so interesting, we talked about life under the communists and if we had more time, I could have carried on talking to her for weeks."

"Trapped with no hope for the future, that sounds like the worst kind of prison." Soon all her stories will be lost because there is no one who cares to record them. It's a sad truth, but people bring nothing into the world and take nothing out, leaving little more than a ripple on the surface of the earth. Only a few have a legacy that survive for multiple generations. "We should start writing down the stories of people that we meet on the road. It would be a little snapshot of reality, of real people's lives." I write the idea down in my notebook for another day.

North of Vilnius, the land is less flat, less boring. Certain parts of it could be mistaken for parts of England if you didn't know where you were. No, Lithuania really isn't a bad looking country at all.

As Sam and I walk on a residential street in Riga, the capital of Latvia, we are a couple of hundred miles north of Vilnius and I can almost remember which way around the two countries are on a map. The streets are wide and the buildings made of heavy stone. It's pretty: a less attractive version of Kraków. Even the thought of that city now fills me with excitement.

"That lady was here last time I came." Sam points out a tiny old woman selling bunches of flowers on the corner of the street. She smiles at the passers by, then raises the flowers to her nose, inhaling deeply. Her face floods with such serenity that you might believe the flowers to be the most delightful thing in all the world.

No one stops, no one buys her flowers.

Sam greets her in Russian and she pulls a newspaper clipping from her pocket to show us an article about herself. I nod, oblivious of the meaning in the words. She doesn't seem to mind.

"That's the same newspaper cutting she had a couple of years ago."

"So this lady just stands here, selling flowers every day, going through the same routine?"

"She does. You'll see her here tomorrow, you'll see her every day you come to this corner. She never moves, she never has more than a few bunches of flowers, she never has a new selling routine." It's not the buildings, it is this woman that is the cornerstone of the city. Everything moves around her, but she comes, rain or shine, day after day.

Despite the calm demeanour of Riga, both Sam and I are desperate to get out of the city. We've been city hopping and we are country people at heart.

Little over twenty miles outside of the city, barefooted we walk onto the soft white sands of Jūrmala, grains of sand dancing across our toes. The beach stretches out for miles either side of us and the sea laps softly at the shore, little more than a pond rippled by a passing boat. The buzz of all the cities in all the world has disappeared and we have found calm.

"Vodka or Riga Balsam?" Oh no, it's that sort of night.

I sip the black liquor of Riga Balsam from its strange ceramic bottle and instantly cringe in disgust. It's a traditional herbal liquor that Sam claims is delicious. It does not agree with my tastebuds.

"That is one of the least pleasant drinks I have ever had the displeasure of tasting. It's like a dirty combination of aniseed and tar."

Surrounded by calm, I feel myself being overwhelmed by the desire to swim. "Sam, do you want to swim?" Sam does not want to swim in the cold water.

I run down to the water in nothing but my pants and leap in, plunging my head beneath the surface. Instantly the breath is ripped from me by icy fingers and my head spins. An evening swim in the Baltic sea is far more appealing from the warmth of the shore. I run back to our little camp and dress in hippy pants and my one hoody.

One on one, Sam and I talk for hours, watching the sun set over the water and cooking pasta on the camp stove. With night comes distant noises and mosquitoes.

"Rich Russians," Sam explains. "They love to come to this place and party." Chinese lanterns float elegantly into the sky and I pull my hood over my head, tying the drawstring. My whole body, except for my face, is covered to protect me from the unrelenting attack of mosquitos. I don't think they make them this big in England.

Behind us in the darkness, we hear a language I don't understand. A large lady has collapsed on the sand and is talking in her sleep. Sam translates her slurred Russian speech.

"I already told you. Just leave me alone."

"Do you think she is going to be OK?"

"Apart from being eaten alive by mosquitoes, I don't think she'll have any problems." We leave the lady with her nightmares and the probable headache that will follow her drinking.

She is still murmuring when we turn in for the night, the same few words over and over, but by morning, she is gone and there is no sign of her presence other than a shallow body print in the soft sand.

Under brilliant blue skies we climb into the Latvian hills surrounded by forests. "I always wanted to try this," I gabble excitedly as we climb into small karts attached to a metal rail. I am a small child about to board a real life alpine roller coaster. The only control I have is a brake lever.

Brakes, ha. I don't need brakes.

I race down the hill, through the trees, around sharp bends.

This thing is going to derail! I am going to impale myself upon a tree. Brakes, I definitely need brakes!

I pull the lever hard enough that I no longer feel under threat of breaking my neck every time I hit a bend, but soft enough to keep my body hair standing on end.

Thirty seconds of brilliance.

In the hot sun, we find our way to a river and I swim while Sam paddles in the shallows. It's so warm, a hundred times more pleasant than the icy sea. I swim across the body of water, battling hard with the strong current. This is a little stronger than I anticipated, I seem to be getting sucked downstream.

Keep swimming.

Is that a whistle? And a megaphone?

Keep swimming.

Exhausted, I reach the other side of the river.

Downstream I see a lifeguard waving for me to go back to the other side of the river. I suppose the coloured buoys meant danger, don't cross this point. While the lifeguard seems unsupportive of my decision to cross the river, he seems even less keen on the idea of leaping into the water to save me if I start drowning.

I need a little break.

I wave to the lifeguard, he doesn't wave back. More words I don't understand blast through the megaphone.

Back I go, swimming hard.

Safely in the slow moving water, the lifeguard stops whistling at me and returns to his little hut.

That short swim was exhausting. I walk into the lone wooden hut near the river and in the unlit bathroom, greedily gulp down as much water as I can before filling my water bottle. Out in the sunlight, I notice that my cool refreshing water is less delightful than I had first thought. It's a dark, reddish brown, so murky that I can barely even call it transparent. Note to self: look at things in light before putting them into your mouth and swallowing them. I pour the rest of the water onto the floor, but my bottle smells funky. How did I not notice the awful smell when I was drinking it? Additional note to self: also smell things before putting them into your mouth and swallowing them.

We are on the side of a small road, surrounded by thick forest.

My head is a rowboat, rising and falling on the gentle ocean swells. Back and forth, back and forth. A storm threatens.

"Do you mind if I sit down for a bit?" I lie on the floor and close my eyes.

A car stops. My stomach lurches at the prospect of being in a moving vehicle. I slump into the back seat.

Don't throw up in the car, don't throw up in the car.

I sleep.

Is this dry land?

I sense the storm has passed, but struggle to my feet and realise my head is still in the row boat, only the water is calmer than before.

In the cab of a Russian trucker, Sam jokes to the driver about my inability to speak anything other than English. They both look at me and laugh. Mocked to my face with words I can't understand, spiders begin to crawl under my skin once more. It's a routine enough occurrence that I don't even need to ask for a translation.

Sulking, I crawl into the bunk bed and put my head down, out of sight for the few hours until we are dropped on the motorway near Tallinn, the capital of Estonia.

Under the darkness of night and having spent several hours curled up in the bunk bed, I have no idea what Estonia looks like when I get out of the lorry. The unpleasant twinge of a mosquito feasting on my blood. Then another. The skies are alive, a swarm of hungry insects. I feel the proteins of the saliva reacting with my body, itching as I run for cover, small mounds raising as souvenirs of the insects' visits.

"Quickly Sam, this is horrible."

On the side of the motorway, surround by either marsh or scrub land, there is no cover. I stop running and jump the motorway barrier then begin assembling my tent as fast as possible to escape the wrath of the mosquitos. They keep biting, over and over, every pregnant female feast another supporter of the mosquito population.

With the tent assembled, we bundle in and pull up the zipper. Sam is on my leg, and his bag is in the way. We struggle to rearrange the interior of our home so that it accommodates the both of us. My arms tingle all over and I rub them viciously, disregarding the possibility of ripping open the uneven surface.

"I don't think I have ever been bitten by that many mosquitos."

The ground is uneven and the itching becomes worse. From outside I am sure I can hear the threatening whine of mosquitos, that dreaded sound signalling imminent attack. Whine, whine, whine, here I come to get you. Or maybe I hear the ones that got into the tent, the ones that will feed on our unprotected faces through the night.

"I am so uncomfortable," I complain. A few metres away, separated only by the low metal railing, vehicles cruise by at tremendous speeds, whooshing, roaring, threatening. "This ground isn't even close to flat and we're on a hill. This is horrible."

"Should we move?"

"For the noise and the uneven ground, I want to move, but I can't bear to face those insects again. My whole body feels like it is full of tiny bugs below the surface, running and tickling. What I'd love right now, would be to get into a cold shower and wash them all away." I think of Kraków, over eight or nine hundred miles away. There is a shower, a comfortable bed, more than one hundred and seventy-three centimetres of tent to sleep inside... that smile. "This is a day where I wish I was somewhere else. Like Kraków."

The conversation is dangerously steered in the direction of Emilia and Sam begins to ask questions. "What did you think of her?" Has he forgotten our previous conversations?

"I liked her. No, I do like her. She is funny, pretty, and very easy to get along with. I feel entirely comfortable in her presence and it's not often that you find all of those things in a single person in such a short amount of time." Sam nods softly in the dark.

"When you go back, how long do you think you'll stay for?"

"A few days, a week. Who knows? I feel after only the three days we were there, I want to spend more time with her and also to stop for a little bit. In the past couple of months, I have rarely stayed in a place longer than two nights."

"I'm not sure what I thought of Emilia." It's an abrupt change of topic and something that I didn't ask to know. "She's not really my sort of girl and I don't find that sort of girl particularly attractive either. I'm more into alternative types."

What does that even mean?

Exhausted, frustrated, itching, I pull my sleeping bag over my head. I don't want to talk, I don't want the mosquitos to eat me, I don't want to be here.

Hold tight.

I have no other choice.

16. Decisions

In a mall in Tallinn, Sam and I access the internet to finalise our upcoming plans.

I read through a hitchhiking forum about how to cross from Tallinn to Helsinki.

'It's not possible to hitch rides with people going by car. If there is an extra passenger in a car or truck, an extra ticket has to be paid.'

A bad sign.

I navigate to some ferry sites and investigate tickets. Why aren't ferry sites as easy to use as flight sites? No service available at this time, please try another time. I want to see every crossing, I don't care what time we have to be there!

At length, I manage to pull up a few tickets and prices. "Sam, the cheapest return tickets I can find are sixty euros each, assuming you book the date and time in advance. If we missed our boat, we'd have to buy a new ticket."

Disappointment spreads across his face. I feel exactly the same. As much as we both want to continue our journey to Finland, neither of us will spend sixty euros on ferry tickets.

We need a new plan.

I log on to my emails to find that there is a message from the Italian farm at which I will be volunteering.

'Hello Jamie. Unfortunately now is a bad time at the farm, I am really sorry but I have two volunteers arriving now and who want to rest here for a long time. I waited for your reply and circumstances have developed considerably since then. I am very sorry but I will not be able to accommodate you this month. But we will keep in touch and if circumstances change and you are available I will write to you.'

Buggar.

I scroll back through the exchange of emails. I was supposed to get there in a few days which would have never happened and promised only to stay for two weeks. This is a sincere apology, but how will I learn about bees and goats now? I wish the Italians good luck with their farm, but even in a ten word email they will sense my disappointment.

"Sam, no more Italy for me."

Here I am again, stuck over. Twenty-five years old with nothing, not even the opportunity to learn about a life I would like to live.

Next email.

'Dear Jamie, I have just noticed you might be travelling to Poland soon. We have a couple of openings for a language immersion programme in Poland where you receive board and lodging in a quality hotel in return for conversing in English with business executives from all over the country.'

I read through the information and browse pictures of the hotel. A fancy hotel in the country and three meals a day, all for speaking English? Plus it's in Poland, three weeks from now. Three weeks to explore the Baltic states, spend time in Kraków, and then have something to look forward to. Perfect.

I email back to say that I would love to take part in the program.

Next email. A message from my father saying that he would like to come and visit me.

I can't believe it.

For the first time in five years of living outside the UK, both sides of my family are visiting me. Maybe they are worried that this time I have gone too far, that it's not OK for me to do what I am doing. I tell my dad the dates of the program and suggest meeting a couple of days later in Croatia. I hear Croatia has nice beaches and as travel is free, it doesn't matter how far away it is.

Next email. The language immersion program has accepted me for the immersion program, that was quick. Can I provide proof of plane, bus, or train tickets to Poland? No I cannot, I hitchhike. I can only promise.

Promises would be nice if they could be believed, but some proof of attendance is necessary as part of company policy. Can I provide a hostel or hotel booking? No I cannot. For the past couple of nights I have been sleeping outside, but often I sleep in the homes of strangers. I can only promise.

Taking me on my electronic word, my place on the language program is confirmed. A warm sense of contentment washes over me. For the next month, I have a loose plan.

"Look at this." I gesture towards images of the hotel. Intrigued, Sam reads through the exchange of emails.

"Do you think I could do it too?" A further month of travelling together.

"I don't know, try emailing."

Within a few minutes, Sam is confirmed to join me on the language immersion program. Then he finds a Latvian farm looking for volunteers. "I've always wanted to improve my Latvian."

I tell him that it would be a great opportunity to practise Latvian if that's what he wants to do. His allegiance switches instantly and the divergence of our paths is confirmed. Together we will turn south, parting ways in Latvia as he goes to his farm and I head towards a girl I have known for only a few days, but think of often.

We walk the world anew, revitalised by our exciting news. Tallinn's old town is full of twisted streets, pointed roofs, and grand windows, all carved from a regal mix of heavy stone and soft pastels. Yes, I like this place very much. Who even cares that I don't speak languages? What does it matter that Sam criticised Emilia? No, none of that matters at all. I have a direction and a purpose and this next week shall be a good one.

As the skies open, we shelter in a hostel bar, playing board games. Two friends hanging out.

"Looks like another fun night." This time, I mean it. We move to a tiny pub and on cramped stools, sit against the narrow wooden bar. Estonian musicians play folk music on the other side of the room, but we can only vaguely hear them above the crush of people.

A group of five Norwegians come into the bar as we are about to leave and persuade us to stay with them. Good company, good vibes, a world of opportunity. Beer flows easily.

Another bar. The three redheaded Norwegians are related, one brother, two sisters. I talk with them, waving my hands in the air, babbling words like a fizzy drink fountain. What great people they are.

They invite us back to their hotel to drop off our backpacks. In the room, I shower and change from my hippy pants and old t-shirt into jeans and a shirt.

"Wow, you look so normal!" one of the girls cries. "I can't even believe that you are the same person."

Putting on clean clothes is one thing, but my long dirty hair is now washed and swept to the side, making it look somewhat more respectable. We turn the music up and raise our glasses once more before returning to the streets. Each bar becomes hazier. I can't remember the names of the Norwegians. I can't remember if I ever asked. These are good people.

The sun begins to rise and the Norwegians tell us that they have to leave. Would we like to pick up our bags so that they can sleep before they catch their ferry? Buggar. We would rather sleep on the floor of your hotel, but that would be rude to ask. We take our bags from the hotel, walk into the full sunlight, and stumble through the city. In another bar, I'm handed a shot and refuse to drink it. It is bedtime. Do you think we can sleep in this bar? No? OK.

I ask Sam if we can sleep on the grass outside the bar. No he tells me, we need to be more subtle. I am so exhausted that it doesn't matter, I just want to lie down.

Victory Park, a large green park close to the centre of Tallinn. Perfect. With the tent set up, I am revitalised. Sam hops off to fill his water bottle while I cook some pasta. It might be dinner, it might be breakfast, most probably it is both.

"Hold this." I hand Sam the small pot of cooked pasta, but it tips over and empties itself upon the floor. Our painstakingly cooked pasta is lying on the grass.

It is too much effort to boil more.

"Five second rule." Together we scoop up the food with our fingers and return it to the pot. Then we eat it.

It is the middle of the morning and we spent the night with Norwegians who turfed us out after sunrise. We now sit in a park eating pasta from the grass.

"This water tastes funny." I look at Sam, a sudden revelation.

"Where did you get it from?" He points towards some bushes behind us.

"From the fountain." We burst out laughing in unison, rolling around on the floor. How wonderful.

We are such a mess.

I crawl into the tent, grateful to sleep on soft ground.

This is my life. My ridiculous, fun, and very ridiculous life. Long may it continue.

17. Wishes

"Get up, get up!" I shout. Someone has just kicked our tent. I scrabble for my clothes and throw them on before rushing through the flap of the tent. Whoever it was has ran away. "I wish they were still here," I grumble. In reality, I do not at all wish that they were still here. The most probable outcome would have been that I asked them politely why it was that they were kicking my tent and if they would mind not doing so. Then I would have got back into my tent, regardless of whether they wished to continue kicking it or not.

Panic over, I am aware that the pain is back. The unplaceable pain somewhere between my stomach and my groin. I walk around, shaking my legs out, trying to rid myself of the sensation. It disappears then bites again. Maybe if I don't think about it, it will disappear altogether.

Sam points to a dot on the map, an Estonian town that I've never heard of, and tells me that it has a beach. Sure we'll go there.

"There is only one type of person I hate," says our pleasant driver amidst a conversation about how wonderful everyone has been during our time hitchhiking. "And that is black people." Sam and I look at each other in silence. Neither of us want to go here. "It's not that I'm racist, I only don't like black people because they cause all the problems in society. Sneaking into trucks, stealing things, robbing people. Actually, all crime is caused by black people."

I feel my hackles rising sharply. "I don't think you can blame any race or nation of people for all problems within society." My interjection is as diplomatic and as level as possible. There is a fine line between pointing out that someone is a massive racist and retaining the lift that they have given you in their car. "Every place in the world has problems and those problems are caused by every group of people."

"Let me tell you a couple of stories. A few years ago I was driving my truck to England and these North African men hid in the back of my truck. The English immigration officers found them and I got fined. I got fined! I didn't know anything about it and they chose to punish me. Then a few months later, I was parked up in my truck overnight and I was robbed. Guess who robbed me?"

Isolated incidents cannot define a people. "I have heard stories of hitchhikers being murdered and chopped apart by the people who pick them up from the side of the road, but that doesn't give me any reason not to trust you. Isn't it fairer to give everyone a chance, just like we were saying before?" My proposal is shot down and we agree to disagree.

Outside the car, Sam and I agree that he was in fact, despite his protests, a massive racist.

"I think the problem," I speculate aloud, "is that there is a lack of awareness and integration. Everyone we've met has been from close to here and looks the same. When someone different comes along, people group together. I've seen similar problems in homogeneous places around the world, sometimes harmless, sometimes less so, sometimes directed towards me, other times not. Where I come from in England is very rural and some people struggle to adjust to what they believe to be outsiders." Over ninety-eight per cent of the Estonian population come from Estonia, Russia, Ukraine, Belarus, or Finland.

In the town of Pärnu, a quiet and peaceful town of wooden structures, Sam and I search for the beach as a safe sleeping refuge. We approach a junction on foot and spy two guys approaching from the opposite direction. They stick out as much as we do, turtles carrying their homes upon their backs. Shall we say hello or shall we pass on by? Everyone else in this town seems to be a resident.

"Hello," calls the taller of the guys. The four of us meet and shake hands. Christoffer from Denmark stands significantly taller than my six foot with long curly hair and a warm laugh. Mikko, Finnish, is shorter than I and more reserved than Christoffer, speaking softly. The two of them are hitchhiking and looking for somewhere to spend the night. Together the four of us search for the beach.

"Where are you guys headed after this?" I ask to Christoffer. Sam and Mikko are in step behind us.

"There's this hitchhiking festival in Lithuania. We're heading there because it starts in a few days time."

"No way! Sam, did you hear that? They are going to a hitchhiking festival." Without having to verbally state the issue, we agree to join them. "I didn't even think things like this existed. How many people will be going?"

"I don't know, one or two hundred maybe. It's still quite a new thing, but they are trying to make it like Rainbow Gathering for hitchhikers."

"That's the peace and love, have-respect-for-the-world-and-everybody-in-it festival, right?"

"Something like that."

What are the chances? Of all the places in all of the wherevers that we could have ended up in, we found ourselves bumping into two fellow hitchhikers, heading to a hitchhiking festival. Thirty seconds earlier or later and we would never have met. Thank you world.

On the beach we pass food and drinks between us, sharing the little that each of us has. I cook Baltic dumplings on the camp stove and one at a time, we eat a dumpling before passing the tiny pot to the next person. Beneath us, the sand is soft and white and stretches out for miles in both directions. There are small dunes behind the lifeguard tower we sit by and occasionally other people stroll along the beach, but mostly we have it all to ourselves. At dusk, we move out of the light wind and into a hollow in the low dunes.

The four of us set about fetching logs and twigs, sorting them into piles based upon their size. We shuffle back and forth from the dark of the trees to our hollow, arranging the fuel around a large hole that we dig with our hands. After an hour of foraging, we have more than enough to keep a nice fire going for a few hours. When the first flames begin to swell and feast upon the twigs, we cheer in unison, feeding the hungry flames. Within a few minutes the fire stands tall, pumping out heat.

The four of us pull off our clothes and race down to the water at high speed, whooping in delight. It's only a hundred metres from the dunes, but the gentle wind nips at our bare skin. Without stopping to dip in our toes, we break the surface of the water, surprised by the unexpected warmth of the protected bay. I close my eyes and let the soft sand rub along my underside, separated from the world by the surface of the water above. My momentum carries me forward without needing to paddle and I let my arms float idly at my sides, preserving my breath. Nothing but the swirling echo of the water fills my ears. Is this how a dolphin feels? Or a manatee?

I break the surface slowly. Beneath the surface, my body is warm and protected from the wind.

A naked pair of legs ahead of me, silhouetted against the almost full moon. They quickly overbalance and fall into the water with a splash.

Above the surface of the water, there is nothing but the moonlight dancing off tiny crests and the soft cooing of our voices.

We are the four naked kings of the world. Except me in my pants. I am the un-naked king of the world.

A camera could never do this moment justice.

We talk in a small circle, exhausting superlatives, before counting down our return dash across the sand.

Racing through the night, the wind nips harder at our now wet bodies. Home we go to all we have.

The fire burns well and we load it up further, its great belly swelling like a well feasted beast. In return, it dries us in minutes.

There we sit and we talk in our hollow, surrounded by dunes, hidden from the world.

The world hidden from us.

After several hours, we cover our fire, hide all trace of our existence, and investigate the lifeguard tower as a place to sleep. Spacious and protected from the wind, it seems ideal until its seemingly consistent use as a human toilet persuades us to look elsewhere.

At the back of the beach is a quiet park. That is where we will sleep. Four strangers.

In the morning, we climb trees. Passers-by look at the twenty-somethings leaping between the branches.

Just a little bit higher I go. A little bit more. That branch will hold me if I move slowly.

It doesn't.

This time I'm falling, I'm really falling. This is the feeling my body knows, a feeling that can go on and on, seemingly never ending.

Yet this time, I know that it will stop.

It stops abruptly on a lower branch which collides violently with my left armpit and my chin.

Ow. My teeth. My tongue. I swing my head away from the thick branch, hanging onto it using nothing but my left armpit. Please don't fall out teeth.

I wipe my tongue on the back of my free right hand. No blood. If it was between my teeth, I would have bitten it clean off.

Gingerly I lower myself down to a thick branch that I can stand on. The left side of my ribs and inner arm are grazed and sporting spots of blood. Far below me, the ground sighs. If not for the branch, it would have eagerly thumped my falling body in bone shattering delight.

I'm still feeling sorry for myself when the four of us split into two groups, promising to meet at the hitchhiking festival in a few days time.

As Sam and I cross a motorway bridge on the outside of the railing, I grip it tight. Below me is a ten metre drop onto hard concrete. My side and jaw still ache, but this time there would be no lucky branch to stop my fall.

One step, two step. Hold the rail with one hand at all times. Do not look down.

I wonder what it would feel like to fall? Wow, I looked. It is a long way down and my stomach jumps. I don't.

One step, two step.

Sam and I are dropped at a small crossroads south of Pärnu. We are heading to another town I don't know and have to turn left.

"Is that two other hitchhikers?"

"That's Christoffer and Mikko." By coincidence, we find ourselves together despite parting several hours earlier. We wave and begin jumping around emphatically, doing everything we can to get a ride quicker than them. It isn't a race, but it is.

We grin when a car stops for us.

A girl, little older than I, jumps out and tells us to wait as she reorganises the car. She throws bags and toys into the boot until there is enough space for one person to sit in the front and one to sit in the back besides her tiny baby in a child seat. We wave once again to Christoffer and Mikko who are still waiting for a lift in a different direction.

"Aren't you worried, picking up two guys?" I ask in surprise. "Especially with a baby. How old is… it?" The child is so young that I have no idea of whether it's a boy or a girl.

"He's nearly six months old now, but no, I'm not worried. I used to get rides a lot too, mostly in Mexico, Greece, and Italy. I once even got a free boat ride from Greece to Italy. You looked like two young guys who needed some help, so here I am." As she smiles, I see that she is wearing a brace. With a soft face and smooth brown hair full of life, she could almost pass for a teenager. "Besides, maybe it's you who should be worried, I only passed my driving test two weeks ago."

New baby, new teeth, new driving license, and two new passengers. We twist through the Estonian countryside, passing small villages interspersed with farmland.

"Wow," I mumble. The girl is on her way to a new job, guiding Spanish tourists around the Baltic region. Her friend will look after the baby while she does all the Spanish tour guiding.

"My husband doesn't think it's such a good idea, but I want to do it. I can't just sit at home and let my life stop to look after my son all day. I want to go out and do things, see new places, so here I am. For years when I lived in Mexico I was free to go everywhere and that's how I have been all my life." She shares stories of exploring the world, working as a chef here, travelling there, sleeping outside when she had to. She is a small girl, wide eyed with wonder, dreams uncrushed by society. A believer in life.

I hang on every word of every story. Everything she has done is what I have been told is not possible. What she is doing, she has been told is not possible. You do not pick up strange men when driving with your newborn baby. In fact, you shouldn't even be driving right now, or going to this ridiculous new job.

Do it while you're young, that's what everyone says. One day you'll have to come back to the real world.

This is my real world. This is her real world.

As our paths diverge, I want to tell her that she is amazing. I want to thank her for being who she is and for not being anyone else, for not letting her life stop, despite expectation. I want her to know that she has given me faith in the world and excitement for the future. I want her to know that she has affected me, touched me.

But she will think I am strange if I say such things. She will think I'm hitting on her or I have an ulterior motive. It will give me a few seconds of awkwardness.

Great British reserve.

I thank her politely and walk away. The words I never said were dancing in my eyes. I hope she saw them.

"Sam, that lady was amazing. I think that she is one of the best people I have ever met."

"Why do you say that? I couldn't really hear your conversation from the back seat."

"It would take me a week to explain. All you really need to know is that she is living her life."

I play gun-dinosaur fights with a kid in the next car. Brilliant fun for all of thirty minutes, but roaring and growling soon grow old. I love kids when I can give them back. Pets are much easier to keep than kids because you give them love and food, then they love you in return. After a few years, you can even get a new one or give it away if you don't want it anymore. People are infinitely more complicated.

We spend the night at the home of Liina, an Estonian girl who greets us warmly.

"I have been training these rats to do tricks," she tells us, taking three rats from their cages, one brown, one with hair as ice white as her own, and one a happy mix of the two.

"And I've been training Sam to do tricks too." She laughs good-naturedly. Apparently she is used to people being skeptical of trained rats.

The three of us sit on the double bed she has offered to Sam and I as the rats run across it. They undoubtedly recognise Liina, but are nervous of two strangers. When they finally grow comfortable with Sam and I, they rush from one side of the bed to the other, over us, under us, investigating us. Never do they step off the edge or make a break to get away.

Liina pulls out a small hoop and holds it out for them to run through, rewarding them as they do. She gets them to stand high on their hind legs to fetch another reward. I stand corrected.

"You have amazing rats. That is something I never thought I would say."

Sam moves to the floor and I sit with Liina, talking into the night. She tells me of her research into training rats at university and how she has now graduated, but doesn't know what to do next. She is trapped and afraid of what will happen, so she has stayed on and continued her work with rats as a post-graduate. Another interesting story.

"Is that what you want to be doing?"

"Not really. I like it and I love the rats, but there is more I want to do. I just worry that if I leave here, something bad might happen."

"I met a girl today…" I tell her of the girl with the newborn baby, the way she explored the world alone, the way she does as she pleases despite everyone's expectations of her. I tell Liina that the nameless girl is someone I look up to and I always will, even though I will never see her again. Where there is a gap in the story, I fill in legitimate details. "For those few hours we talked, that girl inspired me. I will try to be more like her."

Liina fidgets with her fingers, wide eyed in wonder, as inspired by the story of the girl as myself. "This might sound a little strange… but can I hug you?"

"Of course." We embrace for a few seconds.

"Thank you."

"No, thank the girl from the story. I should have done so."

Sam is still sleeping on the floor as I gratefully take the whole double bed to myself. For four nights we have been squashed into the less than one man tent.

In the light of morning, Liina leads us to a bridge in the centre of the town.

"This is a special bridge because when you graduate, you must cross the arch." The footbridge is over fifty metres wide with a concrete arch stretching from end to end and reaching nearly ten metres into the air. The arch itself is only one metre wide.

"And you have done it?"

"Not yet, but it's so high, I wouldn't feel safe. Some people also fell off and others climbed it when they were drunk, so if you get caught it's possible that you can be in trouble with the police." I look around.

"No police and we're not drunk. Let's go."

"It's too dangerous."

I pull off my flip flops and tug at Liina. Sam does the same. "Come on!"

"Oh my god, oh my god!" Liina says over and over as the three of us climb the arch barefooted. We stop on the top to look at the view for a few seconds before Liina rushes down the other side. I can see an awful lot of people. I really hope the police don't see us. We rejoin Liina at the bottom of the arch. "AH! I can't believe you guys made me do that." Delighted, horrified, she bounces around on her toes.

Together we skip to another special bridge.

"This bridge is Angel's Bridge and if you can cross all of it with your eyes closed, you will be granted whatever you wish for. But you mustn't open your eyes until you get to the other side and you mustn't touch the sides of the bridge."

"Whatever we wish for will come true, simply for crossing the bridge? That's a good deal. Can we go back and forth, crossing it all day?"

"No, you can only try once."

The bridge is wide and looks easy to cross, even with one's eyes closed. What should I wish for? I used to wish for fantastical things, for superpowers, to fly, to change the whole world in unthinkable ways. For my family to have limitless success in everything they did, to bring people back from the dead. None of these dreams ever came true, so I realigned my desires. That was when I realised that a wish is a wish. I wished something to happen because it was a dream that I would never pursue. I now wish for desires that I want to follow through on.

I wish for my journey to continue, long and far, safe yet exciting. I close my eyes.

One step, easy. Two steps, wobble. I edge forward, each step less stable, each foot changing direction a little. The planks beneath my feet give no indication as to my location. Shuffle shuffle.

My hip hits something and I open my eyes. The side of the bridge. I am barely halfway across it and have strayed from the centre to the edge.

So much for wishing.

Leaving Estonia, Sam and I continue south, drawn by hitchhiking festivals, Latvian farms, and Polish girls with lilting accents. The light is fading.

Sad eyes, sad face, please pick us up. A lone woman approaches in a small hatchback.

She stops. Thank you lady.

"I don't normally stop for people on the road, but you two looked so desperate."

"We are a little. I know most females don't like picking up guys, so thank you for stopping."

"I felt it was the right time to stop, so I did. My daughter taught me that sometimes you have to trust your instincts. She said sometimes you have to do what you want to do because it feels right and if you want something to happen, you have to make it happen. My daughter is the most positive influence in my whole life, I am constantly improving myself because of her."

"She sounds very wise, how old is she?"

"She is twenty-three. She always will be twenty-three and she will always be the guiding light of my life. She died three years ago." I am rendered speechless. "She always begged me to stop smoking, over and over and I said that I would, but I never quit properly. I only ever stopped for a week or two, but the day after she died, I was smoking a cigarette and right there in front of me, the ash-tray shattered into tiny pieces on the table. No one touched it and that was when I knew: it was her. She was giving me a sign, letting me know that she would always be watching over me, always pushing me to do better for myself. I stopped smoking on that day and I haven't had a single cigarette since. So here I am, becoming a better person because of her."

Immortalised at twenty-three years old, the daughter of this woman will never grow old, will never disappoint, will never fail to fulfil her potential. She will be the best of everything because she could have achieved so much. She is everything and she always will be.

Dare I think that I am a little jealous of how she will be remembered?

18. Cows

"This my house," Kristina says proudly. She is an eighteen year old Latvian and invited us to stay with her in the countryside. Her brother, whose name I couldn't catch, is driving the car. He is only nineteen, but has muscles as big as my legs. We pull into a driveway off the quiet road and approach the house. It's the only house that we have seen for several miles and the nearest town is more than ten miles back.

Kristina's home is an organically sprawling collection of buildings. The house itself is an elegant and skilful construction, well built with care. To the left is an open field with a football goal and to the right is a two-storey barn with hay falling out of the doors. Near the house are a couple of cars and two wooden structures with tin roofs. The larger structure of the two looks as if it has reached the end of its lifespan. Near to it are many pieces of wood that agree, threateningly being assembled into a shed of a similar size. All about the unfenced garden, there are signs of a busy family life, a pile of chopped firewood, an elderly lady performing manual work, toys scattered.

A small dog and two young girls rush out to meet us. Aged six and ten, the girls sport brilliant blue eyes and ice white hair, bouncing with nervous energy. Who are these foreigners?

"Hello," they both giggle, then run off to hide.

Sam and I follow Kristina into the kitchen where a large island is filled with vegetables. All about the room are signs of fresh produce: a full bucket of fresh honey oozes from a large honeycomb and next to that, recently made cheese is cooling under a fly net. Pots and pans on every surface suggest that everything this family consumes is grown in the garden and put together in this kitchen. It warms me from the inside.

A second brother appears, as strong as the first. Two brothers, three sisters, a mother, a father, and a grandmother. Eight mouths to feed.

The ceiling of the house shows exposed wooden beams, structural yet more natural and aesthetically pleasing that modern styling could hope to achieve. Throughout the house, exposed brick elegantly accentuates the care with which it was built.

"How long have you lived here?" I ask.

"Always. My father, he made it for our family."

"It's beautiful." I mean it. This is the farm, the place for goats and bees that I once dreamed about.

Drawn to the young children full of life and wide eyed wonder, we bounce a ball between us. For everything we lack in common language, they make up in cheeky grins. As our game progresses, they grow bold enough to practise the English they have learnt from cartoons and we chatter away in a medley of English and squeaks. In the other room I hear Sam flicking between English and Russian, dependent upon who he is speaking to.

"Where is the toilet?" Kristina points out the front door and tells me to turn right. Her little sister says something in Latvian that I ascertain to mean she will show me where to go.

Outside, I follow the young girl along the wall of the house while a little dog trots behind. I am pointed to the smaller of the two wooden sheds.

Swinging the door open, I find a long drop, a wooden seat with a hole in it. Under the hole will be a big pit where all bodily excrement accrues for a couple of years until a new one is dug. Surprisingly, it doesn't smell too bad. In the door of the lockless hut, a small wooden heart has been carved so that you can see the world outside and shout for someone not to open the door when it is in use.

After tending to their animals, the mother of the family returns to the house. She doesn't speak any English so Kristina translates that we can go to wash in the lake if we like.

"Absolutely."

Six of us bundle into one small car and at alarmingly high speeds, bounce along a dirt track, through a forest, and into open fields. When we stop, we are on the edge of a deep meadow surrounded by trees. Single file, we six traipse through the long grass, our legs becoming wet from the cold evening dew. There is a small wooden hut on the far side of the meadow and there we change. It sits on stilts to protect it from flooding, although right now, the lake is as glass. In turn, we walk down the jetty and leap into the water.

I swim out and out across the lake, my head shattering the perfect surface like a lazy, cumbersome frog. Rolling onto my back, I look up at the sky, out at the trees, listening to the sound of nothing but ourselves and nature. Long wide strokes, I try to form a snow angel on the lake.

At the jetty the two young sisters jump in screaming and splashing. I join in their games, turning head over heels in midair, an inelegant backflip. Landing sideways after a full rotation, I disappear under the surface, my arms flailing. As I resurface, the girls whoop and laugh in delight. Even the children find my lack of agility amusing. The youngest daughter paddles over to me in her bright orange inflatable armbands. Like a limpet, she wraps her arms tightly around my neck, clinging to my back. Now a cumbersome frog with a shell, I paddle around in the shallows. The nervous energy has unquestionably dissipated and the girl accepts me into her family.

The mother laughs as I pretend to sink with the girl on my back. Flapping her arms and squirming away, the girl swims away pouting, disappointed for the game to have ended.

On the jetty we stand and dry ourselves then run across the meadow. The six of us once again cram into the car and for the second time, we bounce up and down the dirt track between fields and forests. In the kitchen we ask to help, but both Sam and I are shunned away. We are the guests and the guests do not have to do anything.

Dinner is served and we are greeted to a table of homemade delights. Cheese from their cows, honey from their friend's bees, and vegetables from the garden. We shovel food greedily into our bellies, taste buds on fire, but try as we might, there is too much for us to eat it all. What a feast, so much better than plain pasta.

At midnight, the house is calm. Almost time for bed.

"Now we move cows."

"We what? We move cows?"

"Yes. No cars and big moon. We move cows." I infer that the cows are rotated between fields every month in synch with the full moon. Tonight is the full moon.

Sam and I follow the family down a dirt track to a cow field. Far from the light pollution of towns and under the watchful lunar eye, we are rabbits in the dark, seers of the night. Like a well trained pack, the family surround the great beasts then leap upon each individual in turn, attaching ropes to their necks. This process is repeated until all the cows have been roped. The mother, the two brothers, and Kristina are all holding cows. So too am I. How did I get a cow?

The fence is dropped and we walk towards the road. Clumsily, the cow barges into me and treads on my flip-flop before dragging me forward.

"Sam, get my shoe!" The cow is too strong to pull back.

"What?"

"My shoe! Get my shoe!" He seems not to understand what I'm saying. Ahead of me the other four cows break into a run along the road, each guided by one of the family members. My cow takes flight and joins the back of the queue, obliging me to run along with it. Shoulder to shoulder we bounce, the cow in a lolling gallop, I jogging in my one flip-flop and hippy pants that flap wildly, dress-like.

Do not let go of this cow, do not let it get away. I am squeezing as hard as I can on the rope, focused on the road ahead.

On the previously deserted road, a car approaches at high speed, its headlights blinding. Do not let this cow get hit, do not let go of the rope. Got to move the cow away from the car. Must not get hit myself.

I am on the outside, the side of the passing car, but we are running down the middle of the road.

I push the cow as we run, shoulder barging her like a football opponent. She ducks my shove and unbalanced, I stumble past her, exposing both cow to car and car to cow. In North America, deer are indirectly responsible for more deaths than any other animal because people hit them at high speed in cars. A cow is much bigger than a deer. If this car hits the cow, I will be responsible.

I keep running, tugging at the cow, incapable of getting myself between it and the car. The car races ever closer.

"Come on cow! Get out of the middle of the road!"

The car is almost upon us.

The cow swings its head my way.

Boom, it sends me flying. I fall into the ditch, holding the rope with all my might. I will not let you go cow, I will not let you die.

Pulling myself up the rope, the cow grinds to a halt as the car passes.

"Let's go!"

We set off at a run, the cow dictating our pace once more. What an incredibly strong creature, I'm rather glad it's vegetarian.

Trotting into the paddock well behind the others, I am relieved to have not broken my cow. The electric fence is raised and the mother disappears to turn the power on. As we sit down to rest, I am breathing deeply.

"I lost my shoe." I point at my foot to emphasise the point. We walk back down the road towards the original field to look for it.

Panicked shouts from behind us.

"What is happening?"

"Cows go. Come quick." We run back to the new field to find that there are no cows in it. At least I didn't lose the cows.

Someone points towards a forest and we run as fast as we can through the long grass. It tickles my thighs and the wetness soaks into my cotton trousers, the extra weight pulling them down. Jump, skip, hold up trousers, jump, skip. The cows are outrunning us.

We catch them when they stop before the forest. A pack of wolves, we circle them once more. Agitated, a cow runs at me, attempting to break the circle.

I am about to be broken by a cow. Broken rib, punctured lungs, this is going to hurt. Arms wide, be bigger than the cow. I am not bigger than the cow.

I leap sideways with my eyes closed as the cow is upon me.

It backs off at the last minute, returning to the centre of the circle. Bit by bit, we usher them across the field, back towards their pen. Occasionally they charge other members of the circle, but never do they actually break it. Fortunately it seems that cows are not brave animals.

The electric fence goes back up and this time we check that the power is on.

I find my shoe embedded in a large cow pat, the undigested residue of plants that have journeyed through all four parts of a cow's stomach. What a wonderful place to find my shoe. I pull it out and carry it back to the house. Now it must be time for bed.

"You sleep inside or outside?" Kristina translates for her mother.

"Outside? Where outside?"

"The cow house."

"Outside!" Sam and I instinctively reply in unison. The two of us and the three daughters head out to the cow barn that we saw earlier in the day and climb the ladder to the first floor. In the narrow torch beam we see a floor of hay, soft and inviting. Blankets are spread across the hay and the five of us fall asleep, the smell of real nature filling our nostrils.

By morning, we have all rolled into a fall in the hay and I am overheating, incubated by the warmth of four bodies around me.

I fetch some water and return to find the two young sisters jumping into the hay.

"They want you to watch," Kristina translates. The youngest girl climbs onto a roof beam and drops into the hay. Instinctively I want to reach out and catch her, break her fall, but she bounces up, giggling, a cheeky grin across her face.

Outside the barn, we kick a football around and eat another mountain of fresh produce for breakfast. Sam talks at length to the grandmother in Russian.

Now we must go. The hitchhiking festival is over two hundred miles away in rural Lithuania, several miles from the nearest settlement, Ambraziškiai, a village of around one hundred people. Effectively we are aiming for one specific field in Lithuania and all we have is an atlas of Europe.

The mother of the family hands Sam and I a huge wheel of homemade cheese, divided into two. My mouth immediately waters despite being full from breakfast.

"Thank you so much for everything. You have the most wonderful place, I love it. I hope someday I can live somewhere like this."

Kristina translates my words and the mother smiles. As we say our goodbyes, the grandmother is tearing up that Sam is leaving. For one day, we were part of the family, we had a home.

The three daughters walk us down the track to the road.

"Do you want to come with me?" I ask the six year old. Her big blue eyes beam and she grins at me, grabbing the hand-drawn sign from my hand. Standing on the side of the road, she holds it up to the first car that passes, her sister having explained the concept to her.

What a perfect little girl.

I take the sign back and tell her that I'm sorry, but I have to go. The smile is gone and she fights as her sister leads her away. They walk back down the garden, hand in hand, towards the little farmhouse made of magic. They wave as they walk, the six year old still fighting to break free and join us once more.

"Let's walk down the road for a bit Sam, I can't stand here."

We walk out of sight and drop our bags to the road.

Another day has passed. A day I will remember forever.

19. Chance

Like a tap not quite turned all the way off, the rain drizzles continuously. It's not light enough for us to stay dry, nor is it heavy enough for us to seek cover. Not that there is any cover to seek. We're at a small junction and all we can see in every direction is fields and fields and fields. Flat nothingness.

In the summer heat, I'm sweating inside my waterproof. I pull it off so that my grey t-shirt turns charcoal, clinging tightly to my body.

Reluctant to dampen the inside of their vehicles, drivers pass us by, pitying us and waving apologetically. Where we stand there is only one road for miles, we are all going the same way. When we do get rides, we apologise to the drivers. Sorry for getting your car wet, thank you for picking us up.

By evening, whoever forgot to turn the tap off properly has not discovered it. The rain has been unrelenting throughout the day, turning us into bedraggled monsters. What started as a fun day isn't funny anymore and we have travelled only fifty miles. I think this breaks a record for the worst day of hitchhiking ever.

We sit in a bus stop in Riga, the rain heavier than before. Entangled in the city's road network, we don't know how to leave it. I ask Sam to get directions in one of his many languages.

An old man explains which bus will take us to the main terminal and from there we can take a bus to Lithuania. Sam explains that we want road directions, we'll walk and get a ride for free. I'm lost in their exchange until the man reaches up and touches my shoulder. Watch, he implies. He picks up an imaginary shovel and begins digging an imaginary hole in the pavement.

"He says that we should get a job like normal people and pay for the bus."

The man pulls a note out of his pocket, slams it into Sam's hand, then marches off, roaring with laughter.

"Did you tell him we were hitchhiking?"

"Yeah, he said it wasn't possible. That's why he said we had to get a job and take a bus."

"Getting a job to take a bus to a place where we would only have to get another job to take another bus to another place, purely for the sake of going to places, would somewhat defeat the object."

"I didn't tell him that."

We are two scruffy young guys sheltering in a bus stop with our whole worlds in backpacks beside us. Rather than free spirited, we look unintentionally homeless.

Another old man, thick set with grey hair and bloodshot eyes, joins us in the bus stop. Sam begins to speak with him. Is that Russian?

"He says that he doesn't know where Lithuania is, but he would like to help us." The man pulls out his smart phone and struggles to find a map application. When it's open, he spends a couple of minutes scrolling around, pointing to different parts of the map, and saying things to Sam.

"What's he saying?"

"He says that he can't see the screen because his eyes are bad." He slips the phone away and pulls a bottle of water from his bag. It smells explosive. He swigs it heavily then offers it to Sam and I. I let the liquid kiss my lips for a split second. It tastes as good as it smells.

"What is that?"

"Moonshine. He also says that you look like one of the characters from Pirates of the Caribbean."

"As much as I would like that to be true, I think you should tell him to get his eyes checked."

The man has a brilliant idea to make some jazz composing software that will make us all rich, but his family don't support his idea and think he drinks too much. He agrees that we will help him and he tries to write his email address down, but in his drunkenness, can't remember what it is. It's OK we say, we'll meet up some other time. He agrees absentmindedly, swigging heavily once more.

Accepting our misery, we spend the night in the home of Sam's friend. While Sam sleeps, I pass the night and morning away with conversation and liquor.

"About fucking time. You snore really bad as well." It's full daylight outside and Sam looks pissed off. Fortunately not the same level of pissed off that he was on the first morning at Emilia's house.

"An unfortunate side effect of too much alcohol."

"I thought you were going to sleep all day."

"No, just a bit. It was daylight before we went to sleep, you shouldn't have gone to bed so early."

"Well I wanted to go to a hitchhiking festival and not just sleep here all day."

"Me too, let's go."

"Now you want to go. It's one o'clock in the afternoon."

"You should have woken me. Besides, we only have a hundred and fifty miles to go, that won't take us long." I leap to my feet and pack my bag in silence. It only takes a minute and I'm bouncing with energy.

Outside we pass the elderly flower lady on the corner. She holds the flowers to her nose once more, inhaling deeply, her face filling with delight. A routine that she must have performed hundreds of times a day for many years. She shows us the same newspaper cutting that she showed us when we last visited, the same cutting she showed Sam years earlier. We smile and Sam tells her that she has lovely flowers, but we don't need any today thank you.

On the outskirts of Riga, we stand in a bus stop surrounded by fields. On the narrow road, it's one of the few places that cars can pull over safely. Ahead of us, a third hitchhiker approaches.

"I don't think we should hitchhike with him, we're on a deadline."

"I agree."

The hitchhiker very formally introduces himself, then puts his thumb out, standing a few metres behind us.

Irritated, we shoulder our backpacks and walk for a couple of kilometres to get clear of him.

Several hours and rides later, we are standing in a small town, almost a village, when he appears again. Once more he says hello, then stands with his thumb out, a few metres behind us.

"This guy cannot be serious," I whisper to Sam. "If there is such a thing as bad hitch etiquette, this is it."

"Should we tell him that we were here first?"

"Yes, you tell him."

"You tell him."

"I'm not telling him. Shall we just move again?"

"Alright."

Two friendly older men come and walk with us, chatting with Sam in Russian.

"They say that they know where we can get a ride. He's a truck driver." We follow the first guy while the second lags behind, stumbling into the pavement railing and tottering precariously close to the road.

"Would you agree that they are both slam drunk?"

"Absolutely."

We turn down the grimy looking bottle of homemade bonfire fuel that they are drinking and try to find an excuse to part company with them.

"They want to invite us to stay at their house. They have a swimming pool."

"Of course they do." The second guy has fallen a long way behind and we stop, saying that we will hitchhike from where we are. I signal for rides while Sam continues trying to persuade the less drunk of the two men to leave. When the second guy reaches us, he has removed his shirt, revealing his big belly covered in yellow vomit. He approaches Sam and grabs his hand to shake it. I burst out laughing and run away from the sickly clutches.

"My hands smell of apples and vomit," Sam complains when they finally leave.

Between choking laughter, I tell Sam, "I think that this is the best thing that has happened since we left the farm." We have travelled only one hundred miles in two days, during which time we have been rained on continually, insulted, and accosted by several drunks. In the distance we watch as the two drunk men cross a field and open an unlocked summer house with a swimming pool. They wave happily at us from the doorway before disappearing inside.

Oh, here we go again.

A couple, little older than us, approach and ask for money or cigarettes. We apologise that we have neither. The male of the duo is an unsavoury looking individual, grinding his jaw and chewing on his lip, bony and shifty. The girl is covered in scars and has almost no teeth. The few teeth she does have seem pointed as if they have been filed. They eye our bags, their minds imagining the treasures that they might contain.

I put myself between my backpack and the couple. Please don't do anything, please don't touch me.

The girl's tongue flicks in and out of her mouth, snake like. The man twitches, blinking heavily, gnawing on himself like a starving rodent.

Come to our house the girl says, her eyes moving between us and our bags. I have as much desire to follow them as I do to hand over all of my worldly belongings.

"This is dangerous," Sam whispers to me in French. Are they going to pull a weapon on us? Will they stab us? Maybe they'll bite us and infect us with whatever life draining, downward spiralling disease it is that they have. Whatever journey they are on, it looks like they are both coming towards the end of it.

"I want to leave," I say back in French. The girl looks irritated.

"Fronseys?" she slurs, followed by a few quick words to her companion, irritated that we are purposefully excluding her from our exchange. After a brief back and forth, the couple tell us they have to get something, but they'll be back in an hour and we will go with them.

Thankfully they leave without our belongings. I'll run away screaming before I follow them anywhere.

A hundred metres in front of us, a police car stops and sets up a checkpoint. "This is a bloody joke," I vent. "The drunk people, the lack of rides, the rain, the scary people. Now this!" I point at the checkpoint ahead of us. "No one will pick us up now, this must be a set-up." The Truman Show feels like real life and I look around for cameras. Nothing.

The first car to approach is pulled over by the police, searched, released, then stops to pick us up.

Once more I stand corrected.

It gets dark as we speed towards our destination in a fancy car. Our driver has less than twelve hours to cross the continent and reach the port in Calais. "Picking people up makes my drive less boring," he tells us. In the front seat is another hitchhiker we've never met before and we tell them that we're trying to get to a hitchhiking festival. "I heard about that. I picked up one of the organisers the other day when I was driving in the opposite direction. He was going early to help set things up. A nice guy, long hair, maybe dreadlocks. Can you say hello to him from me?"

Our driver apologises that he can't take us all the way to the festival: he doesn't have time, but where he'll leave us is only forty kilometres away.

Without warning, a weight drops in my stomach, I am falling again. Those words... he has said them before in a different place, another world. I can't remember when, but I know them. I know what happens next. It's bad, oh so very, very bad.

He brakes and begins to slow the car.

It is coming, a great green eyed monster, wickedness and badness.

My muscles tighten, my heart pumps harder, my breathing rate increases. Fight or flight.

I will fly.

Behind us, cars approach. Is this it, is this the bad thing? I can't remember anymore.

It's pitch black outside the car. Pulled up on the hard shoulder, cars pass at terrifying speeds.

"Come on Sam, come on, we have to go!"

"Calm down."

"I'm going!"

I grab my bag, shout thank you to our driver, and run down the exit slope, away from the motorway. I have to get away, I have to be somewhere else. My eyes roam wildly in the darkness, searching for both safety and danger.

A passing storm, the veil lifts. There is nothing. There is nothing that can hurt us. It's in my mind, it's not real.

My muscles relax, my heart begins to slow down, each breath becomes a little longer. I got away, I am safe.

I wait at the end of the slip road for Sam to catch up with me.

"What was that about?"

"I... I don't know exactly. I just felt. I felt we had to leave. Do you know of deja-vu, when you think you've been somewhere or experienced something before? Well it was that. I thought we'd been there before and that something very bad was about to happen and that the only way I could stop it was to get as far away from there as possible. I didn't know if it was the car or the road, but I had to leave."

"Why? It looked like you were having a panic attack?"

"I don't know, it was just a feeling. Come on, I'm fine now, let's go."

In darkness, we follow the road for an hour. We have drunk all of our water during the heat and frustrations of the day, leaving us both hungry and thirsty. Without water, we cannot even prepare the dry pasta that we have with us.

"If a taxi came now," I muse aloud, "I wouldn't care. I'd give him all these five euros I have on me and I'd say take me anywhere, anywhere where there is some civilisation or somewhere that I can get something to eat or a glass of water. Even a glass of water to cook this dry pasta." Around us is nothing but overturned farmland and high crops. A ditch then a hedge separate them from the road, making the land neither easily accessible nor particularly suitable for camping. Sam agrees that he would give his few euros in exchange for water.

Cars pass at increasingly large intervals of ten minutes or more. It's getting close to midnight and we are almost invisible in the shadow of night without torches. On the rare occurrence of a passing car, we scramble onto the verge so that it doesn't accidentally hit us.

As if by magic, a taxi appears. We jump up and down emphatically, grateful to have found our saviour. With no intention of stopping late at night in the middle of nowhere for two guys who are clearly up to no good, the taxi races past. A tease.

How long can we survive without water? A few days? What about when it's summer and we're walking with heavy backpacks?

No! That's ridiculous. We are not going to die from a lack of water or food in one day. But my mouth is dry and my stomach is rumbling. I have lived a pampered life and I am not accustomed to being deprived of eating or drinking, least of all, of water. What did we eat today? An ice cream that someone bought us. Maybe the last slither of cheese from the farm. Or was that yesterday?

Two guys on a deserted road, late at night. I think of my friends, would they pick us up if they didn't know us? No, I don't think they would. Would I pick us up? Probably not. The thought of two strangers is intimidating from the warmth and safety of a locked car, particularly in darkness. But Sam and I aren't intimidating, we are us. Us in our hippy pants, with our hair too long, hoping to get to a hitchhiking festival which started today.

We step onto the verge as another car passes.

Twenty minutes later, another. We keep on walking in the direction of the festival.

All hope is lost. We have to find somewhere to sleep, I am exhausted.

We wave at another car that most probably can't even see us. It races past, then slams on its brakes, coming to an abrupt stop.

I leap into the air in delight. Someone is helping us. We run down the road as fast as we can.

"Quick, before it leaves. Don't ask where it's going, just get in."

We bundle into the back of the vehicle, arranging the backpacks on our laps next to Lina, a slender twenty-two year old Lithuanian girl with a soft and gentle face. Her parents are in the front seats.

"Thank you so, so much, we are so grateful."

"Oh!" Taken aback, Lina's mother tells us that she only stopped because she thought that we were two girls. For once, our dress-like hippy pants and long hair are positives. We tell them where we are going and they apologise that they can't take us where we want to go. It's dark and late and difficult to see.

"Why don't you come to our summer house? We'll drop you off in the morning," the dad suggests.

Sam and I look at each other instinctively. For the past few weeks of exploring together, everything has become a joint decision. Sam's face says no, we have to get to the hitchhiking festival. My face says yes, let's go with them. "We'd love to stay with you if it isn't too much of a problem," I reply. Sam airs his desires to get to the festival, but without water, I have no desire to walk for however many more hours it would take to get there in the darkness. "It's already late and we'll get there tomorrow anyway."

Against his will, my argument wins.

We leave the road and begin twisting over hills on a narrow dirt track that has been carved below the surface of the grass. The family ask about our journey and obligingly, we explain what we have been doing. They think that we are totally mad.

There is little to see of the summer house in the darkness. Clean air devoid of lights in every direction, I sense nature. Inside, we enter a two storey cottage full of dark woods, open bricks, and an incredible amount of care. If everybody lived in a place like this, the suicide rate would surely not be so high in Lithuania: a mystery I have failed to unravel in this pleasant country.

At the table, we are served cured meats, cheese, and biscuits, but even more importantly, water.

"I'm sorry but we can't eat the meat."

There is an open fireplace, unlit, and a grand wooden staircase. A stylish, black surfaced kitchen is visible at the other end of the open plan arrangement.

"I designed and built this," the father tells us proudly, "so that we could have breaks from the city. We come here every weekend." He has reason to be proud of his hard work.

"It's a beautiful house. I think I would skip the city altogether and just stay here."

With the plates cleared, bedtime is announced. Lina leads Sam and I up the narrow staircase. "One of you can have this room with a bed," she gestures to a closed doorway, "and one of you can sleep here," she gestures to a sofa in the hallway. For only the second time, Sam and I put our fate in the hands of rock, paper, scissors.

"Rock, paper, scissors!"

I win. I feel bad for Sam. Actually, I feel good for me! I have the bed.

"Sorry Sam… well, I'm not sorry, but bad luck."

Sam gets into bed on the sofa and Lina leads me into the room. It's a spacious wooden room with a double bed and large windows. She draws the curtains for me.

"You know, I expected to be sleeping out in a horrible field in my tiny tent tonight, hungry and thirsty. We hadn't planned very well, so I'm really grateful that you picked us up."

"It's not a problem, but really, what my mother said was true. She only stopped because she thought that you were two girls."

"Sometimes you just get lucky."

Our standing conversation continues for several minutes, her about to leave, me about to go to bed, but words are spilling out. It's that moment with a stranger when the socially correct practise is to part ways, but you have more to say to them and they have more to say to you. A lull in the conversation could cause either one of us to end that moment.

"Do you want to sit down for a bit?" I ask. She closes the door to avoid disturbing anybody sleeping and takes a seat on the wooden floor. I do the same. It is warm and smooth, so much better than my too small tent.

"How long have you known Sam?"

"A couple of months. We met on the road, hitchhiking near Denmark and met up nearly three weeks ago to explore together for a bit."

"I thought you had known each other before you started because you seem to know each other quite well."

"After three weeks of spending every waking minute with a person, you get to know quite a bit about them and vice-versa, both the good and the bad. These travel relationships are always very intense. Someone you have never met before becomes someone that you spend a huge amount of time with, then you both head off in different directions and you never quite know if you will ever see each other again." I try and work out the maths quickly in my head. "I've spent, what, maybe… twenty days, so… four hundred and eighty hours with Sam. When you live in one place, that would take months, most likely years to accumulate that much time with one person. Being able to meet so many people and become close with them has probably been the best thing about this journey. I have rarely ever had that experience in my life except when I'm on the road, that's probably why so many people travel long term. It's not about seeing the places, it's about connecting with people. Life normally gets in the way."

"That's a really nice idea, but I never thought people did things like this.

People need a way to survive as well." I nod in admission, my own future in doubt. "How long will you and Sam continue together?"

"Not long. After the hitchhiking festival, he is going to Latvia and I will go to Poland to stay with a girl I met." I explain about the language immersion program and meeting my family in Croatia a few days after.

"And then, do you think you will do this forever?"

"Forever is an awfully long time to imagine."

"Then when do you think you'll stop?"

"When I don't want to do it anymore. Or maybe when I run out of money. I travel very cheaply right now, never paying for transport or accommodation, but I buy food and drinks as I go. The short answer is that I don't know what happens after this next month." Airing these thoughts both convolutes and clarifies these troubling questions that have been swirling about my mind.

"Do you think you will ever live in just one place?"

"Maybe. I have this little dream that one day I will keep bees and goats somewhere quiet in the countryside. I don't know if it will ever happen, maybe I will never get around to wanting that. Maybe it will never happen, even if I want it." Each of these questions is taking me back to the same problem, what am I doing with my life? I literally have no idea!

We swap stories for another hour until there is a shout from downstairs in Lithuanian.

"My mother says we are keeping her awake, I have to go to bed now."

I wish Lina goodnight.

In the morning, I pull open the curtains and gasp. "Wow!" In front of me are rolling green hills that lead down to a lake.

Lina and I walk down to the lake together. There is a single cottage on another hill, but other than that, there is nothing but green. Green hills and green trees. From the jetty, we leap into the water.

"Would you like to swim across?" she asks.

Sure I would. Side by side, we paddle across the lake, continuing our conversation from the night before. Talk of farms, of cities, where we both might be in several years, whimsical ideas that appear fleetingly. Then we swim back.

Lina's mother serves a hearty breakfast of pancakes smothered in liquid jam and curdled milk, Lithuanian specialities.

We pack our bags to leave. No drunks, no being harassed, no standing idly on the side of the road. I was not looking for anything at all, but I think I've found it: another enchanting place as magical as the farm, but ever so different.

What will happen when this is all over? Where will I go? I think back to my tiny Korean apartment, a year of being trapped in a big, flashy city every day. A nightmare, it sends shivers down my spine and I push the thought from my mind.

20. My Dirty Cow Pond

From Ambraziškiai, a quiet Lithuanian village of little over a hundred people, we have followed wooden signs along a rough farm track for several kilometres. We pass a rustic farmhouse on our right and approach a slope ahead. There is a large tree under which people sit in small groups. This is Hitch Gathering and I am the new kid at school. A day late, everybody probably knows everybody. Sam and I gingerly walk up the slope.

A giant man with a pink mohawk bounds down the slope to greet us.

"Hi guys! Welcome. I'm Paul, let me show you around." Thank you Paul.

Paul takes us up the slope, past the large tree, and through a sea of tents.

"You can put your tent here or you can sleep in the barns over there." He points at two large, open doored barns to our right. "If you go past the barns, you'll find the toilet. Well, it's just a hole, but that's the toilet." He grins boyishly. Gesturing to a single-storey farm building with a wooden door on our left he announces, "That's the kitchen area and common room." Behind the barns is a forest and behind the kitchen is a field. "Let me show you guys the swimming pool."

We leave our backpacks on the ground and pass a few groups of people sitting around, chatting, playing ukelele. Across the sloped field we find a small cow pond in a low. Around us, the land is hilly and lush. Someone has constructed a small jetty consisting of a single plank of wood and the water is dark brown, almost black.

"I have to go," Paul tells us, "I'm a book."

"You're a book?"

"Yeah, there is this library project going on today. Instead of taking out real books, you take out people who talk to you about their speciality. You can ask them anything you want and then they put you back and get out another book."

"What is your book about?"

"The good green stuff, marijuana." Another cheesy grin spreads across his face moments before he disappears over the hill.

We find Christoffer and Mikko in the barn, our friends from the beach in Estonia who told us about the festival. Despite only knowing each other for a single night, it feels like being reunited with old friends.

After the people library there are juggling classes and impromptu lectures on a huge variety of topics. Freeganism, hitchhiking at night, veganism: most topics are a little outside the normal realms of society. I look around. This whole place is far outside the normal confines of society. It's a world I had always hoped existed, but was always told wasn't possible.

Taking three crab apples, I try to remember how to juggle. From one hand to the other they go, sometimes falling so that I have to pick them up again. Ahead of me, a bearded Canadian guy is showing others how to juggle. The lower half of his clothing is an impressive medley of badges from across the world, hand sewn to his garments. A distinguished traveller.

"I like your shorts," I tell him as he shows me how to throw one ball higher than the others then how to cross hands mid-juggle. I throw one apple high with ease, but drop them each time I try to cross my hands. Giving up on juggling, we sit on the floor and talk for a few minutes. Without boasting, he tells me stories of hitching across almost every continent and how he has lived his life on the road for the past few years. Inside him is a calmness, a contentedness with life. I can see it in his eyes, something absent from most people living through a busy life in a busy world. This must be what it truly means to be a free spirit.

I realise it without realising it: this guy in front of me embodies everything that I want to be, how I want to feel about my life. I watch him as he moves easily about the group of people, taking time with each individual, touching all of them as he touched me. Call it an aura, a personality, an anything you like because the name doesn't matter, but whatever it is, he's got it and we all feel it. I am grateful for the brief interaction.

A free spirit.

Outside the kitchen is a large bucket for money. If you have money, you put some in. If you don't, you don't. All food is communal and vegan, meals made for everybody by whomever volunteers first. Every evening the owners of the local shop arrive to sell alcohol, tobacco, and snacks. The hundred or so hitchhikers take it in turns to cook, eat, and clean. Politely we shuffle along the queue, take a small serving, then come back later for seconds if there is more to go around. Food is never left uneaten. At night I sleep in the barn, kept warm by the bodies around me in the hay. There are people who have been on the road for years, others who have travelled without money for years, several who describe themselves as home-free rather than homeless. From Europe, both Americas, Asia, Oceania, most parts of the world are represented. A modern day eclectic collection of hippies, nomads, and free spirits.

My eyes are open.

With Paul the friendly giant and Kate, a bubbly English girl who hitched to the festival alone, I hitch into the local town and swim in several of the lakes.

Kate's long dark curls straighten when wet as we sunbathe on the grass beside the lakes. The people of the town watch us in wide eyed bemusement.

"I don't normally get picked up by women," says Paul, surprised as a woman picks us up on the way back to the festival.

"In all fairness, you're nearly seven foot tall with a pink mo-hawk. That could be a little intimidating."

"Oh yeah." Despite his appearance, Paul is the BFG, soft and calm. He wouldn't hurt a fly.

Back in camp, we overhear someone boasting of going further, faster, and cheaper than everyone else. No one cares. "It's not a competition," says a voice from the crowd.

After a couple of days, the crowd begins to disperse. I want to see the festival through to the end, to not miss a thing, but I am drawn to Kraków, over five hundred miles away. Tomorrow I will go.

Anxious, I toss and turn through the night, overheating in the nest of human bodies, my clothes damp and uncomfortable. The rain has been drumming on the tin roof all night and my body is tired, but my mind won't rest.

I step over bodies, escaping the nest and creeping through the darkness quietly. Kate is sitting alone, watching the rain fall. Her dry hair has returned to its naturally curly form and she wears loose fitting trousers, not dissimilar to my hippy pants.

"Can't sleep?" I ask.

"No."

"Me neither. Do you know the time?"

"About five." From outside, light creeps through the gap in the barn doors where Kate sits. I take a seat next to her.

"I was meant to be leaving today, heading south, but the weather doesn't look very promising." The skies are grey in every direction.

"Me too, I have to fly out of Budapest in a few days." We agree to leave together when the rain stops.

When Kate returns to the hay, I venture into the rain and dash to the common area. A Russian girl, the only one awake, makes me porridge and we sit together, communicating in hand signals. I wash the cooking utensils to say thank you for breakfast.

After dashing through the rain, my clothes are more wet than damp and the cold is chilling my body. There is no sign of the rain relenting and I feel my itchy feet ready to leave. The longer I wait, the more things I will find that tempt me to stay. I search around for my book and find it on a wooden table. I must have left it outside, it's wet and the pages are stuck together. A couple of guitars sit silently in the corner and I pick up the blue one. I wish I learnt how to play. I strum the three chords I know in an unmelodious lack of harmony, then put the instrument back down. Like an advocate of peace handed a gun, I know not how to wield it.

My face twitches, my toes jiggle, my fingers dance to a soundless tune.

I want to go, but still the rain beats down, still people sleep.

I run from the kitchen to the barn.

No one is awake.

Back to the kitchen, still empty. My clothes are uncomfortably wet.

Why is everyone sleeping?

Outside the window, the rain beats down as hard as ever. I look across the open field, towards the swimming pool, the dirty cow pond. Hiding at the bottom of a fall in the land, it is invisible from where I stand.

Anxious energy is overwhelming me, jumping beans in my belly.

I strip down to my pants and stride into the driving rain. Huge droplets explode on my bare skin, the wind pulls away my warmth. Across the field, long grass nibbling at my ankles, down the hollow, towards the pool of water. Every muscle in my body is tense, a wall against the cold. The world has disappeared from view.

I walk onto the tiny jetty, the plank of wood reaching over the pond. It takes only two steps to reach the end and the plank bows beneath my weight.

Here I stand.

In every direction I see only slopes of green, the interior of the hollow. Before me is dark water.

Slap after slap, the rain drums upon my skin. It's cold, oh so cold. Each chill heightens my senses, brings my mind to life.

The wind cannot reach me here.

I close my eyes. Take a deep breath. Open them. Exhale.

I am still here.

This is Lithuania. This. Is. Lithuania.

I lean forward and dive headfirst into the water.

Warmth, glorious bathwater, washes away my anxiety. Is this the warmest I have ever been?

I glide under the surface, the water filling my hearing and my sight. I cannot even see my hands in front of me.

Surfacing, I roll onto my back.

All around, the black surface of the water is a million tiny dancers, a billion explosions, a trillion sounds all at once.

Uncountable noise, oh so loud. The roar of raindrops in my ear, against my face.

I float. I swim. I float. I swim.

This is Lithuania, the centre of the universe. Inside my body flows rich, sweet chocolate.

This is my dirty cow pond and there is nowhere else in the world I would rather be.

21. Peace

Sam and I shake hands briskly then walk in opposite directions. We have explored together for over three weeks.

Topless and shoeless to prevent my clothing becoming soaked in the rain, I begin south. Practical.

Kate and I spend the night in a Polish field and arrive at Emilia's apartment in Kraków the following evening. We walk through the large wooden doors of her building, across the high room, and up the stone stairs. Emilia's door stands before us.

Will she be pleased to see me? Did she say I could visit again out of politeness? Is it completely inappropriate for me to be here?

"You knock," I say to Kate, fidgeting with my bag strap.

"Me? This is the girl you want to spend time with." Regardless, Kate knocks on the door.

Maybe she isn't in? Maybe…

The door opens.

Head tilted through the widening crack, her smile lights up the dim hallway. She has been waiting to see me after all.

I introduce Kate to Emilia and she walks in through the narrow hallway. Emilia stops in the doorway just long enough to slip me a kiss and tell me that she is happy to see me. I am happy to see her.

At the kitchen table we pull up seats and share tales of our past few weeks.

I babble words excitedly. "We met a girl with heterochromia iridum today, eyes that are multiple colours. She was fiddling with her lipstick and painting her nails as we drove, long blond hair towards us, then she turned around and it was like magic whirlpools in her crazy eyes. From pastel blue to a dark, almost indefinable shade, the colours swirled."

The eyes, always the eyes.

I make eye contact with Emilia across the table. Her dark, mysterious eyes lock with mine.

"And today we were picked up by a Russian trucker and told him that Kate was escaping from her evil husband. He didn't seem to care, just laughed along and fed us apples. Like all the best people in the world, he was the good kind of crazy.

The only unfortunate ride today was that of a father who was returning from the hospital after attending the delivery of his fifth child. I commented on how busy the house would now be with five children, but he told us, very matter of fact, that one of his children died so it wasn't quite as noisy as it could have been." I pause for breath. "However, our best ride today…"

"Oh no," sighs Kate, "I knew this was coming."

"…was the closest thing to Borat I have ever known. I think it is fair to say that Kate is a believer in women's rights and this doctor, who looked and spoke exactly like Borat, picked us up. He drove like a madman, swerving all over the place and explaining how his daughter was training to be a doctor." I switch into my poor, but attempted impersonation of him. "My daughter is study to be doctor. But it is very bad idea because she is woman and everybody know woman not clever because woman brain smaller than man brain. It very hard for woman and make brain hurting. I thought Kate might punch him!" Kate laughs along with me.

I want to tell Emilia everything.

Away from parks, beaches, and barns, missing the delights of seas, rivers, and ponds, but most importantly, in the presence of a pretty girl, I am suddenly very aware that I have only taken one shower in the past ten days. "Do you mind if I take a quick shower?"

Every moment that Emilia and I have alone is a stolen moment. We are foolish teenagers, entangled in each other's arms.

Tonight I do not need to think about where I will sleep, where I will find food, or who I will spend time with. There is a soft mattress, a fully equipped kitchen, people I am comfortable with. It is all before me and after months of unfamiliarity, I have found a few days of comfortable sanctuary.

Kate and I walk the streets while Emilia is at work or studying. We sit in the park where I watched the moneyless street performers with Sam, dance down cobbled streets admiring the huge stone buildings, and tiptoe through churches, enthralled by architecture built without finance in mind. Every step makes me fall further in love with the town. Even the bustling marketplace filled with medieval architecture is so handsome that I cannot help but feel affection for it. Polish people welcome us warmly and every new path we take is a new urban adventure. Yet within the very city centre, without the noise pollution of vehicles, everything seems calm.

Two days after arriving, Kate leaves for Budapest and I wish her luck on her lone journey. A lone female hitchhiker, five years younger than I, she will go far in the world.

In a dimly lit basement bar, I open a wooden chess board.

"This piece is called a rook," I explain. "Or castle. It can move horizontally or vertically through as many empty spaces as you wish. If you reach your own piece, you must stop. If you reach the opponent, you can take it." I proceed to explain each piece in turn as Emilia listens attentively. Like a blank notebook, she soaks up all the information and we are soon playing a full game.

"You beat me again!" she pretends to whine in her lilting accent, candle shadows dancing across her face, her fringe falling forward.

"Of course I did." I feign arrogance, hiding how impressed I am. Despite it being her first day of chess, she gives me a good game.

Hand in hand, we walk into a movie theatre to watch the new Batman movie.

"I still think I like Batman more than you."

"Did you ever have a costume?" I counter.

"No, but I'm a girl. I would have had one if I was a boy."

"That's a poor excuse. I had a Batman costume and I even wore it to school. When my Mum gave it to me, she made me promise not to jump out of the window when I wore it because it wouldn't make me fly. Another little boy did that and broke into a thousand tiny pieces and they couldn't fix him. It was such a silly thing to say."

"Because you wouldn't have jumped out the window?"

"No! Because everyone knows Batman can't fly."

"Tell her how you want her to cut my hair."

"But it's your hair, you have to decide."

"I don't speak Polish and besides, I don't have to look at myself. Get her to cut it however you want me to look. If it looks terrible, I'll blame you, but you'll have to deal with it."

Emilia laughs at me. "You are ridiculous." I love the sound of her laugh.

"Close your eyes," I whisper. Outside the supposed ex-home of Pope Jean Paul II, we have been walking around an open air art gallery. A local photographer transports us from the microscopic world of leaves and insects through to dramatic landscapes in single steps. Each image is a metre high, some with birds I have never seen, others with mammals that I challenge myself to name. Emilia plays my game and closes her eyes. I stand behind her and put my hands over them to make sure she isn't cheating, then shuffle her in front of a woodland scene. The moonlight kisses the outlines of vegetation, a forest shrouded in blue.

"It's beautiful," she gasps as I let her see again.

"Where are you?"

"I'm in the forest in the dark of night."

"Are you scared?"

"No, I am a wolf, I have nothing to be afraid of."

"Take me out of the city," I ask. "Anywhere you want to take me, but somewhere quiet without people."

We walk through a forest, sunlight seeping through the thin canopy, marking the ground with temporary shapeless forms. A cat, a dinosaur wearing a hat, a boat being driven by a monkey. In the light and shadows, there is as much to see as in the clouds.

We walk apart, I see a mushroom. We walk together, our hands touch. We are silent, at peace.

We rush our words, running out of time.

"Let's take the elevator," I say.

"Two floors?"

"Yes." We squeeze into the one person doorless elevator, a relic of communist times, keeping well away from the finger threatening wall that speeds past us.

Precious seconds stolen.

Alone, together.

I wake up, bright sunlight pouring through the large windows. Beside me, Emilia is sleeping softly, her dark fringe hanging over her face. I brush it away with the tips of my fingers without waking her.

Ten days have passed.

Ten days of cooking, of laughing, of walking, of talking, of art galleries, of sharing, of nothing and everything. Of secret smiles and sweet, soft words.

I gently slide out of bed. I don't want to wake her. I want to leave everything exactly as it is, so precious and perfect, so that the image might last eternally in my mind.

Like a ghost, today I will disappear.

Reluctantly I pack my bag. Emilia stirs. She sits up and offers me a sleepy half-smile.

"Is it that time?"

"It's that time." I offer a half-smile in return. How do you smile when you have to say goodbye?

"Let me make you breakfast." I don't refuse.

"This immersion program," I begin at the breakfast table, "will only last a week. I have to meet my father in Croatia a few days after and I hope to visit some places along the way, but maybe, maybe I could stop by here again, just for a day or two before I go south." My feet are itchy for new stomping grounds, yet my mind is entangled with Emilia. With her here and me on the move, we are faced with impossibility. She would never come with me and I could not stop in one place. Am I prolonging the inevitable, clutching at straws? Why is it that we human beings struggle to let go?

"You know that you are always welcome here, I would be happy to have you stay for as long as you want."

"Then I'll leave some things to pick up on my way back."

After breakfast I sort out what to take and what to leave, then hold Emilia tightly. Is this the dizzy lights of a bright summer romance or something more?

"Goodbye."

"See you later."

"Yes, that's what I meant."

I walk down the cold stone staircase. Alone. How I intended to be.

The door gently clicks shut when I am out of sight. It feels like someone slammed it in my face. Is this the end?

22. You Are Not a Robot

I tip my head back, holding my arms wide, admiring the stars far above me in the cloudless sky. The dawn is fast approaching and they will be gone soon. I stand on a barge, a floating dance floor, speakers calling out for the sun to join the party. Inside, my body is warmed by the flow of rich, sweet nectar. Or is it the fuzzy warmth of Polish beer?

The music stops and everybody boos. Home time, it's past dawn. Ola, my new host sporting fiery red lipstick that compliments her brilliant blond hair, leads me to a breakfast bar. We eat, take a bus, climb fences, walk through vegetable patches, and finally make it back to her apartment on the outskirts of Warsaw, over two hundred miles north of Kraków. There are four hours until I have to be back in the centre of the city to attend the complimentary tour that is part of my language immersion program.

I wake up an hour after it starts and leap out of bed.

Upon reaching the centre of the city, I walk aimlessly, no idea where I'm meant to be, exchanging messages with one of the coordinators of the program.

Ice cream will save the day.

It's good ice cream.

Still can't find them. Probably just keep walking. After all, how big can one city be?

I find the group in front of a fancy turreted building, listening to a tour guide. The majority of the city is modern due to destruction during the war, but we are in the old part of the city. I'll just stand here and finish my ice cream, two hours and forty-five minutes late. Only fifteen more minutes of the tour to get through.

I lag at the back of the group and a couple of participants come over to introduce themselves to me.

This is really good ice cream.

Tour over, a little round of applause, we head into a restaurant to be treated to a free lunch. I sit down and mumble a few hellos to the people around me. I don't really feel like eating or talking. I think I'd rather be snowboarding. Or sleeping. Or maybe back in that dirty cow pond, that was a good place to be.

Why am I here again?

A bright purple soup is served as a starter. It's cold and has bits of vegetables floating in it. Someone points out that it is made of beetroot.

"That must be why it is purple." Is that the best conversation I can manage?

For main course, a plate of fried cheese. On a normal day, that might be heaven, but today it tastes bland and rubbery. After a few bites, I offer it to the table who descend upon it rapidly.

Every so often I mumble a few words of agreement, conversations becoming more intelligible the longer I sit. Yes, I am returning to the world.

Outside the restaurant, we gather in a small circle. Ten of us. Or twelve. The number doesn't matter, we're just there, some people.

Polite conversation flows gently as each stranger waits for another to make a plan.

"How about a beer in the sunshine?" someone suggests. It's a beautiful day with clear skies and the thought of being in the sun appeals to me. Besides, I have no other plans for today.

A tiny American girl marches across the group and thrusts her rigid arm towards me, shaking my hand formally. "Hello, I'm Leah." She is one of those girls who clearly works out and has a body to prove it. Long golden hair surrounds huge sunglasses that obscure most of her face.

"Hello Leah. I'm Jamie. I was late." Way to go making friends.

As we walk to the bar, Leah tells me a very formal account of how she got here, something about her family, possibly her grandparents. I concentrate fully on putting one foot after the other and not tripping on the cobbles, disinterested in the monotone syllables. Why is the sun so bright? I wish I had big glasses to cover my face. Maybe I should ask to borrow them from this girl.

We take seats around a wooden table, shielded from the sun by a large umbrella. This is better.

Leah lifts up her glasses, revealing a well defined face. Nice... angles. Sort my head out! I try and physically shake the daze of last night's drinking and sleep deprivation away from me. Walking, talking, and even thinking seem difficult.

I look again. Sweet little lips, a perfectly smooth complexion, a mole on her cheek, and large dark eyes. She does have an awfully pretty face. So very pretty. Next to her, I am a mess. She wears a delicate, white summer dress, sits with good posture, has tanned skin and great teeth, another wonder of American dentistry, but above all, she carries herself with elegance, almost an air of disconnectedness. Everything about her is so planned, so well thought out. A well oiled machine, a purpose built robot. She worked hard for this image and physically, she wears it well.

I on the other hand, am wearing the first item of clothing I grabbed hold of. I struggle not to slouch in my chair and nothing about me is planned out. I couldn't even manage to arrive on time for the tour I had known about for the past couple of weeks. Not that I like tours. Maybe I was late on purpose… no, I definitely wasn't late on purpose. Just like I wasn't late to my A-level exams on purpose, my route into university.

Lateness precedes me.

Although our chairs are mere inches apart, there is an invisible barrier between Leah and I. Despite her physical perfection, she has a psychological forcefield keeping everyone at bay and although I can hear her words, I know that we live on different planets.

I agree to a beer, then leave the table to stretch my legs.

Immediately the short walk does me good and I feel refreshed. I am over the hump of tiredness and know that I will be fine for the rest of the day. Even the sunshine doesn't burn my eyes anymore. It's as if a cloud of haze has been lifted from around me.

"Why did you come here?" Leah asks upon my return to the table.

"I got an email inviting me to come." Saying that I'm here because I don't have anything else to do sounds as if I don't know what I'm doing with myself. It's best not to let people know about that.

"Were you in England before?"

"No, Estonia. I was supposed to be going to work on a farm in Italy, but my plans were changed. Here I am. Eventually."

"You were late because you were in Estonia?" In her mind she goes through a well thought out list of events preceding my arrival, purely for the sake of organising thoughts and getting things straightened out in her own head.

"Actually no, I was late because I was dancing on a boat until the early hours of the morning and then I got lost. I also had to make an emergency stop for ice cream." Taken aback, Leah checks me out twice as if to say, 'are you messing with me? These things don't happen in my well thought out list of events.' I throw her another curve ball intended to really knock her out of her well planned world. "You see, the truth of how I really got here is that I have been hitchhiking around Europe for the past few months and haven't paid for accommodation once. This seemed like a more comfortable gig than most, three meals a day, a bed in a hotel, so I said yes." Her face is expressionless. I have failed to get a rise from her. Sitting upright, hands folded, listening to my responses, she asks a few questions about where I've been. All of the questions are recited in that same clearly spoken, well pronounced, monotonous voice. She establishes the facts: where I've been, where I've slept, how I get a ride.

Finally, with the interrogation over, the first flicker of a smile offers sunlight through the impenetrable wall between us. "You must be crazy! I would never do that in America. You don't know what it's like there, you'd get chopped up and all kinds of crazy-bad things would happen to you."

"And eaten by tigers or attacked by unicorns. Yep, sure, you guys live in a crazy place."

The smile disappears, the distance between us increased once more. "Are you being serious?" I give her my most serious face.

"I don't know America, but I met some American hitchhikers last week and they didn't seem to have a problem with it. Would you hitchhike in Poland?"

This brings her back to life, her psychological forcefield lowering its death charge ever so slightly. "Are you kidding me? I don't even like walking around the streets by myself. This is the furthest I have ever been from home."

"What's it like, your home? Peaceful and loving, happy and safe?"

"Not exactly." The forcefield returns to full strength, her words delivered flat and level, absolutely measured, completely monotone. She has moulded and mastered almost everything about herself. I don't know people like this in real life: perfectly formed, yet cold and distant.

As the glasses empty, a second round of drinks are ordered without protest. My brain has regained full functionality and I am able to walk and speak just about as well as I ever have been. Leah tells me about her grandparents a second time, how they came from Poland, how she just graduated from university, how she wants to learn the history of Poland, how she booked a tour, how she found a hotel on this site that I've never heard of, how she is on a two week break and wants to learn about where she comes from…

"Where your grandparents come from," I correct her.

"America is a new country, we all say our roots are where our ancestors come from."

"If we go back far enough, we're all from the same place. Where does it stop?" I feel myself interlocking horns in constant battle, pushing her to the edge, searching for a real person under the facade.

Somebody suggests we go for food and most of our group disperses. Should I go to a restaurant with my already dwindling funds? Most definitely not, I must go back to Ola's house. But I don't feel like going back yet. Besides, she said she'd meet me in the city later this evening if I was still here.

I mingle with the reduced group, five of us in all, separated from Leah as we walk down the street. Two Brits and three Americans.

We head down a flight of stairs, towards a basement, and into a pierogi restaurant.

"Do you know what pierogis are?" I ask Leah when we're seated. We sit opposite each other at one end of the table.

"Stuffed dumplings," she replies as if it's the most obvious thing in the world.

"Of course, you are Polish!" I mock. Still nothing.

"We eat these every year." She looks around the restaurant we are in. "I think

I came in here yesterday by myself."

The five of us look through the menu. Traditional pierogis are available stuffed with combinations of onion, potato, cabbage, and ricotta cheese, but there are fillings I had never thought of. Blue cheese delights and fruit fillings topped with sweet cream instead of the traditional sour cream.

"I'm not that hungry," Leah says aloud, resting on her elbows. Is this a subtle invitation, her way to invite someone through the barrier, the monotonous lack of expression?

"Me neither, we can share a plate if you like?" A subtle way of saving money.

"But I'm vegetarian."

"Me too."

"None of the guys I know are vegetarian." On the tip of her tongue is something else, but she swallows the words.

We agree to share food, no longer on different planets, just different continents. Taking it in turns to pick different fillings from the extensive menu, we order a plate between us.

Why am I sharing a plate of food with this girl I've just met? Why am I looking for the real person beneath the surface of this well controlled, planned out persona?

I return to the earlier question that she subtly sidestepped. "So, you were saying before, your hometown isn't that friendly. What's not friendly about it?"

Her stare sizes me up, assessing why I'm asking her this question, why I'm not talking about something easier that allows her to rattle off a well-practised answer. She does this thing with her tongue, moving it behind her teeth as she thinks carefully. "For a start, my job... I work in a home for children with severe difficulties. Some of them are born as drug addicts because their mothers were addicts, others are too abusive to be in a normal school. Most of them will stay in the home their whole childhood and when they turn eighteen, they will be moved to another home for adults. At work I never know if I will get attacked verbally, physically, or both."

I look at Leah. Perfectly formed, the size of a small pixie, receiving beatings from teenagers is not befitting of her. "What do you do if a seventeen year old attacks you? Surely some of them are bigger than me, let alone you."

"We have procedures to try and make it as safe as possible for both the children and the staff..." That was the practised answer. She hesitates before continuing. "...but when I'm faced with a six-foot-two teenager who gets angry because he can't talk and you don't know what he wants, it gets a little difficult... they scare me."

"And this is what you will do for the rest of your life?"

"It's what I wanted to do for a long time. I studied psychology to get here."

Another rehearsed answer. Once again she thinks for a few seconds before continuing. Can she trust me? She isn't the trusting type. "Right now I don't know what I want. I just graduated and I already have a job at this place, so it makes sense to stay. A lot of people are really struggling to get work in the US, so it isn't as simple as just finding something else."

"OK, so your job sucks. What about the place you live, where was it again?"

"Boston. It's a good city, really nice actually, but it's still a bit intimidating. I come from Detroit which has its bad parts, but I lived in a nice area there."

"Do you feel safe in Boston?"

"Every night when I walk home from work, I walk with my keys between my fingers, my hands clenched into a fist. If someone attacks me, I want to be able to fight back."

Blatant honesty for the first time.

But her life is not a life for anyone.

When the food arrives, we cut each parcel in half before rating how good they are. I tell Leah that my selections are better than hers and she offers the glimmer of a smile before retaliating that she chose the best. Increasingly often, she peeks her real self out before retreating behind her wall once more.

Across the rest of the table, beer and conversation flow. Five strangers.

"I have to go meet some friends now," the program coordinator announces, "we have an early start in the morning." The minibus is leaving the centre of the city at ten a.m. It's the first strict deadline that I have had to make since I started hitchhiking, a hundred times more important than the tour that was arranged purely as a reward for taking part in the program.

Out on the street, we prepare to split up, but I have nowhere to go until Ola joins me in the city. "Anyone fancy one more drink?" I ask. It's beginning to get dark.

"I don't know how to get back to my hotel," Leah frets. "I'd like to come, but it's getting late and I should go back."

"You could always take a taxi later." Someone asks which hotel she is staying in and then tells her that it isn't far. A taxi wouldn't cost much.

"I don't know what the taxi drivers are like here, I should probably go home now." Someone else tells her that it isn't a problem. "I've never been out of the US by myself, I don't really feel comfortable."

If there was daylight, this girl would be scared of her own shadow.

Torn, Leah is a small child, defenceless and afraid, drifting over an unknown ocean in a fragile wooden dinghy and waiting for somebody to save her. She wants to stay out with us, but won't do so unless someone reassures her that nothing bad will happen. "I'm pretty sure nearly half of all lone females make it home safely when taking taxis in Poland," I mock.

"Oh come on, you wonder why I think I should go home now?"

After several hours of probing, I am done with looking for the real person. She has to make the choice. "You have two choices: you can go or you can stay. But if you stay, you have to let go and stop fretting. You have to try to enjoy yourself or at least pretend to for the sake of everyone else around you."

She looks at me discerningly, that same look she gave me when she told me I was crazy.

For unfathomable reasons, I see that her mind is already made up. She chooses not to follow every survival instinct that her brain demands of her, but instead, to stay out with us in the big, scary Polish city. "OK, I will try to relax." Her eyes open wide at the admission and she takes a deep breath as if she realises the mistake of her words as she speaks them. It's as if the words slipped out without her permission.

The other two leave so that John, a confident American, Leah, and I, are the only three left from our initial group. As Leah walks in front of me down a busy alley, her summer dress flitters in the wind. Elegant, she floats like a fairy, the soft steps of a dancer. On her back, below her right shoulder, is a tattoo. The silhouette of a ballerina. The words 'Always with me in my hand,' surround the silhouette. Leah could be the tiny ballerina in that picture.

The tiny dancer.

Through the alleyway, we find hoards of people drinking openly in a small courtyard, surrounded by bars and corner stores. The Polish 'no drinking in public' rule is strictly enforced and this oasis is the first place I have visited where the rule is not adhered to.

"This looks like a perfect spot," I gesture to a space on the ground, large enough for the three of us to sit.

"You want to sit on the floor?" What she really means is, 'you want me sit on the dirty floor like an uncivilised being when I am wearing a perfectly lovely white dress and we could quite easily go into a bar and sit at a table like normal people?' Something like that.

"You made a promise to let go. It's summer and we should be outside." Resignation spreads across her face, a look that tells me she wishes she was back in her hotel. With an inaudible sigh, she sits on the dirty floor in her clean dress and as she does so, her whole being is transformed. It's as if she has fought and battled constantly with her wall for all her life, fighting hard to keep people out, but by sitting on the floor in a pretty summer dress, she admits that she is not a robot.

I head inside to grab some drinks and receive a call from Ola. I tell her roughly where we are and she says that she will soon join us.

"So, what do you both think of Poland so far?" I ask as we pass a bottle of wine between the three of us.

"I love it here," John begins, "I love all of Europe." He lifts his iPad into the air to take a photo of the bustling activity around us, then takes a photo of the three of us on the ground.

"It's so old," Leah adds, "I never imagined how wonderful it would all be. We don't have cities like this in the US."

The excitement of the evening is contagious. We share stories of how wonderful Europe is and what we want to see.

"I can't wait for tomorrow," Leah jabbers, her monotone and well paced defence mechanism overruled by a starry eyed girl living out her dream of visiting Poland. "The hotel in the country sounds so lovely and I can't wait to see the Polish countryside. I am going to try all of the food, then go home and tell my grandparents all about it." Real emotion, real thoughts.

Now she smiles.

And laughs. Like a bird released from a cage after a lifetime of captivity, it is a precious laugh, rarely heard.

For these sacred few minutes she is a real person. Her whole body shakes with laughter, almost awkwardly, as if she has forgotten how.

Ola and her friend join our outdoor wine picnic, Ola wearing that glorious red lipstick once more. "We are going to a party in the forest later, would you like to come?"

After a couple of hours in the courtyard, John excuses himself to meet friends, but Leah is torn. She is smiling, she is laughing, she is having a good time. She is a real person, but she has not yet forgotten who she was. "I really would like to, but I think I must go home now. It's already later than I intended to stay out." I sense the impenetrable barrier threatening to emerge from the ground once more, winding upwards to encase her in a world of safety.

Stay away wall, let this happy person stay with us.

"Oh come on!" Ola cries. "We'll get you home." Ola's warmth and good nature shine through in everything she does. That radiance shatters Leah's forcefield like a cannon ball through a single pane of glass. I can almost hear the shards skipping upon the floor.

Disengaged from autopilot, Leah chats openly with Ola and her friend, telling stories of the US and how much she loves Poland… after only two days.

I see before me a tiny golden haired ballerina full of smiles and words and a love of the world. She is glowing and rainbows dance upon her skin.

It is just two days since I parted with Emilia. I think of her smile, her lilting accent, her everything. It is still there and I feel it as strongly as I ever felt it.

Yet before me, Leah lights up the night. Two mutually exclusive feelings that have no bearing upon one another.

The world vibrates as we approach the forest. Beat, beat, beat, speakers so loud that they make the very forest dance.

Around the forest, which is actually a park, is a circular metal fence. At the entranceway, stewards issue tickets. A single dirt road leads into the park and we step off the road to let a large food van pass ahead of us.

There is a step on the back of the van. The van is going into the gig. The gig for which you need tickets. Tickets cost money and I don't have much.

I run and leap onto the back of the van, landing on the step with nothing to hold onto.

What have I just done?

The driver has no idea that there is a freeloader on his van and I have no idea how long it will be before I fall off. I lean against the back door, hoping not to overbalance as it bounces on the uneven ground. The stewards shout something at me in Polish as they watch me pass. I wave. Yet all I can hear, drowning out the noise of the epic speakers, overpowering the sound of the van and the shouting, is Leah cackling. Her uncontrollable, unmeasured, definitely not monotone laughter vibrates through my chest as easily as dolphins leap from the water.

A thousand captive birds released from their cages, it warms my heart.

She is not a robot.

23. Lateness

I can't believe it. I am such a failure.

It is ten fifteen and all I had to do was get to the bus stop by ten. The one place I have had to be at a given time in the past few months and could I do it? No, I couldn't. Twenty-five years old and I can't even get myself where I am supposed to be. And that pain is back: that unplaceable pain somewhere between my stomach and my groin.

I can't decide which is worse, the physical pain or the pain of being that guy. I am that guy. I am the one who turned up two and three quarter hours late for the three hour tour, I am the one who missed the bus, I am the one who is completely incapable of organising himself. Despite not booking a hostel, despite not booking flights, despite everything, I made a promise, a promise of trust. I have let them down and I have let myself down.

In the kitchen, Ola asks if I would like breakfast. I would like breakfast. We're nearly an hour outside the city and even if I left now, I would never make it to the minibus in time. In fact, it has probably already left.

I should check my phone.

Three missed calls, two messages. 'Jamie, where are you?' 'Jamie, please call us, we have to leave now.' Sent five minutes ago. I can't bear to face them in a conversation. 'Sorry, running late, won't make it. Is there a bus I can catch?' Within seconds, I receive the name of a small village I can't pronounce and instructions to walk a few kilometres from there.

I sit down and enjoy a leisurely breakfast with Ola, losing track of time. If I don't look, maybe it didn't happen.

"What will you do now?" Ola asks.

"I have two choices. I try and get there or I don't. "Quite honestly, as nice as the week in a hotel sounds, I'm not sure if I can face turning up late again. I might just head south today. I don't even know how I would get to this place, it's a country hotel about sixty miles away from Warsaw."

"I can take you to the train station if you want. They have buses there too, so maybe you can find something."

Do I want to go? Do I want to be 'that guy' in front of all those people? Or should I just skip it? Surely I can't just go back to Emilia's already and I'm not meeting my family for another ten days. What about the little ballerina, a hidden person so real that I already feel I've made a friend? That alone presents reasons for and against going.

I try to weigh the reasons up, but it's an impossible sum. Best to shut down everything, not think about it, then go with whichever idea screams loudest and longest.

In the shower, the language immersion program leaps forth, shouting over the flow of running water.

"OK, let's go to the train station," I say excitedly when I'm out of the shower. My decision is made, I'm going.

In the car and at the last possible minute, buzzing with energy, I change my mind. "Drop me on the road instead. Hitchhiking is cheaper and probably faster than public transport."

We drive a short way out of the city, then stop on a small road. It leads directly to the village close to the hotel and I am sure it won't take me long to find a ride. I thank Ola for her fantastic company and pull my backpack from the back seat.

"Actually, I think we should go a bit further, then you will have a better place."

"Really, this is brilliant already. I don't mind getting a lift from here, I'm sure it will be easy."

"No, no, come on, I'll take you a bit further." Once more, her warm persona and easy words win over.

We talk as she drives. Then we talk and talk and talk some more, the culmination of several days in each other's company. Our flowing words carry us all the way to the country hotel and through the large iron gates surrounded by white stone walls.

"I guess I'll get out here."

Around me are several large white buildings with wooden window frames and grey roofs. Spacious gardens stretch in every direction, but where are all the people?

I am the naughty kid who is late for school, the one who has arrived after the morning bell has rung. Ola, my only safety net, drives away and leaves me alone.

I walk around the white structure to my left and into a small garden where a few unknown people sit at wooden picnic tables. I turn around and walk towards another white building. Inside there is a large hall, but like most of the grounds and buildings that I have encountered thus far, it is empty.

I walk aimlessly until in the distance I see people moving around. Could that be where I am supposed to be?

As I pass a couple of vaguely familiar faces from lunch yesterday, they look at me with surprise. Oh, it's you. I hadn't expected you to actually make it. I clearly made a wonderful first impression.

My stomach tightens as I pass Leah. Despite barely having any sleep, she looks as perfect as ever and offers me silent acknowledgement of why I missed the bus. Raving in a forest until dawn seems so far away from the placid world around us.

"Jamie, you made it!" Ben the organiser is pleased, maybe relieved to see me. I mumble an apology. "Don't worry about it, several people were late so we've only been here for an hour anyway. Please, come and get some lunch." He leads me into a spacious dining hall. "You can take as long as you want."

Symbolising my lack of timekeeping, I sit alone at a table that seats over twenty people. It is elaborately laid with a white tablecloth and silverware. Just a few minutes ago, this room was full. I gorge myself on Polish delights while outside, I hear the start of an introductory activity. Speed friending. You have three minutes to meet, greet, and talk with a member of the group, then the buzzer sounds and you switch to the next person. It's the embarrassment of meeting people you know nothing about, intensified and replicated over and over again.

When Ben said take as much time as I wanted, did he actually mean it? Could I actually just sit here and miss the whole activity?

When the interest in twiddling my cutlery around the remains of my lunch has entirely expired, I return to the group outside. They are arranged in two rows, either side of benches. The Polish language participants are on one side and the native English speakers are on the other. Each time the buzzer sounds, the natives shuffle down one space and start a new conversation with another new face. Ben tells me to join in at the end of the line.

"Hello, nice to meet you. My name is Jamie... I'm twenty-five years old. Where are you from...? I'm from England... No, I don't actually live there right now, I'm spending some time in Europe... I lived in South Korea before... South Korea, near China and Japan, do you know? I was an English teacher... Yes, I do miss my family. I have four brothers... What do you do...? I do like Poland, it's a very pleasant country with friendly people... Pleasant? It means nice... One more week maybe... Sports. I like all sports..." And so on and so on and on and on and so.

When the activity is called to a halt, I can barely remember what my own name is, let alone the names of the people I just met. There were university students, sixty year old business men, those who wanted to learn English for fun, and those who needed it to develop their careers. Ben's introductory speech informs us that from eight in the morning until nine at night, we will have a program to follow that is split into one hour blocks. There is a two hour break after lunch. For the majority of the day, we will be paired in one-on-one situations, free to roam the fields and gardens for an hour as we talk with our partner before returning to pick up a new one. There is a dirty lake to explore with a dirty old pedalo and if we want to walk out of the hotel grounds, there are farm tracks to follow. All meals will be eaten together, Polish participants and native speakers sitting alternately, and a couple of times a day, there will be group activities. The last hour of each day is designated as a game. After this, the bar is open and we can do as we please.

During the final hour session of the day, I am paired in a one-on-one conversation with Mateusz, a young Polish actor. He flicks his blond hair to one side and smiles cautiously, occasionally removing his thick framed glasses to clean them.

"Jamie, this is so hard for me. To speak English all day. It is, how do you say…" He laughs nervously.

"Very difficult?"

"Mmm, yes. It is very difficult."

I immediately take a liking to him. His English is good, but his confidence, lacking. Each careful movement and twitchy gesture is a part of him, suggesting the experience of having to speak English for twelve hours a day may soon overcome him.

"Jamie, Mateusz, time for dinner." We are twenty minutes late as we walk into the dinner buffet. I appear to be building quite a reputation.

After the evening activities are through, I sit at the bar. Almost everybody is there and the Polish language participants mostly form their own little Polish speaking groups, grateful for the respite after a whole day of constantly speaking English.

"I saw you have some tattoos," I say to Leah as she comes to the bar beside me. She is wearing jeans and a white vest top with a pink cardigan. Simple, yet elegant. "There is a large one near your shoulder, a ballerina silhouette. Does it mean anything?"

"It's the lyrics for an Elton John song. I got it because I used to always listen to that song with my dad. Do you like it?"

"I know the song, I like it."

"I meant the tattoo. Do you like that?"

"Not really, I've never been a fan of tattoos." Leah's mouth opens wide with her eyes, somewhere between a smile, surprise, and outrage. In the comfort and safety of a nice hotel, she is in an environment that she knows, but more than that, last night's conversations seem to have lowered her barriers sufficiently so that the spice of dance has been added to her previously monotonous speech and expressionless actions.

"I can't believe that you would just say that. Did you really just tell me that you don't like tattoos after looking at mine?"

"I did, but it's personal taste. Nothing lasts forever, so apart from scars, I try not to permanently stain my skin. How many have you got?"

"Four. And I love them all because they all mean something to me from different times in my life."

"As long as you like them, that's all that matters." I turn back to the bar. "How about something Polish?"

Those of us closest to the bar take sweet cherry shots of a blood red liquor. It disappears like innocent fruit juice.

After the bar closes, most people leave for bed. Just Mateusz, Leah, and I remain.

"Jamie, Leah, I am really having problems. Today it is too hard and I have many, many, many things to do." Mateusz gestures flamboyantly with his hands and unintentionally with his facial expressions. "Before this started, I thought, Mateusz, should you do this? Is this the right time? And I was going to cancel, I said no, I will go another time, but my boyfriend, he said to me that I must go now, that I must do it, or I would never do it. So I have come and I am here, look, you see me, but… oh my gawd, it is so difficult. My…" He taps his head?

"Head? Brain?"

"Brain! My brain it is to like, boom!"

"Your brain feels like it is exploding?"

"Oh, yes yes! That is beautiful, that is soooo beautiful, you understand all of my words. Tell me again." He takes a notebook out and transcribes the phrase.

"My brain feels like it will explode."

"Explode?"

"Boom!" I spread my hands and fingers wide.

"To explode, boom?" Mateusz copies my gesture.

"Something like that."

The three of us are sitting on the floor of the porch outside the locked bar and this time, Leah didn't protest about sitting on the dirty ground. A small entrance light offers enough visibility for us to see the outline of each other's faces.

"So Leah, please can you tell me, why have you come to Poland?" Mateusz's voice rises up and down like a song.

"To teach English and to see where my family came from. I have always wanted to come to Poland and now I've finished university, it was the perfect time." Leah's long hair is kissed softly by the light above. Whispers of gold. Her lips move perfectly, every word well formed. They are small and delicate, like the rest of her being. As she talks about Poland, there is a glint in her eye, a fire that I would never have imagined only yesterday. She becomes animated, telling the story of why she came to Poland, of her first days in Warsaw. Is this the same story that I heard yesterday in monotonous, discordant tones? I think that it is, except this time it is full of emotion, of desire, of life.

For each concern that Mateusz has, together Leah and I find a solution. There is an openness, a simple honesty within him that is so rare in the world. Without even having to vocalise them, his elaborate body actions give away his feelings. For hours we sit, just the three of us. Mateusz tells us of acting, of standing up on a stage in front of hundreds of people, of performing on TV shows and films that will be watched by thousands.

"That sounds terrifying," I confess. "When I was in school plays, I always played the part of the musician. I would normally be the sound of the donkey, clapping two coconuts together to recreate the sound of hooves on a dusty road. In my final year of first school, I was away for casting day. I got cast as Angel Gabriel and I had one line to speak in front of all the parents. I cried so hard that they nearly let me skip my part."

"No, but Jamie, for me acting is like life. To be up on the stage in front of those people, it is the most exciting. What you do, your hijacking…"

"Hitchhiking."

"Yes, high-tacht-king, that is, oh my gawd, I can't believe it. It is the most terrifying thing."

"It's just one stranger you have to speak to, not a whole crowd of them with the expectation of being entertained. It's like talking to me now."

"No, because to talk to you now is very easy."

"Exactly. Hitchhiking is just the same." I truly believe that standing upon a stage, putting yourself in front of people as an entertainer, is one of the most terrifying things that one could possibly do in life.

When we walk to bed, the only sound around us is that of the insects in the night, clicking, chirruping, living their busy little lives. Across the garden, we pass the forest that surrounds the dirty lake and Leah shudders as we pass.

"You don't want to go for a walk in the forest?" I joke.

"I couldn't think of anything more terrifying."

The three of us return to the safety of our separate rooms in the clean hotel with locked doors and light switches. The night cannot touch us here. I have a single bed in a room that I share with a friendly Scottish guy.

Unexpectedly I find myself walking into a kitchen. Is this my family home? Or is it somewhere else, I can't tell? A faceless girl is in the room with me. Even the colour of her hair is imperceivable. Black then blond, then both at the same time. A pregnant snake slithers into the room menacingly, its grotesque underbelly bulging with offspring. The girl runs behind me for protection and I grab a chair to fend off the snake. It leaps at my ankle and I kick at it hard. Beside me, drawers spring open and large stag beetles fly at me, each bearing a tiny human face. The snake explodes, baby snakes sprawling across the floor, all aimed at…

Gasping, I sit up in bed.

It's almost morning.

I shower and prepare myself for another day of continuous conversation. My brain is already spinning. Looking around the room, there is no sign of either snakes or insects.

'Look forward to seeing you soon,' I message to Emilia. It's the first thing I've said to her since we parted ways. It's almost true, I do look forward to the one last time we'll see each other, probably never to see each other again.

Yet in my heart of hearts, I know that years have passed in the three or four days since we were together.

24. Tiny Dancer

The rumbling skies open and we run for cover. An hour ago, it was a beautiful sunny day.

On a short break between conversation classes, ten of us stand under the spacious porch of the dinner hall, admiring the speed with which the storm has approached.

A distant flash, a dull groan of nature.

The wind throws the rain at us and we retreat further under the protection of the overhanging roof.

A brighter flash, a louder roar. Louder and louder, the storm grows furious as it approaches.

A bomb on our shelter, a train wreck inside my head, the sound of a whole ocean inside me!

My ear drums explode as I leap for cover, the crack of thunder so deafeningly loud that the lightning must have struck directly overhead. Around me, people are on the floor, others hold their heads in their hands.

I am clutching hold of Leah, protecting her, hoping she will protect me.

"Sorry, that caught me by surprise." I quickly release Leah's tiny frame as people gabble like turkeys. Did you hear that? Oh my god it was so close! I thought it must have hit us.

Truly, it was one of the loudest sounds that I have ever heard in my life. Only once before do I recall hearing something louder, another crack of thunder several years ago. Shortly after that occurrence I found a smouldering tree close to where I had been cowering.

Satisfied with our terror, the storm passes overhead, each flash less intense, each eruption of the clouds a little quieter. The wind relents and the rain ceases. Then the clouds disperse.

Is there such thing as a flash storm? That may have been it.

At lunch, I instinctively find myself taking a seat beside Leah. "You can't sit here," she whispers, "we have to sit next to Polish people." I move to the next empty seat.

Still we gravitate.

After lunch I tell more stories about myself in well paced English, speaking as slowly and clearly as possible. In exchange, I listen to the stories of others, to what they do and why they want to learn English. It's like the friend dating game except that each date lasts an hour. I take one student across the lake in the pedalo to avoid the monotony of walking the same paths as before. The storm over, we paddle slowly from one end of the lake to the other, careful not to fall in. The water looks darker and dirtier from the surface.

In the evening, conversations pass from person to person and when the bar closes, Mateusz, Leah, and I, are alone once more. A natural trio.

"Stop me if I've said this," I instruct, saying the same thing for the tenth time. It is day three and I can't remember who I've said what to. My brain is becoming scattered from the continual and sometimes inane conversations. We talk to practise talking, covering as much content as possible, invariably returning to the same well covered topics and knowing that each conversation lasts only one hour before the next arrives.

"I have one yoke." I am on the far side of the lake, walking with an older Polish man. His words are awkward and he often says things I don't understand.

"A yoke, like an egg yoke?"

"No, a yoke, like haha, a yoke."

"A joke!"

"Yes, I have one yoke. I would like for you to tell me if it is a funny."

"OK, go ahead."

"There was a fishing man who go to catch the fishes in his woosh-woosh. Boat!"

"A fisherman."

"Yes. The fisherman, one day get a very special fish. This special fish say to fisherman, you fisherman, can have one... one dream, one want..."

"A wish?"

"One weesh. Anything or everything of all of the world that you wants. But there is something. When you get one... weesh... your neighbour, he will get two. If you have one house with five bedroom, he will get two house with ten bedroom. If you have one million dollar, he has two million dollar. The fisherman, he thinks." We have been walking for several minutes of the yoke. "You understand?"

"Yes, I understand. The fisherman has one wish from the magic fish."

"But his neighbour, two times. Do you know what he wish for?"

"No, I don't. What did he wish for?" He urges me to make a guess. "A new house?"

"No, the man hate his neighbour and said fish, kill my eye." He starts to laugh hysterically. I smile and force a chuckle. "The secret, is really, he say take my..." A gesture to the crotch.

"His testicle?"

"Yes! Because neighbour get two times, so bye-bye!" Another roar of laughter. Again I force a chuckle. The awkwardness of the situation makes me cringe. "Is no funny? Why you no laugh?"

"It is funny," I did try to laugh, "but telling jokes in another language is one of the most difficult things to do. When you can tell and laugh at jokes in a foreign language, you know that you have mastered it. A good friend once told me that when he was learning English, he would laugh louder and longer than anyone else when he first understood jokes, even if they weren't particularly funny. Now he speaks fluently, he doesn't laugh so loud." Now he laughs less like a crazy person.

Our circuit of the lake is complete after many minutes of the fisherman joke. The conversation is stunted and I try hard as every topic is directed towards another long joke.

As we rejoin the group, I catch a precious few seconds with Leah.

"I've been listening to some jokes for the last hour."

"Did you hear the one about the fisherman?"

"I did." She nods, knowingly. Ben rounds everyone up and we are off again with new partners.

By the end of the day, I am exhausted by conversation roulette.

At the bar, we talk with the bar staff, two of the girls giggling as they point out Mateusz across the room. They know him from a TV show. People disperse, the bar becomes quieter, then it closes.

I walk back towards the accommodation with Leah, overcome by tiredness.

"Let's go on an adventure," she says, taking my hand in hers for just a second and pulling at me. There is that glint her eye, the glint that says I am alive and I have never been so alive in all my life and I am a real person. My hand falls back to my side.

"It's late and it's dark. Besides, I thought that you were scared of the dark." I am so very tired.

"I am. But you'll keep me safe."

Say yes more.

Side by side, we walk across the hotel garden and into the forest. Under a canopy of leaves, the darkness is complete. The birds are not yet awake and the insects have stopped buzzing for the night. All we hear is the padding of our feet upon the carpet of fallen foliage.

"Are you scared?" I ask.

"Only a little." I will keep her safe.

"Did I tell you, I grew up in the forest? Not like Mowgli raised by wolves, but in a house in the forest. My father lived there for most of my life and every night as a child, I used to check each door lock and window mechanism to make sure that the world outside couldn't get in. I was terrified of what might be lurking between the branches. In the day we would run and play outside, but at night, our playground became a place of monsters and the unknown. Right now though, I feel at peace."

"I can't believe I am actually doing this. I am in Poland, walking through a forest at night. Can you even see where we're going?"

"Barely. If you look closely, your eyes adjust to the path. If we keep following it, we should reach the lake."

We reach the end of the path and find ourselves at the lake. Untouched, it is a mirror reflecting the stars in the clear night sky. We walk to the end of the wooden jetty and sit down on the damp wood.

"What can you hear?" I ask. "Listen carefully." Instinctively she looks away, concentrating on the sounds around us.

"Nothing."

"You hear the sound of quiet, an explosion of silence. No wind, no birds, no people. Nothing at all. This is the darkest hour of the night, a sacred moment of peace when the whole world could be sleeping and it is only us who are awake." In this moment, no one else exists in the whole world.

"Would you sit out here alone?" Everything is so peaceful and there is nowhere else that I would rather be, but I would not be here if it was not for Leah. I would not be here if she didn't want to come on an adventure, if she didn't want me to protect her.

"I don't know," I answer honestly. "I feel safe because you are here. And I feel safe to keep you safe. The mind can play awful tricks when you are alone. It makes you afraid of things that might not really exist."

"You hitchhike, you sleep outside, you are one of the craziest people I have ever met. What are you scared of?"

"Those are just words… I have a list of things that freak the hell out of me… The truth is, I have always been afraid…"

"Of what?" It's an innocent question, genuine interest. I had no idea that my internal battles could be so glaringly unnoticed to those around me.

"It's not something I like to talk about. I am trying my best to get over those things." She has opened herself to me and involuntarily reciprocating, I feel my barriers opening to her. Words threaten to gush forth as she waits in patient silence, watching me with stardust filled eyes, the tiny dancer on the jetty. "I think it started nearly two thousand years ago…" Does she really want to know? Do I really want to tell her?

"How so?"

"As a child, I went to a Church of England First School. I'm not religious, nor are my parents, but I went to this school because it was the closest to my mother's house. It was a nice school, less than fifty students in total, but many of the teachings were based upon Christianity. For the first few years of my life, I had been looked after very well and shielded from everything that could harm me. Then I went to this place full of strangers, more strangers than I had ever seen. They told me things that I had never known. I am ignorant of the ins and outs of Christianity, but they told me that if I didn't adhere to strict codes of behaviour or if I broke a certain set of rules, I would be damned to burn in Hell for all eternity. Then they showed me pictures of naked men and woman impaled upon tridents wielded by grotesque beasts. Being only four years old, I was terrified. The safety bubble that my parents had built for me was completely shattered. Before this time, I had only ever known the pleasantness of life.

"Before I went to school, I used to bounce into my mother's bedroom with my woollen lamb each morning and feed it the grass from my stepdad's chest. I was amazed that someone had chest hair. That was the sort of kid I was. By the time I started school at four years old, I could pretty much swim, ride a bike, and read and write because I was so well looked after. However, after I started school, I used to lie awake at night, terrified of dying, of someone else dying, and all that might follow: images of Hell filled my nights. During my first few months of school, I had to be physically restrained every day that my mother dropped me off. I didn't want to live in that scary world. After positive reward, fear is the most basic element of power. One day people will learn that they get more from one another by offering incentives so that they can both win. That aside, I think that is why I first got scared."

"First? What happened after that?" As if all of my words were held safely in a balloon, I feel the plastic rip apart and they come tumbling out, one after another, everything I never thought I would say.

"After Christianity came dinosaurs. It was a natural progression. The indoctrinations laid upon me taught me to be fearful and while my mother was pregnant, we went to the cinema to watch Jurassic Park, so I suppose that made me about five years old. The T-rex, the velociraptors, they were all intimidating, but that wasn't what got into my head. There was another dinosaur, this tiny dinosaur that a man threw a stick for like it was a dog. It brought out these big frills around its neck and then started spitting poison at him. I couldn't open doors in case that dinosaur was behind them waiting for me. Then there were ghosts and cannibals. Everywhere I went, I thought I was going to be eaten or attacked by something. Then came germs, possibly the worst of all because they were an invisible enemy. Everything had to be clean. If my hands touched the table during dinner, I had to get up and wash them. If something touched my food, I wouldn't eat it.

"The blue van in the forest, that man with the beard, the part of the street without lights, radiation from mobile phones, cars, orange moss that caused asthma, knives, aeroplanes, not being able to get to the toilet when it was needed, people who climbed though the windows at night, teachers, walking around objects in the opposite direction from which I came, touching the ground with only one hand, stepping on cracks and inciting bad luck. Fruit that wasn't the right colour, fruit that might have insects in. Insects and dirt. Pieces of dirt that looked liked insect eggs. Dirty insects. The possibility that a poisonous spider had crawled into the bananas and been transported all the way back to the supermarket where I helped my parents shop, setting the house on fire, talking to people, fire, not fitting in, standing in front of the microwave when it was opened. Sharks, people laughing at me, talking to people. People." I stop for breath. "Sorry. I didn't mean to throw all that at you." I blink, long and hard. What have I just told her?

"It's OK, I would have had no idea. How did you get over these things?"

"My parents helped me a lot, but these problems were in my head and most of them were irrational. Sometimes we have to conceptualise something in order to deal with it. As an awfully shy and nervous teenager, I looked at my fears and I realised how much they were inhibiting my enjoyment of life itself. I had realised that no one could keep me safe forever and one way or another I would have to learn to deal with them alone. That's not an easy path, but I think you have to accept that you are afraid in order to deal with being afraid. It's OK to be afraid, it keeps you safe."

"But how would you conceptualise fear itself? I know that I'm scared of hitchhiking for example, but I don't think that I could ever get over that."

I think for a moment. You could conceptualise fear in a million different ways for a million different benefits. My little pink ghost springs to mind.

"Fear is a little pink ghost that has the ability to change into any form more terrifying than your worst nightmares could even dream up. He can cripple you, taking everything. When he is around, you are falling constantly, a bottomless journey of no end. You have three choices of how you can deal with this little pink ghost. Firstly, you can run and you can hide. He will always be chasing you, he will always be looking for you. One day he will find you. Secondly, you can punch him in the face. Fear roars at you, you roar right back. It is a simple matter of who roars loudest. And lastly, you can embrace him and you can hold his hand. You walk with fear and you accept him for the little pink ghost that he is, always knowing that he is there, but keeping him in your sight."

"And now you hold his hand?"

I shrug dismissively.

In silence, we watch the stars on the unbroken mirror of the lake.

"Has anything bad ever happened to make you afraid?" Leah asks tentatively.

"No. I have broken my back and I have had stitches in my head, but I'm OK. Everything is OK. Everything will always be OK. Until it's not."

"I suppose so. Do you want to know something?"

"Sure."

"This might be the best week of my life."

"You've only been here for a few days."

"That doesn't matter. You couldn't understand my life in America. If you could, you would understand why this is the best week of my life. I feel that I have lived more in these past few days and spent more time with good people than in my last many years of living in the US. There are a few special people that I miss, especially my family, but besides that, I have so much more here. Even in myself, I feel that I am a different person, a happier person, a person who smiles and laughs and talks to people."

"I see that. On the day we met, you had this invisible wall around you. As polite and friendly as you were, it was as if you had the words 'fuck off' plastered to your forehead, warning everybody to keep their distance. Even the way you talked, a monotonous stream of dialogue, was devoid of life. I have to confess that when I first met you, I didn't really like you that much at all. Talking to you was more of a challenge than anything else. I was probing to see if there was a real person inside: I'm happy to see that there is."

"I know," she sighs. "Sometimes I feel as if I really am walking around with the words 'fuck off' plastered to my head, keeping everyone out. You are one of the first people to ever get through that and certainly no one has done it so quickly." She looks across the lake longingly. "Everything is better here, I wish I didn't have to go back."

"Then don't go back."

"What?"

"Don't go back. What have you got to go back for?"

"Everything. My life! There's my dog and my job. I have loans to pay. My family. My apartment and…"

"You have those things only if you want them. With the exception of family whom you should always go back for, everything else is up to you."

"But it's complicated, there's…"

"Stop, I don't need to know why it's complicated. It is only as complicated as you make it and only you can choose what you do."

"What would I do here?"

"I don't know. Be alive?"

We sit in comfortable silence once more, thoughts rolling through our minds.

"It's cold," she whispers.

"Very."

On a different night, with a different girl, in a different world, we'd be grateful for the cold so that we could cuddle for warmth. But this is not a different night and this is not a different girl. We sit on a damp dock overlooking a grey lake somewhere in rural Poland. There is nowhere else in the world I would rather be.

We're so close, a million miles apart. I can hear her breathing. I can feel it.

What if we touch and we can't let go? What if we hold onto each other and shut the world out because it's big and it's scary and this is where we were meant to be and nowhere else in the world would be right and we could keep each other safe just by holding on?

We don't touch in the silence, we do anything but let our bodies meet. The morning wind awakens, softly rippling across the lake, bringing another chill as we sit side by side. I want to offer her my jumper, wrap her up in it and keep her warm. Without it, I would have to leave within minutes: minutes that pass as moments while anonymous hours fade into the mist.

"I think we should go inside," I finally say and the magic wavers. I can bear the cold no longer. For a few more precious moments we are on the dock and as we climb to our feet, I am terrified that the moment will shatter into a thousand billion pieces and be sucked into the ground in the way that a desert insatiably swallows water, never to be seen again. But it doesn't. The sacred moments continue as we walk down the wooden boardwalk, soft feet on wet boards. We approach the forest, the impenetrable darkness offering us sanctuary from the world. Together we enter.

"If you had told me a week ago that I would be outside in a forest at night time, I would never have believed it." I know. "Everywhere I know has street lights. I don't think I have ever seen darkness like this."

"You cannot fight the dark, it comes around once a day. Better to hold its hand and walk with it. Only when you are outside of it is the dark unknown and only when it is unknown can it be scary. You cannot come from a city and really know the darkness. In your world, the dark is the back-alleys and the secret corners of badness that the light cannot penetrate. Every city searches for perpetual luminescence to keep the people safe from the things that they don't want to know because the light is our dominance over nature. Look at us sun, we don't even need you to survive because we make our own light. I have been scared of many things, including the dark, but when you are in the heart of darkness itself, there is nothing left to fear." I want to tell her that with her by my side, I am not afraid of anything. Anything except telling her that she makes me less afraid.

We walk on.

The soft sounds of our feet on leaves are joined by a single bird high above us, the first to rise in the pre-dawn hours. I look up and see only black and wonder if the little bird has ever been afraid of the dark.

Leah breaks the silence. "Can you hear it?"

"I can."

"I wonder what he is saying."

"Good morning world."

She stops at the door to her room, hands numb, fiddling with the key in the lock.

"See you in a few hours," she says, her back turned, the magic broken.

I walk on by. "Goodnight," tiny dancer.

25. Ice Cream

Leah glows. A night light that has been with me all my life, a box to hide secrets.

How did this happen?

The two of us are sitting on a sofa in a large function room, listening to a friend playing piano.

"Where will you go after this?" Leah asks me.

"South. I'm meeting my family in Croatia. Before that, I'll stop in Kraków. I left lots of my things there at a Polish girl's house."

"Just a random Polish girl?"

"No. A very lovely Polish girl I was with before I came here. I was going to visit her again after this week." I feel that I can tell Leah anything. And I do.

Ben calls the group together and we divide into pairs once more.

After the day's activities, we are in the bar. Around me, every brain seems to be scrambled by the constant requirement to talk. Conversation is stunted and each individual takes a few minutes of being switched off to fully function once more.

Tonight there is a buzz in the air, a sense of excitement unlike the other nights. People come to the bar quicker than normal, the bottle of sweet cherry liquor is emptied, and the bar staff are continuously kept busy for the first time. Ben looks on in dismay.

"Don't forget to be up nice and early tomorrow," he calls to everybody, removing himself from the situation.

When the bar reaches closing time, it is still full. One more hour is granted.

When the hour is up, everybody stocks up on bottles of beer. The bar is locked and the party moves outside. A security guard approaches. We can't sit out here, we are too noisy and there are guests sleeping.

All of us funnel through the empty piano room and into a dining room. There is a large wooden table and around it, more than ten of us sit. A pack of cards appear. A game starts. Drinks disappear.

My head spins a little.

Leah's head seems to be spinning more than mine. She has let go of her calm demeanour and may soon lose control of her basic motor functions.

"Everybody drink," somebody calls. Everybody leaps to their feet, then climbs onto the large wooden table, clinking cans and glasses in the middle. Behind us, the door opens and the security guard reappears. He looks at us, bemused, gestures for us to get off the table and puts his fingers to his lips to request quiet because other people are sleeping, please and thank you.

I put out my hand, help Leah off the table, then leave the room.

Here I am, in the bathroom, my outline fuzzy in the mirror. Looking back at myself, I see my eyes are glazed. That look of someone who isn't quite there. Someone who is not capable of making rational decisions.

I put myself to bed.

Light fades at the end of the day. Mateusz and I walk through the forest and past the lake, only to find a second lake. There is a forest on our right and we walk upon a small dirt track, alongside the straight edged lake. It looks manmade. Large tyre tracks in the mud suggest the passing of a tractor or three. At the end of the second lake is a third.

"Let's sit here," I suggest. No one else walks this far, no one knows where we are. We are completely isolated from everything and everyone.

"Mmm, this is very nice." An emphatic nod of the head.

"It is. Look at that." I point across the third lake. The sun is beginning to light up the skies with pinks and oranges which are reflected across the surface of the water.

"My problem now Jamie, is I don't know what to do next. Do I do more classes or theatre, or this wonderful thing?" I am pulled into a world of possibilities and listen attentively, actually caring about the outcome for him.

"You simply have to choose something and go with it for a little bit. If you don't, you will end up debating forever and never going anywhere. I don't know what it is that you should do, but do something. Here I am, hitchhiking, but this isn't my life. What is important for me now is that I will always remember these days and the people I spent them with. People like you, people like Leah. There have been days by myself and days with others, like this week, where I sat up almost every night with you and Leah, not to mention all the other people here. These are all days that matter to me, days not to be forgotten."

"Me as well."

"I think that you have too much choice right now. Sometimes there is too much choice in life. I like to think of it like ice cream."

"Ice cream?" Mateusz imitates a child licking ice-cream, thrown by the apparent change of topic.

"Yes, choice is like ice cream. If you go into an ice-cream shop and there are five flavours, vanilla, chocolate, strawberry, mint, and pistachio, which one do you go for?"

"Strawberry, it's my favourite."

"OK, so you get your strawberry ice-cream, you eat it, you're happy. I chose vanilla because I expect little from it and it always exceeds my expectations, making me happy. I could get chocolate, but I know that simple chocolate is never as good as I hope it to be, so I would feel cheated. Now think of this. You go into an ice cream parlour and there are one hundred flavours. You can choose triple strawberry, strawberry kisses, strawberry surprise, strawberry sunset, raspberry and strawberry, strawberry ripple, summer fruit explosion, strawberries and cream, red fruit extravaganza, or a strawberry stacker. Which flavour do you choose?"

Mateusz laughs. "Mmmm, that was so quick! Again please, I forgot."

"My point exactly! There is too much choice and you never know which is best. Whatever flavour you choose, you will be disappointed because you didn't pick a different one. In this situation, I would be drawn to chocolate and no doubt I would pick something named quadruple chocolate truffle, only to find that it was little better than the plain chocolate, leaving me dissatisfied. I should have gone for vanilla." Mateusz laughs again, that almost nervous, but growing in confidence laugh.

"This is ice cream. I am confyoo-said."

"Confused. What I mean is, don't overthink things. Choosing something is better than choosing nothing. It will never be perfect." Trying to help someone else with their life decisions helps me forget that I cannot even make my own. If you can do something well, do it. If you can't, tell other people how to do it. Something like that.

Mateusz's phone rings.

"Oh my gawd, Jamie, we are thirty minutes late again."

We walk back for dinner in twilight, the remnants of a beautiful sunset behind us as we mull over what flavour of life ice cream would taste best and how many different flavours we have to choose from. There are always too many.

26. A Tiger

"I'm sad," she tells me. "I don't want to go back." Her eyes are almost watering, the hint of tears.

"Can I get you a tissue?"

"No," she laughs, the free bird not ready to be put back in its cage. "Look what has happened to me." She wipes her eyes with the sleeves of her cardigan. "I never cry, literally never. I haven't cried for years."

"That doesn't surprise me." As sad as she is, not one tear has fallen. Has she forgotten how to cry?

We sit on the porch of the bar, cross legged, facing one another. Everyone else has gone to bed. Mateusz as ever, was the last to leave. Am I here because I find sleep elusive or am I here because Leah is here too? Why is she here?

"When I said this was one of the best weeks of my life, I meant it. And that was a few days ago. Tomorrow is the last night and I don't want to go because when I go, I'm alone and I only have three more days in Poland and then that means I have to go back to America." I want to reach out, to touch her, to tell her that it's going to be OK, that she doesn't have to go back. But I can't because it would all be lies.

She is falling and I cannot catch her.

"Wherever in the world you find yourself, there are good people. With an open mind and half a smile, you will find them, regardless of whether you are in Poland, America, or any other part of the world." After the past few months, I believe this to be true.

"I don't want to. There is nothing that you can say right now because I am here and this is where I want to be. You don't understand how my life is in America, you don't understand how I am a different person every day here to the person I was back there." I want to understand. "Jamie, you are one of my favourite people I have ever met and nothing you do or say could ever change that." My heart flutters, a butterfly in the wind. I don't want to change that.

"Let's move inside."

We walk through the garden in silence.

Sitting on a sofa, side by side, her dry tears have gone away.

I decide to play one of my favourite games. "If you could wake up anywhere tomorrow, where would it be?"

"Right here," she replies without hesitation. Good answer.

"So why are you leaving?"

"It's complicated." I don't need to know.

"How about this one. You've lived a good life and when you get to the end of it, you get told that your reward is to pick what creature you come back as. As you've already been a human and you can't be the same thing twice, what do you pick to be next?"

"That's a hard one."

"You can be a bird and fly, a fish to breathe underwater, anything at all that you want. But if you don't decide in five seconds, you will come back as a maggot."

"Hey, that's not fair. I don't like birds, so not a bird."

"Five…"

"And fish are slimy."

"Four, three…"

"It's too hard, I need more time."

"Two…"

"I am not being a maggot."

"One…" Leah reaches out and tries to put her hand over my mouth. I see it coming and catch her wrist just before she silences me. "Zero! You are a maggot. You had the choice of all the creatures in the world, but you couldn't decide in time, so that is your fate."

"I've changed my mind, I want to be a tiger."

"Too late, it's over." Her wrist still rests in my hand. "What about this one? You're a billionaire. You can do anything you want in the world. What do you do every day?"

"I'd go to South America."

"Forever?"

"Not forever." Her hand rests upon my knee, my fingertips upon her wrist, my grasp released entirely.

I daren't breath, less I move us.

Our eyes lock.

We look into each other, neither of us acknowledging our touch.

"What else would you do then, besides visiting South America?"

I shuffle on the sofa. Our fingers intertwine.

We both look away.

"I would…"

It doesn't matter.

We gravitate.

My eyes are closed as my fingertips trace the side of her profile.

She's so small. She's so small.

I open them, an inverted blink, the silhouette of golden hair ahead of me, her face invisible in the darkness.

I can feel her breath upon my face, upon my lips.

Tiny dancers waltz upon my skin.

Another blink, our lips touch.

Boom, boom, boom plays the music inside my head.

We cling tightly to each other, our bodies intertwined, our lips meeting again and again.

Let us hold onto each other forever in this moment, let us shut out the vicious world.

Let time itself, cease.

Let us be.

I open my mouth to tell her that she is one of my best friends in the whole world.

The words don't come out.

27. Sorry

Tomorrow, we leave. I might never see any of these people again. The very thought ties my stomach up in knots.

How could I never see these people again? Mateusz, I know his elaborate gestures, his nervous smile, his honest words. Leah, I know her glow, her laugh, her greatest fears. I know her everything.

How could I not see her again?

Around a bonfire we sit, singing songs in Polish that only half of us can understand. Beside me is Mateusz.

Leah emerges from the bar to hand me a glass of beer. A pinch upon my skin, a pang of delight. As she sits inside with those who don't want to sing, she thinks of me.

"For the shots you bought me." She disappears as quickly as she arrived. Tomorrow she will disappear forever. I can't bear to sit with her.

If I don't look, maybe it won't happen.

The fire reaches its peak and Leah reappears. Another drink. She is still thinking of me as I think of her.

As the embers die, she appears a third time.

"We are coming inside now." Tonight is our final night, whether I accept it or not.

The buzz of easy conversation flows inside the bar. One week of constant interaction has formed friendships that will far outlive the week. Every face is familiar.

The bar closes.

A group of us migrate to the jetty, clinging to the experience of the past week. It is the same jetty where Leah and I sat alone just a few nights before.

We want to watch the sun rise, to experience the whole of the night, to not waste our last seconds.

The jetty is damp and around us, the lake is covered in mist so thick, we can barely see the water a few metres away. When I walk to the forest, using it as a bathroom, the sight of my friends is obscured. It's like walking through the clouds except I always hoped they'd be softer, like warm candy floss stuffed pillow cases.

Obligingly, the sun arrives, burning off the dark and the mist all at the same time. For every step higher the sun climbs, we can see a little further across the lake. Someone has put on music and we listen to it through the dawn, each body silhouetted, each face kissed with golden highlights. If this was a movie, this is where they'd shoot it, right here in this moment of serenity, of nature and beauty.

With the sun up, the lake is glass, the trees are full of fairies, and each of us glows. I walk down the dock once more and look at my friends from a distance, people who were strangers only a week before. If I could take that image of them sitting on the end of the dirty wooden jetty above a dirty lake and burn it forever into my mind, I would. There isn't anywhere else I would rather be right now than where I am. How many times have I thought that now? I have lost count.

Soon the people burn off too. One by one they all disappear until as ever, we are three. Mateusz, Leah, and I. All week we speculated on swimming and here we find ourselves by the lake in the last few hours. I grab Leah. She wriggles and screams in my arms as I pretend to throw her in. She doesn't know it, but I wouldn't do it. She truly believes I'm crazy.

I'm not crazy unless crazy is crazy enough to try and live.

Mateusz leaps into the lake, naked. Escaping my grasp, Leah leaps in fully clothed. I take off my jeans and t-shirt, leaping in after the both of them.

Rather than disappearing under the surface of the water, my feet embed themselves in sticky mud. My head is not even wet, yet my breath is sucked from me by the cold and the three of us scrabble back to the jetty. Leah struggles to get out and I hold up her feet, helping her out of the water.

My hands are numb. My feet hurt.

On the jetty, I put my clothes back on and so does Mateusz.

"Here, wear this," I command Leah. "I'll be fine in a t-shirt." I hand her my red hoody.

The three of us fall asleep, side by side on the soggy jetty.

I can barely move my fingers as I awake. We've been sleeping for only an hour, but every digit is stiff. The cold runs deep within my bones and my body aches. The back of my t-shirt is soaked through.

Leah is one side of me and Mateusz the other. I shake them both awake.

"Wake up." My voice is brittle, it might shatter at any minute. We have thirty minutes until the final few classes.

I drag myself to my feet. The sun tries to thaw me, but only the outside is warmed. Will I ever be able to get warm again? Each step is a dull pain, each movement a seismograph, shaking, shaking of cold. My fingers can't operate my shoe laces, so barefoot I walk through the forest and across the garden.

Goodnight Mateusz. Or is it good morning? He goes to his room in one direction, leaving Leah and I to return to our own separate rooms.

I shuffle up the stairs, dragging one foot after the other.

At her door, we touch. Or we don't. My mind is as clouded as my movements.

I let the shower run at a low temperature. It scalds me.

Lower still. It chills.

Under cold water I turn the dial up, little by little.

Life returns to my body and when I step out of the bathroom, I am late again.

We take the bus to Warsaw and the group splits up, hugs served upon the pavement. I stand awkwardly, unsure of where to go. One moment I am part of something, then I am not.

"Come with me," Leah says as if it is the most obvious thing in the world. How perfect, how treacherous. I should be returning to Kraków, but I don't even have the balls to message Emilia and tell her I'm not coming. We haven't spoken all week. Maybe she doesn't want to know.

One more day.

She has all my things.

Like a guilty puppy, I traipse after Leah and into the hotel she has booked. Out of sight, I wait behind a pillar while she checks in. Around me, people in suits walk with briefcases, nibbling on croissants and macchiatos from the black marble cafe. The front of the hotel is an ocean of glass and I watch the streets from the rising glass elevator that Leah activates with her keycard. I am wearing my hippy pants, scraps of material flapping from my backpack as I turn.

In the room are twin beds, white linen and freshly pressed towels on each. I lie down to read while Leah moves about, putting something here, arranging something there. It's the first time we've been allowed to be alone since we met, but we remain in opposite corners as if our gravitational pull has reversed. We're here, finally alone, but we shouldn't be.

"What will you do when you get back to Kraków?"

"I… I'm not sure. All my things are at Emilia's house, but I doubt she'll want to see me."

"Well, what do you want to do?" She applies no pressure either way and if I want to walk away now, I know that she won't try to stop me.

"Again, I'm not sure. If I think about Emilia, I feel the same as I ever felt. She's just as smart and funny and pretty as the day I met her. I am still attracted to her, but the complication was meeting you."

I finally message Emilia to tell her that I won't be in Kraków for a couple of days. She says OK. I tell her something happened. She says OK. I tell her that I'll speak to her when I get back. She says nothing.

In the public street, Leah and I move close together once more. She links my arm as we walk.

We eat dinner with friends from the week past, we go to a bar. Ola joins us in her glorious red lipstick, but we are tired. She smiles when she sees me with the girl she took dancing in the forest. We search for a nightclub, but can't find one. The sun comes up and everybody disperses. I crawl into a white linen bed.

Reluctantly the next morning, I board a train to Kraków with Leah. One way or another, I am going back. It is ever so convoluted.

Leah is too afraid to hitchhike and I could have left her at the station, simply walked away and continued upon my own path. I could have justified it by saying that I can't afford to take trains, that I have to be somewhere else, and it would have been true. But I don't and I didn't and I wouldn't and I won't.

She has fallen asleep on my shoulder. An American sitting opposite us, refers to her as my girlfriend. It's easier not to correct him.

In Kraków, the streets are tainted. I walk a hasty line, looking over my shoulder. I message Emilia to tell her that I'm in the city, but staying with a friend. A half-truth. She tells me I can pick my belongings up from Tomasz, her roommate. She doesn't want to see me, she doesn't want an explanation. Without me having to tell her, she knows. That is how well we resonated with one another: she understands me without me having to say anything at all.

Another night passes with white linen sheets and Leah heads to a tour of Auschwitz.

"Are you sure you don't want to come?"

"I can take nothing positive from other people's suffering." Across the city, bright yellow placards advertise fun days out at the end place of millions of people. I have no right to indulge in such an experience.

I message Emilia once more to ask if she'll leave my belongings outside the door. I will simply take my things, then quietly disappear.

'I don't care.'

Does she not care to return them? Have I just lost my things? Not that there is anything valuable other than the opportunity to say goodbye.

'I don't care about seeing you,' she clarifies.

I walk the whole of the city, nearly an hour to her house, enter the large wooden door, ascend the wide stone steps, and knock on the small door of her apartment. I know all of this so well. She opens the door to the dark hallway. There is no secret smile, she no longer lights up the room. I don't know this part so well.

I hand her the cake I bought for her on the way. "I got you a fruit tart."

I blush as I give it to her. Oh, here's a fruit tart to compensate for everything. Now everything is OK, right? I almost want her to be angry at me, to shout at me, to knock me down. She does nothing of the sort.

I sit on her sofa while she busies herself with papers on her desk, sitting on the far side of the room, facing away from me.

"I'm sorry." It's all the words I have. I never meant to hurt her, but I see sadness in her eyes. On this day of mourning, the room is chilly. Something large and dark is lurking in the corners, but neither of us want to draw attention to it.

"It doesn't matter." Still she asks no questions.

I try to engage her in conversation as I move to the floor, collecting my belongings. She moves from the papers to the computer, dismissing my attempts at communication.

"You can keep this book, it's too heavy to carry, but it's one of my favourites." Ironically it's a copy of Norwegian Wood, a Japanese novel about loss and a young protagonist who falls for two very different women. At the door, I awkwardly try to hug her goodbye. "Are we still friends?"

"You don't get it, do you? We never were friends." She delivers the words matter of fact, disconnected.

Not angry. Exasperated.

"What were we?"

"We were a great summer romance and I was happy to have found you. Those weeks I waited for you and the weeks you were with me were a wonderful time for me. I always knew that you would go, but now you've ruined it. You've made me doubt myself over the last few days and I don't like feeling this way. You go away for ten days and you meet someone else, leaving me here. I don't want to speak to you anymore because it upsets me. This is why we'll never be friends."

She never even asked to know what happened, she simply knew. How could she just know, can she read me so easily? "Maybe I don't get it."

When I said sorry, I should have told her what I was sorry for, that I was sorry that I could care for more than one person. But that is not what she wants to hear because here I am, walking away from her with someone else. In life, to choose one wonderful thing over another is so very difficult. We are creatures of an indefinite world, a world where no choices should be black and white.

I open my mouth to speak, but no words come out.

I want to tell her that she shouldn't feel sad, that she is as attractive and everything else that she has ever been, that my feelings towards her haven't changed, that I still feel it, I really do. I want to tell her that we meet other people not because we stop caring, stop feeling, but because life isn't black and white, because it's digital not analogue and we can feel for multiple people at the same time, independent of one another, but all to varying degrees. Emotion is not a tap that is turned on or off at will. I want to tell her that this must be the way of the world because if it wasn't, we would all have the same number of friends and they would all be of equal value and we would all have one lover and then never be able to care for anyone else ever again. Not even a little bit. We would die from sadness if that love wasn't reciprocated, curled up in a ball of tears upon the bathroom floor, but we don't, we pick ourselves up, sometimes slowly, and we fight to survive. We learn to love someone in a different way and to a different degree and that is what makes us human.

She walks me to the door in silence.

I am a flailing fish and I am drowning. Every word or lack thereof, serves only to gall her further. I respect her enough, so very much in fact, that I walk away and say no more, hurting to have hurt someone I care about.

She closes the door on me for the very last time. The latch clicks. It's over.

Did she pause on the other side or simply walk away? What did she feel when she heard that click? Anger, disappointment, sadness? Or an overwhelming sense of relief that it is over?

Here I go again, doing what I have learnt to do, whatever first comes into my confused mind and screams loudest and strongest, throwing all reason and sensibility out of the window. Even if it doesn't work out, at least I will only have myself to blame.

28. Goodbye

"You won't get on the plane, I know it. You will have the escalator moment and you will stay." I feign indifference, pretending not to listen as Kasper, Mateusz's boyfriend, predicts that Leah will stay in Europe. "Look at you two, you are too perfect to leave." He is strong and tall with dark hair, an imposing figure beside Leah who says little.

From the corner of my eye, I watch her smile nervously. She looks so perfect.

Having returned to Warsaw on the train, blowing more of my precious funds to spend more time with two new people I care very much about, we are in Mateusz's apartment.

"What is the escalator moment?" Leah asks innocently.

"The escalator moment is the final moment of the movie…"

"In the airport…" chimes Mateusz.

"When the girl goes up the escalator…"

"Then comes back down because she cannot leave." The moment that makes one's heart stop.

Impossible. That only happens in movies. She has a life, not one she enjoys, but a whole life in America. I would never ask her to stay. If she was to jump and to fall, I might never forgive myself for persuading her to do so. Better to shoulder only the responsibility of my own actions.

I excuse myself and walk out to the balcony, letting the gentle breeze rustle my hair. Unlike the city centre, the suburbs are quiet and green at this hour.

"I have a job, a new apartment, my dog, my family…" Leah's words drift from the living room into the open night, the list of things that force her to go back to the US. A city she has outgrown, a job she hates, an uninspiring life. For ten days, free from the constraints of society, free from the expectation of others, she has been a free spirit.

We are all free spirits, deep down inside. Except that our eyes become clouded and we forget. It is awfully sad to forget.

The four of us eat dinner and sip red wine. The last supper.

Every smile, every laugh is genuine, but at the tip of each word is a snag, a little pull back. This is the end.

Back in the spacious apartment Leah rented, she takes a bath, asking for a few minutes alone. I stand on the balcony twelve floors up and look out across the city. There are so many people, rushing by at the speed of light, never stopping to take a moment and breathe, never taking a moment to listen with their heart and to look with the wide eyed wonder of their innocent selves. A business deal here, an appointment there. Optimise this, market that. What does any of it matter? I want to freeze everything with my magic watch, keep it just as it is.

Leah joins me on the balcony in a towel. I hold her tightly and close my eyes.

In one week I have shared more with this girl than most people in my life and in return, she has done the same.

Outside the apartment complex, we wait for a taxi to whisk her away to the airport.

There is nothing left to do or say.

It pulls up and my hands are shaking. I pull her tiny body into mine, hold her one last time, the soft scent of intoxicating perfume. Even her hair smells of meadows in the spring time. There is a stone in my throat, so large, I can barely breathe.

"Goodbye," she says. "Thank you for everything." This time a tear rolls down her face, the first in many years. That beautiful, oh so beautiful wild-eyed fire begins to dim. To a stranger, she is expressionless, but before me I see the sadness in her eyes, in her tight lipped smile, in her lacklustre movements. She is returning to the real world, the world of routines and unrealised dreams where she will be a robot once more. From these few days, I can see into her mind, sense her thoughts. I know her more than I know myself. Just occasionally, time is not the most important thing in the world. But our time is up.

I swallow the stone. These will be the last words I ever speak to her.

"For me, this world is more real than any other. The hitchhiking, the lack of job, no home, few plans, the nothing except living from one day to the next, always excited for what comes next. The real world doesn't start when you finish university or get a proper job. The real world is now and it is happening every day. What is happening to me now is more real than anything I have ever known. I will remember every single day of this journey, especially the ones that I have spent with you. I don't really have a point... in fact I haven't thought this through at all... but I want you to know that you can do anything you want to do. I've seen you, the person that I think is the real you... it is the real you. I don't think you let many people see that." She nods in agreement, silent tears now streaming down either side of her face. "When you go back to America, all I ask of you is to know that you are not stuck, that you don't have to live your life for other people in a way that makes you miserable. Some people need to see others suffer around them so that they can mask their own misery, but you can see past that now. Do your job if you learn to love it, live in your city if it feels like home, but when those things no longer feel right, jump. Jump and don't look down." I never thought I would tell her that. "Just… be you… be you more than anything else in the world. Because you are wonderful."

The stone chokes me once more and I hug her, pass her a handwritten note, then turn away.

The taxi whisks her away and I follow it down the street, her tiny hand waving as she disappears around the corner.

She is gone.

My final words that she will read alone, the note I passed her as she left, it read:

> *'Dear Leah,*
> *Never stop chasing happiness.*
> *Never stop being that amazing person that you are.*
> *Life is scary.*
> *Sometimes you have to jump and sometimes you have to fall before you can succeed.*
> *Aim high.*
> *Only you can help you (this is a great person, you showed me this already).*
> *Jamie*
> *P.S. In case of last minute escalator scenes / discussions about changes of flights with airlines, call this number…'*

My phone number was the last line of the message.

I stand alone on a quiet street, a large love heart spray painted on the wall in front of me. Red silhouetted in black and white, lovely and disgusting, I scowl at how pretty it is. I want to wallow in my sadness, let it engulf me, swallow me, then quietly slip away.

I blink heavily, but I do not cry. Maybe it is I who does not know how. There is a weight, heavy upon my heart, and I am falling once more. Falling with no end, wishing for it stop, but it won't stop and I know it won't stop and I will keep on falling. I should cry. Maybe I would if I was a different person. I am not a different person.

I want my family around me, to lie in bed, to have them bring me food and not have to get up. To spend the day reading books and to get lost in the magical world of imagination, the friendly place full of dragons and monsters, not this scary place I have inhabited for the past twenty-five years. I want my parents to cook for me, I want to play football in the garden, I want to take a walk on the beach with my dogs. I miss those crazy dogs.

Would it be better for me not to know? Not to know what the world is like outside the tiny bubble from my childhood, not to become bored, not to want more? Would I take it all back for that simple, blissful ignorance? Would I erase everything if I could go back?

I don't think that I would.

I wish I could stop falling.

I walk and I walk then I walk and I walk some more. Directionless, my mind the remnants of a volcanic eruption.

A large apartment block painted with red balloons looks down upon me. Up they float, away and away, higher towards the clouds with no safe way down. One day they will burst and they will come crashing back down to Earth. I am a red balloon.

I sit on a bench and call my dad who will be meeting me in a few short days.

"Hi Dad."

"Jay! It's so great to hear your voice. Are you OK?" One thing with my dad is that rather than asking how I am, he asks if I am OK.

"I am always OK," my voice falters. Today I am not OK.

"You don't sound very OK. We'll be there in a few days though, I'm really looking forward to it."

"I am too. I know you weren't sure exactly what date you would come, but I'm free now if you want to come sooner."

"Jay, what's wrong?"

"Nothing is wrong. I just don't have anything to do right now, that's all." The whole world is in front of me and I have lost the desire to live in it. I could be anywhere, anywhere at all, but I want to be nowhere and doing nothing. "I'll see you in a few days. Send me a message to let me know when you'll be arriving and I'll be sure to get there too."

I end the call and watch the ground beneath the bench. Safe, unchanging ground, so comforting.

I check my phone. One hour to her flight, no escalator moment.

In the Warsaw train station, I sit with my headphones on, countless people moving around me. I am a statue fixated on one thing, the large white clock with black hands that race around at dizzying speeds, watching over the train station. I don't want to catch a train, I want only to watch the seconds tick by. My headphones drown out the sound of the people, but above it all, clear as day, I hear the click, click, click of the clock taunting me. I should be on the road, heading south, but a part of me, a bigger part than I can account for, keeps me glued to the seat. Surely she can't just leave? Surely she can't return to a strangling life devoid of possibility? She couldn't, she can't, she wouldn't, she won't.

Thirty minutes until take off.

I check my phone. Nothing.

How is it that a clock can move at such speed? It defies the laws of nature itself.

Fifteen minutes. Nothing.

Ten minutes.

Five minutes.

Time.

I log on to the internet and check her flight. It has taken off. The ground is crumbling beneath me. Right now she is somewhere high above me, speeding away at six hundred miles an hour.

Maybe this is when I should cry. Instead, I feel nothing. No longer am I falling. I am a coffin, cold, hard, and empty inside. I want to take my sleeping bag and lie down upon the floor, just for a day or two until I feel better. I hate all these people around me, why can't they all just go away and leave me alone? I am already as alone as I could be.

I know that the people won't leave, not until it gets dark, then I'll be thrown outside into the streets.

For thirty minutes Leah has been in the air. By now she must be nearly three hundred miles away.

My phone, checked hundreds of times, my phone that let me down, must be switched off to save battery.

Three missed calls from an unknown number. A message?

'Its leah. i changed my mind.where are you?'

Letting out an audible yelp, I drop my bag and leap into the air. For a moment I pass through the ceiling and into the clouds. With my headphones still on, I dance to the music as strangers watch me. I want to hug them all, for them to dance with me. How happy I am that they are all here, how glorious everything is. I love you clock, I love you train station. I love you most of all, poorly punctuated text message.

"Leah, I'm in the train station," I gasp into the phone.

She walks back into my arms, fire dancers in her eyes, and I squeeze her once more. Her touch is the warm shower after being naked in the snow, dying in the cold.

"Oh my god, oh my god, I can't believe it, this is the craziest thing that I have ever done, absolutely the craziest."

"You know what it means?" I grin mischievously. "You're about to try hitchhiking. You already cost me two train tickets I couldn't afford."

She nods eagerly, the girl who called me crazy. She is jumping with both feet, not looking down.

This is our escalator moment.

As my heart pounds, all I can hear over and over again is a little tune, humming away.

'She's so brave, she's so brave.'

29. Monkey

"Do you regret it yet?" I ask.

"Not at all."

I drag her oversized red suitcase towards the bus stop.

"I'm surprised they even let you bring this much stuff on the plane." The bag is so heavy that she can barely move it by herself.

"I told you, I'm supposed to be moving apartments. I brought things from my old place to take to my new place."

"Of course. It makes perfect sense to carry everything from Boston to Poland and back again. In England, we recently developed these strange mechanical beasts known as cars that we use to carry around our things. It has revolutionised the way we live and no longer do we have to transport everything by aeroplane." I grin mischievously.

"Alright, you only have to put up with it for another week or so." Despite not getting on the plane, Leah has changed her flight rather than skipping it altogether. She will fly out of Croatia, offering us precious extra days together. We have three nights until we meet my family, over eight hundred miles away in Croatia.

"Are you nervous about meeting my family?"

"Of course I am. Little over a week ago you didn't even know who I was, now you are introducing me to your family."

"It's all about timing, it just worked out like that." Yet I feel no hesitation. She is meeting my family, that's how it is.

We leave the city on a bus, this time with tickets, I want nothing to go wrong. For my whole month in Poland I have barely ever bought a ticket and instead, disembarked when I saw ticket inspectors climbing aboard. I stamp it in the onboard ticket machine and stand casually, not having to look over my shoulder.

"Where do you want to get off?" Leah asks. I peer out of the window at the road signs.

"One more stop I think." We are heading south to an unknown destination, our trust in the online network of strangers who might invite us into their home for the night.

Where we don't get off, the ticket inspector gets on. I smugly hand over my ticket. Look at me Mr. Ticket Inspector, first time you stop me and I have a ticket.

He looks at it, nods, then gives it back. Conversely, he shakes his head at Leah's ticket and doesn't give it back.

"What's the problem?" He points at her ticket. It isn't stamped. "Leah, did you not push your ticket into the machine?"

"I did." I thought so, I watched her do it. In Poland you push your ticket into the machine and it stamps it with a time and date, validating it for a given period, dependent upon which ticket you bought. An unstamped ticket is classified as invalid as it hasn't been activated.

"Don't worry about it, I'm sure he will understand that it's a genuine mistake." I pull the receipt from my pocket and show him the time and date. Two tickets, bought forty minutes ago. Mine stamped, Leah's not, because she didn't push it all the way into the machine. The man shakes his head.

Come on Ticket Man, it's obviously a genuine mistake, just look. He shakes his head again.

The bus pulls up at the stop at which we intended to disembark. Two large, bald guys step onto the bus and forcefully escort us off it.

"Get off my arm," Leah snaps, pulling away from the thugs. Dressed in dark clothing, they could be anyone at all and they load our belongings into a car that was following the bus.

"We could run for it," I speculate, knowing the men understand no English, "but we would lose all of our things." I have no real intention of running, but I'm frustrated and powerless to do anything.

The men drive us to a car park and when we get there, Leah is frog marched to an ATM. I try to get out of the car, but the door is locked. I can't see her anymore. Who are these men and where have they taken her?

"Hey, you, let me out." I pull at the handle, but the man in the driver's seat shakes his head. I am a prisoner. "Let me out!" I wind down the window, but it stops less than halfway. One of those locks to prevent children or maybe criminals from escaping. I will escape. I try to push my head through the window.

I'm getting out, I will not sit here when Leah has been led away by these thugs, I will…

I see Leah walking back across the car park towards the car, the bald man close behind her. I settle back into my seat. The driver is still pissed off that I was trying to get out of the window, but now I seem content to remain inside the car, he stops shouting at me.

"Creeps," Leah snarls. "This dickhead stood over my shoulder, breathing down my neck while he made me get out money. The first ATM didn't work so we went to a second and a third before I got cash, then he took it all."

"How much?"

"One hundred and thirty złoty."

"About twenty-five pounds, not too bad." That sum of money could last for a week or more on the road.

The thuggish men drive us to the bus stop we were going to get off at and unload our bags from the boot.

"Well done guys, really great job today. You made the world a safer place by fining us for a genuine mistake. You can sleep well in your beds tonight, congratulations for just doing your job without applying any common sense. Without pillars of society such as yourselves who upkeep the word of the law, civilisation would surely crumble and collapse." I am as bitter as the old man who has been left behind by society and trampled by the world.

But I deserve it. For every bus I've black-ridden, for the sadness I have caused, I deserve so much worse than humiliation and a monetary fine.

I realign my thoughts. Beside me is a girl who has dropped everything for this adventure and when I think of that, all else is irrelevant. The fine was inconvenient, unpleasant, but we are alive, so very alive. Sometimes bad things happen. We accept them, we move on.

Our first ride is a kindly pregnant mother who speaks perfect English. I sit in the back with her young child. Thank you world for delivering this person to us.

Leah bounces around on the side of the road while we wait for our next ride.

"Hitchhiking is amazing!"

"You try it once, it becomes addictive."

What I hadn't anticipated was the effect that an attractive blond girl in short summer shorts would have on my hitchhiking efforts. Alone, I rarely waited more than thirty minutes for a ride, but with Leah by my side, or more specifically, standing in front of me, we catch ride after ride within minutes. Despite not leaving Warsaw until late afternoon and getting tangled up with the ticket thugs, by evening we arrive in Kraków over two hundred miles away. Our final driver gives us bus tickets and tells us to get onto a bus which takes us to the train station.

Leah winces. "I'm nervous to hitchhike at night."

Involuntarily, my eyebrows leap like billowing parachutes in an accusatory gesture. "We said no more trains."

"I know." She twitches nervously, a sign of true fear.

"This is a luxury. You are only scared because there is another choice. There will be times that hitchhiking is our only choice."

For her sake, we take a night train. I want to keep her safe, I don't want to let her be scared.

"Thank you," she smiles, relief washing over her.

"Just so you know, each of these train tickets cost several weeks of hitchhiking." It's a statement, not an accusation. A simple admission that for someone such as myself, travelling on trains is not an option. But for her happiness through this one night, I am happy to make sacrifices. She is worth it.

Who am I now?

We wake up in Bratislava, the capital of Slovakia, famed by the movie Hostel. What an awful representation. Like in all the old cities of Europe, we are met by antiquated streets and elaborate architecture. A white castle perches high over the city, watching, summoning. Nobody kidnaps us and sells our bodies, no one tries to cut us to pieces.

Leah, desperate to wash after a day without showering, hoses herself down under a small tap in some dirty public toilets. I brush my teeth.

"Stop!" As we walk across a deserted square, Leah is taking a huge arc around a group of pigeons. "You told me you were scared of birds, but this is too much." Her eyes flit from creature to creature, prepared for flight at any second. I take her tiny hands in mine.

"No."

"I won't make you, but I want you to run through them."

"No," she shakes her head. I hold her hands and look straight back into her eyes.

"You can do it. If you want to."

"You don't understand how afraid I am of birds. I have never been near one in my life."

"I am here."

With her hands over her eyes, she shrieks and runs through the crowd of pigeons. They take to the sky all around her. As soon as she has passed, the majority of them reassemble in the same huddle.

"I can't believe you made me do that, I have always been terrified of birds."

"I didn't make you. I merely suggested it."

To feel proud of someone, you have to have an emotional attachment, to care about them deeply. Of course I don't tell her, but I am ever so proud of her.

From the look of contentment she wears, I know that she is proud of herself.

Inside a small toyshop run by Shaggy from Scooby-Doo, we pick up everything and test it out.

"Do you want me to make badges for you guys?" Shaggy asks in an American accent. How did an American end up owning a toyshop in Bratislava?

"Yes please." We immortalise our bus fines in wearable jewellery and wear them proudly for the world to see.

My phone bleeps and I read the message aloud. 'Hi, my name is Jakub. I live 40km from Bratislava in a small village. I can host you if you like.' Leah twitches once more. Hitchhiking, birds, now sleeping in the home of a stranger, all in twenty-four hours. This is quite a canyon leap from her well-planned, comfortable life.

"You guys need somewhere to stay?" Shaggy asks, overhearing our conversation.

"We might. How come?"

"I might have space at my place. Then again, I might not." After deliberation, it seems more likely that he doesn't have space at his house for us.

We take Shaggy's number and hold a private picnic under the walls of the castle.

Across the city, we follow trails of graffiti, speculating on what each one means, how long it took to create. Once more the sun shines brilliantly and Leah wears her face covering glasses, only this time I know the pretty face and soul that lie behind them.

Beside the ruins of an old stone church, we are completely alone. I take Leah's hand and spin her around, dancing in the street.

"Why did you come with me...?"

"Because I trust you." As simple as that. She trusts me. From a girl who trusts almost no one but herself, I take this as quite a compliment.

"What do you want to do tonight? Whatever you want to do, I will do too."

"Well... what do you think about this Jakub guy, is this normal?"

"I posted my number online so I can't check out anything about him. Maybe he is the most lovely person in the world, but equally, he may be a complete weirdo." We settle on heading to his house in the early afternoon so that we can investigate, then we will decide whether or not we'll stay with him.

It's all for her and I don't mind one bit.

Jakub, as it turns out, is not an axe-wielding maniac, carefully luring us into the countryside. He is a recent graduate of a British university, smaller than I with blond hair and a face that is harmless and smiling, a face that is immediately likeable. He picks us up from the station and drives us to a metal tower in the forest. Large and rusty looking, it looms high above the trees.

"There is no way I am going up that," Leah protests.

"Trust me." She does.

Four ladders we ascend, stopping on each platform to admire the view. The structure sways gently in the wind. Leah's eyes are wide with terror, but here she stands beside me at the top. What a girl.

"That way," says Jakub, pointing back where we came from, "is Slovakia. And that way is Austria, just a few kilometres away. If you look in that direction, a little bit further, you can see Czech Republic." Sometimes it is easy to forget how small Europe is. On my short journey I have already traversed through fourteen different countries. Coming from a nation where many states are larger than the average European country, Leah is overawed and her wide eyed terror is replaced with wide eyed wonder and delight. In this moment, she is no longer fearful of heights.

Back on the ground I ask Leah if she thinks Jakub plans to murder us in our sleep and she agrees that he probably won't. We will stay with him tonight.

"Jakub, we only came so early so that we could see if you were a weirdo. We've decided that you're not." He seems amused at the notion.

Slovakian style, we are then taught how to drink. Despite being far smaller than I, Jakub knocks back drink after drink and my head is clouded once more.

"That's amaazin!" I cry. "You'ra hitchhiking. Alla tha way through Iran and Pakistan, alla tha way to India? Thas amaazin!" I can hear myself slurring, but my mouth seems to have taken control of itself. I repeat my words before my brain has time to stop me. "Leah, deed you... wheras sheee gon?"

Half my size, I follow the trail of red wine across the hard floor and find her in bed, a part-full glass on the bedside table. When she wakes up to rejoin our party, there is nothing but arms and legs. Not a sprawling mess, but a collection of disjointed limbs.

A spider monkey.

"Come ere, bed fur you." I pick her up and carry her tiny self back to bed. She clutches at every post, every table, every corner that she can, laughing hysterically. What a fun game we're playing. On the bed, she reaches out for the bookshelf. "Oh no you dunt." Within seconds she is asleep and I return to Jakub.

By morning, she has forgotten everything.

"Good morning little monkey."

"What?"

"Don't you remember me putting you to bed last night and you clutching at every single thing you could?" Her face tells me that she doesn't remember.

"You're kidding me?"

"No Monkey, I'm not."

Monkey, it has a nice ring to it.

Entering Budapest that very same day, I am overawed as we travel across an intricate bridge, surrounded by elaborate architecture on one side and a monument topped mountain on the other. The pastel buildings, the decorative roofs, the perfect skies: this delightful entrance to a city is like no other I have ever experienced.

"This is the most beautiful city I have ever seen," I proclaim boldly within minutes. Where else would I rather be, but right here? Nowhere at all.

We knock on another unfamiliar door. It opens just a crack. "Wait here," says the single eye that peeps through. Inside, there is a large group of people quietly gathered around a table. The Eye reappears, revealing a full body that leads us to an empty apartment. "There isn't a mattress, but you can sleep on the sofa bed."

"Monkey, this is wonderful," I gush when we are alone. A whole apartment to ourselves with a balcony so that we can stand outside and look down upon the city.

We climb to the monument atop the mountain and look down on the city as the sun sets. What an unlikely looking pair we are to passers-by. I in my loose fitting hippy pants and an old t-shirt, she a pretty blond girl with fashionably short shorts. I watch her as she climbs steps, as she takes a photo of the city. She is the sort of girl who turns heads.

We power round the city, stop for dinner in a restaurant, and rush home for a few hours of sleep.

There is a knock on the door at six in the morning, but I am already awake.

I open the door cautiously. "Hello?" It's The Eye, the owner of the apartment.

"I'm going to bed now." Devoid of personality, he must have been taking or making drugs all night long.

"Bed? What have you been doing?"

"Working." A dealer then.

"OK, well thank you very much, this apartment was really lovely. We're just about to leave so here's the key."

"Put it under the mat when you go."

"OK, we'll do that. We've put everything back as we found it. Really, thanks again."

"Bye."

"Er, OK. Bye." He has already disappeared.

Today is the day my family arrive. We have seven hours to reach Zagreb, our meeting point, a mere two hundred miles away. With the last of our Hungarian currency, I buy some bread from a bakery and give it to a homeless man, leaving us without food or money until we reach Croatia. No problem, we'll be in Zagreb in a couple of hours. Except that we're not. When a ticket inspector boards the city bus that we use to exit Budapest, we disembark and walk for two hours. One black-riding fine is quite enough.

Since a recommendation at Hitch Gathering, I often use a '20km' sign. Everyone is travelling twenty kilometres and it gets people to stop, even if they aren't going in the same direction. Realising the power of my little blond Monkey, I put the sign away. Ride after ride, we are just ninety miles from Zagreb with three hours to go. I can't wait to show my dad how great hitchhiking is. Although I have been on the road for several months, he still doesn't believe it is possible. However, he also chose to drive the thousand plus mile journey because he is afraid of planes and justified it by saying that driving was easier. A curious mind indeed.

An hour passes in the hot sun. No one picks us up. Then another. Leah heads off in search of food and water, complaining of feeling nauseous while I pass out on the side of the road, my headphones on.

Someone is shouting. A policeman. I can't hear... my headphones.

"Hello," I say as innocently as possible. Is hitchhiking a crime or am I being questioned because I'm lying beside a deserted junction, miles from civilisation? I am alone. The Monkey must still be looking for food and water.

He barks a few words of Hungarian. They could be either angry or friendly, I have no idea.

"I go Zagreb." I put my thumb out to show I'm hitchhiking. It seems that when speaking to people with whom I don't share a common language, my English deteriorates into a malformed language consisting primarily of keywords and simple verb forms. "Is problem?"

"Here OK. Downstairs," he points at the motorway, "no OK. OK?"

"OK." I hope that he'll give us a ride. Instead he speeds off, leaving me at the deserted junction, confirming that I cannot legally stand where all the traffic seems to be passing.

After a third hour of sunbathing, a van drives us two miles and drops us at the next deserted junction. There we wait until my dad calls. He is in Zagreb.

"Just keep going," I tell him, "I'm on the A4." I try to play off how bitterly disappointed I am that we didn't get to Zagreb before him. A luxurious four by four takes us halfway and we meet in the middle, fifty miles short of Zagreb. Dropped at a service station for the first time in many hours, Leah rushes in to fill up her water bottle and invest in peanut nutrition.

It isn't until my dad has hugged me that he finally believes I am real. With my father is the eldest of my little brothers, twenty-one years old and a full two inches taller than me with significantly darker and longer hair, accompanied by his girlfriend who is even smaller than Leah.

"This is Leah," I say to my family, "but I have decided to call her Monkey. You can do the same if you want."

Nonplussed, my family accept that I have brought along a young, attractive American girl and together we head towards the coast.

Tonight I will gorge on gourmet food with familiar company and have a comfy bed to sleep in. Tonight, I still have My Monkey.

30. The Promise

Millions upon billions of tiny pebbles, light in colour and smooth to touch, make up the beaches in Croatia. The rest of the shoreline is dominated by jagged cliffs, erupting high from the clear water. It is with good reason that Croatian beaches are famed as some of the most beautiful in Europe.

From beach to town, from glorious sunshine to thunderstorm, from great food to great wine, we explore the Croatian coast. Each day we stay in a small rented house and then investigate ancient ruins, walk the markets, or swim at the beach. One of the wonderful things about seeing family so sporadically is that you never waste time sitting around watching TV until another day is through and you have to go to sleep, just so that you can repeat the process again the very next day, but we've already forgotten what day it is because they are all the same.

The first dinner we ate was upon a small veranda, a storm attempting to invade, the rain spattering our feet, the wind pulling at our food. It was beautiful.

On the second day we were gifted a huge container of homemade wine and try as we might, we couldn't finish more than a quarter of it. In the morning we caught my father pouring several litres down the drain because it was 'rude to have drank so little,' yet we were not allowed to take any with us because that also 'would be rude.'

While most parents find their children perplexing, I often find it to be the other way around.

"Dad, stop the car! There was an old lady selling cheese at the side of the road."

"Oh cheese, that would have been nice. Too late now."

"No it's not, just stop and turn around." The road behind us is completely empty and we are driving through the rocky countryside, sparsely decorated by hardy trees.

"Dad has a thing," my brother explains with a grin, "about turning the car around. He feels it is the opposite of progress, so he just keeps going forward."

"We have nowhere we need to be, please turn the car around." A simple shake of the head tells me that this isn't possible.

By the middle of the day, the natural beauty of Croatia conflicts heavily with human destruction. Abandoned homes riddled with machine gun fire serve as a startling admission of a conflict that raged as recently as the early nineties, a time when I grew up safely in rural England, threatened only by imaginary cannibals and venom spitting dinosaurs.

"Look at that, would you just look at that!" my father cries over and over again in despair. He is genuinely outraged by the ghosts of atrocities that we are witness to. I sit quietly, knowing nothing of the history of the war.

There are conflicts occurring daily across the world, but we turn off because we don't want to hear. We don't want to know about another bombing or shooting in the same place as before. We want new bombs and new shootings in unexpected places. Only then can our interest be held.

I have actively avoided the news since I left home, close to a decade ago. I always found it too depressing.

At Plitvice Lakes, we walk from one turquoise pool to another, along clifftops, across small wooden boardwalks, all surrounded by huge white cliffs. The constant rush of water echoes through the valleys and between the trees, the sound of hundreds of waterfalls, more than I have ever seen in my life. This is one of those special places in the world unlike any I have ever known. Each time we walk near the edge of a cliff, my dad drops to the floor with his hands upon his head, imploring us to get away.

It is the final day before Leah leaves and for the past few days, she has been accepted into my family. Both of us have loved every minute, shared experiences that will always be remembered. For close to three weeks, she has been my shadow and I have been hers.

How do you cut away your shadow?

Placing my hands upon the wooden safety railings and swinging my feet into the air in an attempted semi-handstand, I balance precariously as I look down a sheer, rocky cliff face. Other than the short rush I get, this balancing act serves no purpose.

I overbalance. I tip forward.

Everything moves so slowly. The wood under my fingers, the smell of the waterfalls, the horrified silence. I feel everything.

I kick back, but I am too far gone.

My head goes over the edge, my body follows. I kick out with my hands, as hard as I can, spinning in midair, clutching the railing with my fingertips. The white cliffs, the pools below, the jagged rocks that will break me. I see them all spinning around me.

I hold my breath, bracing for impact, but as I fall, my toes catch the edge of the boardwalk and my fingertips clutch at the outside of the railing. Just enough toe to support my bodyweight. In my mind I looked like a gymnast agilely twisting in midair. In real life, I know it was a different story.

I am on the wrong side of the safety railing, standing over a large drop.

My dad didn't see, but everybody else looks at me with their mouths open. That was real danger, something that I should be afraid of, yet it lasted only a second and only an impulse reaction saved me. I look down at the drop. I might have survived, I might not. I probably won't do that again.

"Don't tell Dad," I whisper, "it would just worry him."

Sometimes the most innocent of accidents, the safest occasions of all, are the ones that catch you off guard and take away everything. Why is it that I have always been afraid of dinosaurs?

This is it, the day Leah leaves.

I start up the car. Two hours to the airport. My family are spending a second day at the lakes, allowing us our final precious minutes alone with each other.

"Music, Monkey?" She nods, choked for words.

I pass a hitchhiker without stopping. We can't share our last few minutes with a stranger.

"There is no escalator moment this time," she tells me. "You know that right?" This time it is my turn to nod. "I have my student loans, I have…"

It's all been said before. This time it is real. She is actually going.

I blink and we're at the airport.

With the bag dropped off, we sit in fallen leaves outside the terminal, our gazes locked upon one another, a million miles away. The foreboding darkness of the world rests upon our bleeding souls.

Terminal, what an appropriate name. A slow, incurable end.

I blink. "It's time."

Each step is a step closer to the end. My feet become heavy, I don't know if I can make it. Part of me is dying, part of me is already dead.

I hate you airport, I hate every airport in the world. Goodbyes shared with strangers on their holidays, excited to be rushing off to a foreign destination, coming home after a week in a new place. Loudspeaker announcements, grey tile floors, big yellow signs. Trolleys overloaded with suitcases.

Amidst the chaos, the crazy goings on, I hold her tightly.

"I'll come back, I promise I'll come back," she says sincerely, looking me directly in the eyes. "It might be six months, maybe a year or two, but I'll see you again. I couldn't not ever see you again."

I try to smile, to tell her that it's OK, that I'll see her again, but my smile is sad and forced. I want to believe her, I want her to come back. I don't want her to go. But the escalator moment has passed. "Six months from now, a year, who knows where we will both be."

I let go.

One of my best friends in the whole world walks away through the dull security gate, joining a line of holidaymakers. She waves, disappears, comes back to wave again. And again and again and again.

She must go. So too must I.

I turn, she turns, our paths diverge.

Finally, a tear falls.

Two mornings after My Monkey leaves, my family leave too, dropping me at a service station where I am picked up by a psychedelic Russian rock band. They drive me all the way to Budapest where I join them for a gig and find them a free night's accommodation.

I will never be alone, but I can never stop missing the people I leave behind.

31. Routines

Budapest, one of the prettiest cities in all of the world. I walk the large stone streets, barefooted, people giving me funny looks as I pass. Irate, a construction worker runs over to me and begins shouting at me in Hungarian, his face inches from my own.

"I don't want to wear shoes today, thank you. Please leave me alone."

I have found a bed in a hostel. In exchange for one or two hours of work, five days a week, I can sleep for free. I walk the city every day, up and down nameless streets, sometimes alone, sometimes with guests from the hostel.

"Try this, it's the most unhealthy food in the world, but it's really, really good." If someone says do something, I do it. I order a lángos, a heavy bread dough that is flattened and deep fried then smothered in sour cream and grated cheese. It is disgustingly tasty.

What next?

"I want to show you a ruin bar."

Sure, why not? I have nowhere else to be.

I follow each recommendation, some better than others.

What am I doing here?

"You have to see the cemetery, it is so beautiful."

I walk through the most elegant and respectful cemetery in the world, elaborate statues, odes to the deceased. It moves me deep inside, but not to tears.

I wake up, a concert cellist practising next door. In the afternoon, she hosts a small orchestra in her living room to perform an impromptu, open air concert. That's nice. Very nice.

An Australian girl arrives on a vintage bicycle, a basket on the front. She cycled from Berlin, nearly six hundred miles away. That's a long bike ride.

"Are you Jamie?" she asks. I tell her that I am. We met the same person in the Czech Republic and she recognises me from my stories. My stories that have stopped.

Where next?

More Australians come and go, stopping a few days, then moving to the next party. West to Oktoberfest they head, the world's largest fair, famed for participants' excessive beer consumption.

I am still here.

I sit on a bridge over the huge Danube river, listening to stories. "Many years ago there was a young man who loved to travel, spending exuberant amounts of his family's wealth partying and meeting young ladies. This was back in the day when Buda and Pest were two cities separated by the Danube. Upon hearing that his father had become ill, he rushed back to see him, only to find that bad weather prevented him from crossing the river. Every boat refused to take him in such awful conditions and when the storm finally cleared, he arrived home to find that his father had died. He then decided to use his large fortune to build a bridge so that no one else would suffer such misfortune. That bridge over there," she points up the river, "is the bridge that he built."

Truth, oftentimes less interesting than fantasy, is at times best left undiscovered.

Armed with reckless disregard for everything in the world, I climb the huge bridge structure in the darkness, the wind trying to throw me off. On a strip of metal just a metre wide, I look down at the road, cars passing a death-fall away. I float above the city. At the lower reaches, a friend slips to the ground, leaping back up with blood running down his face. Someone else jumps into a fountain fully clothed.

"You are The White God," a voice calls over and over again, bowing to a white cat. He walks with an umbrella, his best friend, talking to it through the night.

More new people, more walks.

Streets, alone together. Waking and walking this elaborate outdoor museum, each night returning to the same place to make the same beds and do the same thing over again the next day.

How many days have I been here? How many will I stay? Why can I still feel that pain?

32. Jump

"What would you say if I was to come back?" Leah asks through a shaky Skype call.

"I don't know," I respond, caught off-balance. I hate playing hypothetical games when you want them to be real life. "Do you want to come back?"

"Yes, I miss it. Ever since I left Europe I realised that this wasn't the place for me."

"You knew that before you left."

"I did, but I didn't have a choice."

"You would still come back if you had a choice?"

"I would. I would come back today. I'd leave my job, my apartment, and just get on a plane if I could. I don't know what I'd do with this little guy though." She lifts a tiny black sausage dog in front of the screen who, full of boundless energy, proceeds to attack her face with affectionate, slobbering kisses.

"If you came back today, I would still be here. But I have to move on soon."

"I know that. I wish it wasn't like this."

"The job is up to you. If you don't like it, you should quit, regardless of all else. The dog, what you'd do next, everything that follows, that is up to you too. If you come back here one day, come back because you want to come back for yourself."

"I would be coming back for myself. I want to come back for myself because I never do anything for myself. But having you there would help."

It is idle talk. Impossibilities defined by the world of American student debt. I end the call feeling even more deflated than before I spoke to her.

It is time for me to move on, I can't mope here forever, living on lost memories. I browse the internet, looking at maps. Christoffer, the tall Dane I met in Estonia, messages me to ask if I want to go to Africa. I do. But I have little money, a couple of hundred pounds at most. He is in the same situation.

Say yes more.

Yes, I tell him, let's go to Africa.

This might be the biggest decision of my life.

Another Skype call.

"Monkey? Hello again."

"I've done it."

"What?!"

"I jumped."

"You did?"

"I did."

"Really?"

"Yes."

"Oh!"

"Oh?"

"I can hardly believe it."

"Me neither, but it's true."

"Good."

"Are you happy?"

"Very."

"Good."

"When?"

"Next Saturday."

"Wow. To Budapest?"

"Yes."

On a whim, leaping for happiness, she has decided to leave a secure job and a stable life in search of something more. A something, for the meantime, that we can do together. What an irrational decision, to walk away from the safe bet. I am not a safe bet, this is not a safe bet.

Struck by lightning and befuddled, I am floating somewhere between dreams and reality. I hope above hope that this isn't one of those wonderful dreams that I'll wake up from, crushed that my reality is so much worse. I always liked scary dreams the best, because they are the ones that I am happiest to wake up from.

No, this is not a dream. I must tell Christoffer that my plans have changed and then I must wait for My Monkey, the girl who has given up everything on a whim, daring for adventure.

She is the bravest person I have ever met in the world.

33. Forwards

I run out of the hostel, I have to catch a bus. Why am I always late? I have had weeks to prepare for this day, but could I get myself up in time, could I get myself to the airport? No, of course I couldn't. That would be far too reasonable.

Sweating, I board the bus and drift in and out of the fairy world all the way to the airport.

There it is.

The large clock tells me that I am thirty minutes late. Thirty minutes!

I watch every passenger walking through the magic glass doors, the portals to the other side of the world.

Where is she, where can she be, why is she not here already, has she already gone? I bet that's it, I bet she already left, she already headed out of the airport and into the city. What a bloody brilliant plan, arrive late at the airport to surprise her after arranging to meet in the centre of the city when she has given up everything and flown across the world.

A tap on the shoulder. "Oh, you!" Only with my arms wrapped around her do I finally believe that she is real. I hold her tightly, as if I never want to let her go again.

"I told you that I would come back for you."

I never believed her. Or did I always know that she would?

Elated and dizzy on the rich, sweet nectar of life, atop miniature folding bicycles we cycle across the city through the night and into the morning. We are our own superheroes, we are the emperors of the world, we are.

"Watch me!" I yell, leaping up kerbs and back down them, pedalling on rocket fuel.

I am invincible.

Head on, I leap up a particularly large kerb. Except that I don't. My front wheel appears to have connected with the kerb and the bicycle has stopped dead. I however, have not stopped moving. I am the rockstar leaping off the stage and into a non-existent crowd, I am the skydiver without a parachute. I vaguely notice as I travel over the handlebars, headfirst towards the pavement, but sadly my body doesn't seem to realise what is going on. Not a protective arm, safety roll, or any such evasive action: just a mild turning of the head so as to prevent peeling off my face. I'm aware of my shoulder striking the ground, followed shortly by my left elbow and knee. My head stops and my feet somersault through the air, overtaking the rest of my body.

Now I stop moving.

Pain. Those unfunny bones take control of all sensations.

I hold my breath, trying not to breath. Every movement hurts.

Someone is cackling. Someone finds it hilariously funny. I raise my head to see that Leah has almost fallen off her own bike in fits of laughter.

"You, Monkey. You have a very funny laugh." She radiates elegance, except when she laughs. A natural, wild, makes-you-want-to-laugh-too sort of laugh. "I'm glad to see that you have a sense of humour as dark as mine." I inspect my elbow and knee. Both are already swollen. "I normally never bruise," I whine out loud.

Look after me nurse Monkey, make me better.

"Is your head OK?" she finally asks when she is capable of breathing once more.

"My head didn't even touch the ground. Everything else did." For every snowboard, ski, football, and general life tumble that I've ever had, only once have I hurt my head. I took on a batting cage and lost. Five stitches to the back of my head in exchange for an awful lot of blood. I will have a raise across the back of my skull for the rest of my life, but it seems that some people get lucky. The day I wrote off my first car, there wasn't the slightest impact upon my shocked body. I choose not to question this, but to accept it and be grateful.

"Where do you want to go?" I ask. The whole world is in front of us.

"Anywhere and everywhere." The look in her eyes tells me that this is the absolute truth. She is alive and she is ready for anything, daring to dream, to let go, to take a chance on life.

"How about we go back to Jakub, the Slovakian guy you first Couch Surfed with? He seemed like a nice guy."

"Let's do it." We look at the map together. "Then can we go to Prague? It's all in the same direction."

I hesitate. "I don't want to go to Prague." It's beautiful, it's wonderful, but I can't go back right now.

"Why? Of all the places in Europe that I could go, England and Prague are the two that I want to visit most."

I reluctantly agree that we can go to Prague on the condition that I don't have to enjoy it. Only for her.

In darkness we stand on what remains of the Hungarian, Slovakian border. Surrounding us are desolate, uninspiring buildings that once served as border controls, regulating the flow of people in and out of each country. With the introduction of the Schengen Area, twenty-six countries with a combined border, the inter-country border controls have been abandoned. The cars can barely see us in their headlights as they pass.

"Are you scared yet Monkey?"

"No, I have you to look after me."

My only shoes rip apart as I perform a celebratory dance in Jakub's town, happy to have completed another leg of our journey. Now all I have are flip-flops.

Jakub takes us to the ruins of an old castle and we climb high, looking over the Slovakian countryside. Without shoes, I stumble barefooted onto a snake and yelp in terror. Poisonous or not, I do not want to be bitten by a snake.

In the village pub, a humble stone structure with simple furniture, a fight breaks out. A man battles ferociously with a chair, kicking it across the room and glaring as it skids along the floor. He shouts angrily and looks around the room. My lizard brain leaps for the door, we have to get out.

"Don't worry about it," Jakub assures us. Sure enough, the man soon passes out on the table and gets sent home by his friends who then send free drinks to our table for the Monkey. With a tiny frame not fit for Slovakian drinking, I sling her over my shoulder and carry her home. She weighs almost nothing.

I tell Jakub to keep in touch as we leave. His proposed route of hitchhiking towards India may intersect with ours again.

We will head north towards Berlin in view of the approaching winter. It's now or never and without the tent and clothing I passed over to my father, we must soon chase the sun. It's a five hundred mile journey to Berlin by our intended route.

From Jakub's small Slovakian village to Vienna, I am overwhelmed by an endless buffet of eye candy. Quaint streets, delicate structures, and a level of cleanliness that suggests even the streets have been sanitised. There are few cities which emanate such delicacy and beauty. Overawed, I leave my camera on a park bench and return in haste, to find it untouched, a full half an hour later.

Two Czech guys, high on life after securing new jobs in Austrian petrol stations, hand us a large ball of weed on the way to Prague. I thank them politely.

"Get rid of that," I say to the Monkey once they have driven away.

"Get rid of it? Why did you take it, only to get rid of it?"

"To be polite." We crumble the dried plant into the roadside. I am not getting in trouble with police in a country that I don't know. "Maybe it will grow here and in a few years time there will be a large plant for everybody passing by." Truth is relative because you can stand where you like and so can everyone else.

In the beautiful city of Prague, even I struggle to contain my melancholy and it bursts forth in delight at the orange roofed city once more.

"Let's go out for dinner," I suggest. My funds are running close to empty and while most people would react accordingly, some reckless abandon deep within me decides that spending a week's worth of food supplies on a nice bottle of wine and a meal in the centre of town would be an appropriate course of action.

On a bridge decorated with locks, the symbol of lovers who have thrown their keys into the water to entangle themselves forever, I speculate aloud about how many of them regret doing so. "How many of them wish they could take their keys back, cut down the lock, and forget that something wonderful has been lost? Nothing lasts forever, right?!" What becomes of me, of my journey, of the future?

The breeze of a passing metro train soothes my soul. The three route line map, the unusual circles decorating the station walls, the old square trains with their straight line seating, the wind blowing down the escalators, air brushing girls in dresses and turning them into momentary movie stars, the Prague metro itself, it comforts me. Something familiar, something I remember in a fresh world of unfamiliarity.

Leah catches a ride while I am searching bushes for fruit. I run to the road and the driver speeds away, disappointed that she isn't a prostitute.

At a service station, a German hitchhiker gives up his ride for us. "You guys take this camper, there's enough space for both of you and I don't mind waiting a bit longer." We manage to squeeze all three of us into the tiny van, then sleep as we whirl from one city to the next.

In Berlin, we enter an apartment full of things and things and things of no description. Cardboard boxes, papers, disused office furniture. In the large living room, more like a disused storage cupboard, debris obstructs all movement and leaves only enough space for a single mattress. Four of us sleep in this room, three more in the small bedroom, and the owner sleeps on the floor of the kitchen between the fridge and the sink, a space barely big enough for a body. Every time someone goes to the bathroom, they clamber over us on the floor. It's like a dysfunctional squat run by a pleasant but reclusive guy who never leaves.

City to city, we are continually surrounded by urban sprawl, cars moving us from one red dot on a map to another. Every day is a new adventure, every day we do something new together. Every day Leah smiles and laughs like the free bird who never wants to return to its cage.

"I need to leave the city," I confess. The freedom of the countryside, the ability to walk across soft land, the quiet freedom from the constant drone of people. I miss it all. "You would hardly believe where I grew up compared to where we are now. It's so quiet. Maybe I will show you one day."

"Maybe someday, that would be nice." A spark in her eyes, delight at the thought of England.

"But today the world is cold and we must go south, chasing the sun."

One and a half thousand miles away is Turkey. Surely that will be warm. We agree to go.

No plans, no aims, no worries, no bills, no mortgage, nothing I never wanted and all that I did.

The whole world is before us and after Istanbul, the great divide: the road east into Asia or the road south to Africa. My heart skips and my head spins at the possibility of this transient life becoming permanent. No end date, just a Monkey, myself, and the open road. Could I really do that? Could I just keep going and not look back, not thinking about what will happen, travel into countries I know nothing about?

The ground threatens to recede beneath me.

There are few people in the world who truly drop everything in the hope of a great adventure. We don't dare to let go. Do I dare to let go? Beside me, My Monkey shows me the way.

Onwards, upwards, forwards, and beyond. Hand in hand we go.

34. Being Human

"I'm scared, I don't want to go."

"There is no other way to go," I sigh. "Serbia or Romania are the only practical ways to reach Turkey."

"I just don't want something bad to happen. What if…"

"Please, stop. I don't want anything bad to happen. But it won't." American media has portrayed much of Eastern Europe as countries to be feared. Despite pushing the mental boundaries of birds, sleeping in the homes of strangers, and hitchhiking, it seems that the Monkey is approaching her limit. "There is an alternative solution."

"What?" A hopeful look, mingled with dread.

"We don't have to go the same way. I want you to come with me, of course I do, but if you are not comfortable, we can go separate ways and meet later."

"I know, I know, but I want to go with you. I'm just scared."

"It's OK to be scared. However, this is your decision and you must come only if you are comfortable." Despite the sigh of resignation, caught between what she wants and what makes her feel safe, I know that our fate is sealed. She would not choose to part from me already. We will travel my path, but not quite all of it.

The selfish part of me reels at the compromise, resenting the loss of absolute control over my journey. As with life, everything is a balance. I have chosen this compromise, to travel with this girl rather than continuing on my egomaniacal way. She is my choice, my freedom. Do I regret it? Not at all.

At the Hungarian border, the police pull our banana truck over. Their eyes light up when I get out of the cab sporting hippy pants and a backpack decorated with shreds of material. Leah is wearing a rainbow striped headband and both of us are in flip-flops. The police pull my bag open, checking every fold, every pocket, as they look for drugs. They know that they will find something forbidden. But there is nothing to find. With less enthusiasm they pull apart Leah's bag then leave us to reassemble our worldly belongings.

Our last stop in Hungary is Szeged, a southern city a few miles from both the Serbian and Romanian borders. We spend the night at the home of some medical students, slaving away for years and years to become respectable pillars of society, securing their futures. I am envious of their dedication.

"What will you do after this?" they ask.

"I don't know." There is no long term achievement to what I'm doing. I chase nothing because it is better to chase nothing than to follow something that isn't worth following. We must always chase nothing or something. Keep moving, keep going, keep doing, don't stop. Most of all, don't let your thoughts catch up with you. When you continually outrun them, you never have to deal with them.

Why hasn't that pain gone away yet?

Arriving at the Romanian border, we are shifted from one vehicle to another, the drivers implying that the vehicles are being sold, not wholly within the confines of the law. "This is the way in Romania, this is how we do things. I wouldn't recommend for you guys to be here, doing what you do. If you want a lift, people will ask for money. That's if they don't do something bad to you first. This is a dangerous country, I can't wait to leave. My friend says he'll get me a job at the docks in America. As soon as I get my visa, I'm out of here and never looking back."

I feel Leah squeezing my hand tighter, everything she fears coming to life.

In a tiny village, we search an uneven, rocky path for the home of another stranger who has invited us to stay. Grizzly stares follow us from dilapidated buildings, the village oppressively silent and devoid of movement. Around us, endless fields stretch out, broken only by flocks of geese and the occasional lone tree. A teddy bear, its stuffing ripped from its belly, lies upon the worn track. I approach a group of young children and try speaking to them in English. They run away, back to the safety net of their homes.

"Don't worry Monkey, we'll be there soon. This is a nice little village isn't it?" The look on her face says that this is not a nice little village, this is not where she wants to be at all, that she hugely regrets coming to Romania. I take her hand in mine.

Walk with me.

At the house we eventually find, we are greeted by geese, chickens, pigs, cats, dogs, rabbits, and ducks. Everything has a purpose, everything provides something. I am saved. This is the good side of life that I had been looking for, something I can take pleasure in and share with Leah.

"Isn't this great?"

She looks around. "I don't like all the flies."

A tiny kitten, little bigger than my hand, leaps onto my plate, stealing plum dumplings and hissing.

"I don't feed the cats so that they kill the rodents for me," our biker host tells us.

We hitch into the local town, walk around, then hitch back in darkness. An elderly couple pick us up. "No money, no dinero," we say, making it clear that we have nothing. They drive us back to our temporary home then turn around expectantly. I have a couple of pounds worth of Romanian currency in my pocket and only a few hours before I leave. I hand it to them.

They babble back and forth, tensions escalating, voices rising until they are almost shouting.

"Come on," Leah whispers. She pulls me out of the car and we rush towards a dark pathway, hiding in the shadows of a tree. We are invisible in the absolute darkness. After several minutes, the car pulls away slowly. I regret giving them anything at all.

In the light of day, a new ride runs out of fuel. A lit cigarette hanging from his mouth, he tops up his tank from a fuel canister. The burning ash drops into the stream of flammable liquid. Is this how it ends, blown up on the side of the road because of a lit cigarette?

No. On we go. I laugh nervously as I recite the story to Leah. She is not impressed.

The cold rides south with us, one step ahead. With one sleeping bag and no tent, we have to find somewhere warm to sleep each night. When I'm cold and tired, Leah buoys my spirits. When she is afraid, I hold her hand. Like an uneven see-saw, we battle to balance out the scales, to keep the other going.

When I am happy, so too is she. When she smiles, I smile right back.

Our last ride in Romania is a car with two fridges strapped to the roof. How very fitting.

Enter Serbia.

Just metres over the border we wait for an hour, no one stopping to pick us up. We realise that we have made a mistake, we are standing between the two border controls. No one would pick up a stranger at this inconvenient point. We cross the second control point and find ourselves on a quiet road. Apparently we have entered Serbia at a tiny border crossing, barely used. Hardly a car passes. A few parked trucks sit idle, their curtains drawn as the inhabitants rest for the night, far from home.

It gets darker, it gets colder. Ahead of us the glow of the nearest town is not even visible. It could be hours until the next place of sanctuary. We knock on a parked truck. Can we come in please, if only to sit in the warmth for a few minutes? No answer.

I wear my only jumper and trousers. And my flip-flops. I am in need of shoes.

We both sense it, the elephant in the room, but say nothing.

This is getting dangerous.

How resistant is the human body to the cold? The wind bites our backs, wild and fast as it races off the barren fields.

A small pixie of a man appears, darting from one lorry to another, inspecting us from a distance. What does he want? He edges closer and closer until he stands on the other side of the road from us. Then he crosses to speak with us in a language other than English, thus one I don't understand.

"Autostop, Belgrade," I tell him. Belgrade is the next big town along the road and judging by our map, little more than a hundred miles of countryside lies between where we are and the city itself. He motions for us to follow him.

"What do you think?" I ask the Monkey. "Do you want to go with him or not?"

"Do you think he'll drive us where we want to go?"

"I know as little as you. It's too cold to stay outside though and his face seems friendly enough." Desperate and shivering, there is nothing else for me to base my decision on.

We weave between the parked trucks, avoiding large puddles, and climb into a truck. There we sit for a while until he fires up the engine and begins driving. Warm air, so delicious, oozes from the vents. We traverse darkness, seeing nothing but a few metres of road illuminated by the headlights. There really would have been nothing for us if we walked.

A town finally appears, small, run down. In the huge lorry we twist through the dimly lit streets until we reach an unsealed track, narrower and darker than other streets in the little town. At the end of it we find ourselves in a lonely dirt car park, empty except for one other truck. The headlights illuminate creepy silhouettes, the bony fingers of bushes dancing in the wind. Engine off, our driver makes a call. This is not Belgrade.

The driver pulls something from the glove compartment. Was that money? What are we waiting for?

A car pulls into the otherwise deserted car park, a small hatchback with heavily tinted windows. Our driver climbs out of the lorry. Two men appear from the shadows somewhere to the right of us. The group of men converge towards the car.

This is it. This is my promised experience, the terrible thing that everybody tried to warn me about. Adrenaline pumps yet again, but this time I'm not falling.

I'm flying.

I have a pretty young girl, someone who gave up everything to be here, someone who is one of my best friends in the whole world. I will protect her.

My senses run in overdrive, the world slows down around me. Or is it I who has sped up?

The promised moment approaches, how desperately exciting. I take the pixie trucker's passport, scribble down the passport number and his name, then slip the note into my pocket. My bag that was previously on my lap is moved to the bed behind me. Better manoeuvrability. I put my own passport into my pocket and advise Leah to do the same. We need nothing but ourselves. From this high position, I have a good kick at anyone trying to enter the vehicle. Regardless, I lock the doors, studying the gear stick and controls around the driver's seat. I am sure I can drive this thing if it comes to it. The key is still in the ignition.

"I'm scared," Leah whispers in a small voice.

"I've got this, I'll keep you safe. I'm not worried." The last part is a lie, but I have something to fight for. Hairs on end, I bristle like a mad little puppy, unaware of how insignificant and incapable I truly am. "Do you regret it yet?"

She shakes her head in defiance, her body shaking with fear.

Brave girl.

For her...

The two men from the shadows walk right on by. Our driver exchanges something with the hatchback driver. The car speeds away.

Only our truck driver is left in the once more deserted car park. Alone, a simple smile on his friendly face, he walks back to us. Flicking the mechanism, I unlock the doors.

Dare I say that I am almost disappointed? This was my moment to be a knight in shining armour, to live life on the edge. But promises have not been fulfilled. After months on the road I have not been mugged, attacked, or mistreated in any way. Have people lied about the evil state of the world? Are people really good after all?

I rub Leah's knee excitedly.

"See Monkey, I told you everything would be OK. Everything is OK. Everything will always be OK. Until it's not." My hands are still shaking. "That not is not today."

Using hand signals, we laugh and joke with our driver, the man we thought had sold us out to some undesirable fate. He feigns disbelief when we point at the map, showing him our route and that we hope to reach Turkey. All smiles, we shake hands when our paths finally part, richer for the experience.

"Do you see Monkey, do you see?"

"Do I see what?"

"You, I, them, us, it doesn't matter. No matter where we go in the world, no matter how brash, abrupt, or downright negative someone might at first seem, it is entirely insignificant. It doesn't matter where we come from, where we grow up, or what our ideals are in life, what matters is that there is something, a small unwatered seed of sameness that we have with every human being on this planet, even the people you hate. That tiny, sometimes imperceivable seed is different for each person, but somewhere, maybe deep inside, it is there, it is lurking, it is waiting to connect. We forget that some of the time. If we were all to remember, there

THE BOY WHO WAS AFRAID OF THE WORLD

would be no racism or prejudice in the world. There would be no wars and fighting. It is hard not to hold preconceptions of others because our cultures teach us to do so. One day, when the media stops separating us into groups and clans based upon where we come from and which god we follow, we may get a little closer to collectively understanding that we aren't as different as we like to believe. We all bleed and breathe, love and dream. Just not in exactly the same way. We are all human."

Today, the world is my best friend and all of the people in it are new friends that I haven't yet had the pleasure of meeting.

35. The Three Musketeers

"Monkey, that's really rude," I scowl between gritted teeth. "They are breaking hitch etiquette."

"Go and tell them then."

"Tell them? I can't tell them, they should just know." Two hitchhikers have turned up and aggressively try to catch rides directly in front of us. My Great British reserve keeps me tight lipped and tutting. We're the best tutters and queuers in all of the world. If we see a line for something, we stand in it, presuming that there must be something good at the front of it. If someone bypasses protocol and attempts to skip the queueing process, we tut and mumble under our breath.

I tut and mumble to Leah.

Both men catch rides and we take the third vehicle to stop. Yes please, I would like a cold beer and some food, thank you very much. Turkish truckers once again show us extreme generosity.

"Jay?" Leah whispers when the driver gets out of the cab to check something in the back. "Did you see that?"

"See what?" She looks into the mirror to check that the driver is still occupied, then slips out a DVD cover from under a magazine.

"He tried to hide it when we got in." I burst out laughing. The case is a series of graphic pornographic images of slender, young blond girls. With a few more clothes, any of them could at first glance, look like Leah. The trucker returns, oblivious to our discovery, and harmlessly takes us along our way. Despite his obvious penchant for young, blond females, what he chooses to do on his lonely nights is of no concern to us.

For our stay in Sofia, the capital of Bulgaria, I spent hours researching and selecting an apartment to rent for a few days so that I could meet a friend from England. It was a big decision as everywhere else I have slept has been free. Discovering that our kitchen consists of a sink, our four bedrooms of a double bed and two singles, and that the heating is only turned on when the temperature hits minus twenty, I am much aggrieved. As a solution, we are offered extra blankets and use of the toaster in the office. The fact that there are multiple beds in the living room is never addressed. Our great reunion dinner consists of cheese and crackers and I curse the wasted money, resolving to sleep outside and never pay for accommodation again. At least then, my expectations will not be high.

On the last day in the apartment, Jakub, our Slovakian friend, arrives at short notice on his way to India. Happily we are reunited and leave the apartment, spending the night with Sarah and her seven year old son. Sarah is Bulgarian and warmly welcomes us into her home. Together, we climb mountains and walk the city. In a rural dog sanctuary, we pass stinking cages where hundreds of dogs are crammed together, wallowing in their own filth.

"There are more than ten thousand wild dogs in this city and when they are hungry, they go hunting in packs. Sometimes they kill people," Sarah explains. "These dogs have been saved from the streets because there are people who choose to poison the dogs." All around us, signs warn people not to touch the dogs, not to get too close to the cages. Many of the dogs go wild as we pass, jumping and barking.

A husky, beautiful blue eyes, a calm demeanour, a pristine coat high above where he finds himself, stares out at me longingly. Take me away from this place he begs. Against what I've been told not to do, I reach in through the cage to touch him. He nuzzles my hand gratefully, starved of affectionate contact in the rabble of yelping dogs.

"I'm so sorry. There are too many of you to save."

In the same way that I turned off the TV as a teenager and never looked back, I walk away from the dog sanctuary and pretend that it doesn't exist, but just a millimetre below the surface, I know that it is still there and the husky waits for someone to save him. Every dog, every person, waits for somebody to save them.

Over a thousand miles away from the cold of Berlin, we continue east from Sofia. The three of us, Jakub, the Monkey, and I, continue our relationship as it first started: with a large box of cheap wine. It's sour and makes me wince, but washes away the fears of what happens after Turkey, of what the purpose of this journey is, of what the future holds. We put the box in plain sight for all to see. Look at us, three hitchhikers drinking wine for breakfast, surely you want to pick us up. We pass a metal cup between us, inhaling the ghastly liquid, catching a ride just before the blue skies are hidden by dark clouds that empty over us.

Around and around the cup goes inside the car, sip, pass, sip, pass, fill again.

The road outside the car is a small river. My words become tangled. I think I have a wine hat on.

Security guards shoo us away from the entrance of a bank. Why can't we do cartwheels here?

I throw my only footwear into a bin. I don't need my flip-flops anyway, I'll be shoe-free.

"Monkey, you are half shoe-free too." One of her shoes is lost and she is bleeding excessively after stepping on broken glass. I will just rest my eyes. A buzzing wakes me. Leah seems to be cutting Jakub's hair with a small electric razor.

And so the days pass. Shared moments, little memories, conversations upon hilltops, and walks around ruins that mean nothing to anyone but us, each day the three of us learn about one another, each day we become further committed to our journey.

I buy new shoes.

We are The Three Musketeers and nothing can stop us. We jump happily for passing cars as we approach Turkey, the land dry and rocky around us.

At the Turkish border we walk along the motorway for several kilometres, the queue of lorries backed up for several hours, maybe even days, as they try to clear customs. We sidestep truckers, all inviting us for tea, all offering to feed us. A border guard picks us up as he drives past and takes us into Turkey, the first country for which I have had to purchase a visa during my journey. It is the twenty-second country I have hitchhiked in since that day so long ago when my mother drove me out to a small fuel station near my family home. It is the furthest east I have ever travelled without taking a plane.

I bang on the window of the visa issuing guard. He is slumped over on a sofa, clearly riveted by his job.

As we pass, border guards laugh raucously, amused at our hitchhiking attempts. We assure them that it is possible, but they refuse to believe it. Of course I didn't hitchhike around Europe for the past few months, I clearly made that story up to fool you and then came here to flaunt the lie. They laugh in our faces. "In Turkey, no possible!"

One valuable thing that I have learnt is that people can only offer you advice based upon what they know about life and what they would or wouldn't do themselves. Every decision that you make is better made as your own.

We pass six irrelevant checkpoints, each one studying our passports, then allowing us to pass. No wonder the queue of lorries stretches back several hours.

Stopping in Edirne, the first city over the border, domed mosques and minuets stretch into the sky. Vendors sell fruit and spices from large buckets. People move and bustle, more people than I could have ever thought possible to be in one place. Yet there is a snagging feeling, something dragging me down, something bugging me about the place. It's different from the Europe I know, sure it's different, but it isn't that different. I wanted to be transported a whole world away, I wanted to go to a new dimension that I never even knew how to picture. But this is real and it is real life and it is in front of me and my jaw hasn't dropped in awe. Maybe there is another world within the city itself.

We enter one market, then another. People selling piles of things, mostly junk, just like every other part of the world.

Inside a mosque, a woman rushes to Leah, throwing a scarf at her. Cover yourself heinous woman! We admire the elaborate mosaics, the fine detailing on every feature of the interior. Speakers echo loudly through the room, the call to prayer. Along with the majority of the women, we are shooed out of the mosque and into the street. A few covered women are permitted to stay at the rear of the mosque, behind a screen.

"Why are the women not allowed to join the prayers?" I ask to an English speaking Turk.

"It is better for them to pray in their own homes."

"Why is that?"

"It is the will of Allah." The man hurries inside to join the prayers. I have a lot to learn about the world.

Outside the mosque, we look over the city from our high vantage point. Across the minuets, above the domed roofs, we watch the sun set. The world is on fire, a miraculous orange and red glow, the likes of which I have never before seen from a city. My legs dangle from the side of a high wall and Leah chats softly with Jakub. I watch them both fondly, but right now in this moment, I have no idea what they are saying.

My ears are muffled and I am sinking. To sink is less horrifying than to fall, but similarly unpleasant.

What will I find when my head falls below the surface? What comes next? I suspect nothing.

The sun fades and the night engulfs us. Darkness.

I can feel it, unquestionably deep, I can feel it in my bones. This is the end. I just haven't figured out why.

36. Delusions

Istanbul, the heart of Turkey, a city famed for its vibrant beauty. It takes us several hours to traverse the outskirts of the city. Rarely have I ever seen such an urban sprawl.

Kemal, a large Turkish man, slaps me on the back. "Silly boy, I told you to meet me tangential to the metro station." We are in a large open square surrounded by tall buildings and the metro exit is in the centre. I have no idea what he means and despite his generous offer of hosting all three of us for the night, I feel my spider senses tingling at his brash personality. The majority of the Turks who have picked me up in the past few weeks and months have been warm and pleasant, but with Kemal I sense something else, something I can't quite put my finger on. It is something that makes me keenly aware.

This judgemental attitude, assessing people instantly and deciding whether or not I like them based on almost nothing, has developed and grown during my months on the road. When accepting rides or invitations into homes, my intuition is one of the few forms of self-defence that I have. Thus far it has served me well. Only when meeting the Monkey was I hugely wrong. Her invisible barriers had not allowed me to see the person that was inside, not for a few hours at least, but I knocked and knocked until she let me in. The very thought of how different things could be, makes my head spin. What if I had gone to Italy to work on the farm? I would not be here, I would never have met Leah or Jakub. I am grateful for how things have turned out.

Kemal asks if we want to go out to some bars and a restaurant. We explain that we'd like to cook him dinner to say thank you and not to spend much money because we have little, just as we explained in the message online. He is a big man, proud of himself, and trying to be the centre of attention. Despite our protests, we are taken to a restaurant and multiple plates of food are ordered.

"Do you mind paying for this?" Kemal asks quietly. "I forgot my wallet." We foot the bill between us. "How about we go to some bars now?"

"If possible, we'd really like to just sit down and relax, we're hot, tired, and sweaty."

"We'll just look at the bar then decide." Clumsily the three of us struggle into a busy bar with our backpacks on.

Two hours later we are led to another bar. "We really would like to just go back. Like we said in the message, we can't afford to go to lots of bars." Aside from Scandinavia, the cost of alcohol in Turkey far exceeds most other European countries.

"What about the nightclub after?" The three of us look in bemusement at one another: dressed in sweaty clothes and wearing backpacks, we are not well kitted out for a nightclub.

Jakub perks up, putting forward a strong argument for going home. We are saved and I am grateful to him. We head to a bus stop.

"If you all give me ten lira each, I'll add the money to my card and pay for tickets." The machine flashes a three lira charge as each of us boards.

By morning, the three of us are eager to explore the city and wait for Kemal to get up. He told us to wait for him so that we could see the city together. He rises mid-afternoon.

"We'll eat breakfast, then go into the city. I just have to get some things from the shop. Leah, would you like to clean the table in the living room or sort out the kitchen?" The table in the living room was a glass table that got knocked over and has been shattered on the floor for several days. We have all been told to wear plastic slippers so that we don't cut our feet. Clearly one of our trio is going to have to clean up the broken glass.

"I'll clean the table," I say. I get onto the floor, collecting the shattered pieces of glass while Leah and Jakub clean other parts of the apartment. A fourth Couch Surfer, a ghost within the apartment, brings me a hoover. He is from Pakistan and he tells me that it is the first time he has left his own country. As I clean, he reaches down behind me and begins to caress my shoulders. I shuffle away quickly. "Thanks for the help, but I'm OK. Maybe you should see if they need help in the kitchen."

Leah, Jakub, and I, make a quick huddle when we are alone, whispering about how we need to get out of this place. Jakub says the ghost has already tried to massage him three times and I can't help but grin at our predicament. We will leave as soon as possible.

After a couple of hours, the apartment is clean of dirt and glass, and Kemal returns with several overflowing shopping bags.

"Thanks guys for helping out. You know, I used to feel bad about asking Couch Surfers to help me clean up, but then I realised that I can't clean my whole apartment by myself. Here's the bill from the shopping by the way, you can pay me later." Reluctantly, I help him retie the bandage that covers his deep cuts from the broken glass table and we finally leave the apartment in darkness, take a taxi to a bar, then drink beer.

It's all over. I can feel it.

"I have apartments in thirty countries because I don't like to use hotels." "I translate dictionaries into five languages at once so that I learn languages quicker." "I don't read anymore because when I look at a page, I see all of the words at the same time. By the time I was eighteen, I had read about eighteen thousand books and now I can predict the ending of any book that I read, so I find them boring." "When I was twelve, I beat up an adult for the first time. I took him and threw him down the stairs. Now I'm a martial arts Grandmaster." "I once went to South America for a few months, but I don't really remember it and I didn't take any photos. It was a bit of a crazy time." Delusions of grandeur, Kemal throws tall tale after taller tale at us. As far as I can tell, he spends his days flicking between Facebook and Couch Surfing, but at one point he offers me a job with his tyre recycling company. I am dubious of both the existence of this company and of the technology he describes to me.

In the morning, I tell him that an old university friend has invited us to stay. He cooks another meal, opens wine, anything to stop us leaving.

"I'm disappointed," he says, pulling me aside, "I thought you guys would stay a long time and we could have fun together."

"I'm sorry," I tell him, "but I haven't seen my friend for such a long time." Blatantly lying to his face seems far kinder than telling him that we have to leave because of him. He is blissfully unaware of his actions.

Freed from his clutches by mid-afternoon, we run down the street, whooping with delight to tour the city, tasting the magic vibrancy. It's intoxicating, wild, and full of life.

I lose myself, just for a moment, falling in love with the ancient architecture and the cobbled streets.

"I could live here Monkey. I could live here for a bit and I could teach again, I could take a break from the cold, then carry on. Why don't we live here together?"

For those precious few moments, we are caught in the spell of Istanbul and the world is full of possibility once more. Yes, this is what I was feeling: not an end, but a break. There is so much more to come.

37. Acceptance

"I have to go back to England. I'm sorry." I look on helpless as Leah bursts into a flood of tears. "I don't want to… but it's this pain and it's getting worse. Every day it worries me, every day I muse over what is wrong and it keeps me awake at night. I have no health insurance and when I looked at my bank account this morning, I found out that I only have twenty-two pounds in the whole world, not even enough to make an appointment with most doctors. In England, doctors are free. I can find out what is wrong there." She cries harder. "Health is life and life is great. Without it, we'd be dead." She doesn't laugh. "Please My Monkey, please try to understand."

"I… I do understand. I… I just don't want you to go. I don't want to be here by myself. These past few months have been the happiest of my life."

"Come on," I try speaking jovially, nudging her shoulder, "you came here for an adventure, a better life. Not just to spend time with me."

"I know… I do know… but… I want to be… with you too." I can barely understand her between heavy sobs. "And now… now you're leaving… you're leaving… you're leaving me." She closes her eyes tight, trying to shut out the whole world, begging for it to not be real.

"Hey, look at me." I lift her chin softly with my finger. She sniffles meekly, stifling her sobs for a second. "I am not leaving you. This is nothing to do with you. I have to go because I could never forgive myself if something happened to me and what that would mean to my family. Do you understand that?"

"I know that you have to go. I just don't want you to. Please let me be sad."

And it all makes perfect sense. She doesn't want my hollow words, she doesn't want to hear my jokes about plenty more nice British guys to go hitchhiking with, she doesn't want to make me stay. She wants only to be sad in this moment and for me to give her the dignity of doing so.

How badly I want to hold her, to take the hurt away.

For weeks I have pushed the pain aside, but it has become too much. Real physical pain that surely has both a cause and a solution. I hid it behind every precious moment we shared across the continent and now this city. So many moments. The moment I drank pickle juice, only for it to explode out of my mouth in disgust as I threw wild accusations of being fed the worst drink in the world. The moment Jakub asked some security guards for a spoon so that he could eat their soup and in response, they invited us to join them for dinner. The moment we ate so much delicious food, none of us could walk home for several hours and we had to sit and wait for our self-inflicted, gluttonous suffering to pass. The moment we cycled around an island, admiring wild horses under blue skies.

The moment that we said we could live in Istanbul. Together.

There was another moment on the bicycles when I was cycling alongside a girl I didn't know. Her boyfriend dived in-between us and kissed her on the cheek. Screaming in terror, she threw her hands into the air and came down hard upon the tarmac at high speed. I couldn't control my laughter, tickled by the boyfriend's well intentioned gesture that went horribly wrong. But here we are now: she is the girl on the bike and I am the well intentioned guy who has got things wrong. I don't want to hurt her, but she has travelled across the world for me and this is me, letting her crash to the ground as I cycle on by.

Three days ago, I sat with a new friend as she told me that her father had died during the night. I wanted to hold her and to hug her and to say nothing at all because there were no words that I could offer to ease her pain, but I could have been there, me a stranger and she a stranger, but us sharing together in her hurt, if only for a moment. Like a coward, I sat in terrified silence, too afraid to move, unable to comprehend her words. I had told her how very sorry I was. How could I have offered so little?

Now I flail with Leah, unable to comfort her.

"Do you regret it yet?"

"No."

I believe her. With all of my heart, I believe her. If there was a time for her to regret this all, to wish she was somewhere far away, somewhere she knew, a place where one day led to the next, that would be now.

"What do you want Monkey, what can I do to stop you hurting?"

"I want to stay with you."

"But I have to go. I don't want to be sick."

"I don't want you to be sick either."

"So I have to find out."

"I know."

"So what can I do?"

"You do what you have to do." We are going around in circles.

It hits me like a beautiful sledgehammer, Pandora's box full of butterflies.

"Come with me." The solution is so simple.

"What?"

"Come with me." She can hardly believe what I'm saying.

"But you travel alone. I know you already, I know that you do your own thing."

"In a word, you are right. I prefer to be alone, to do my thing. But right now, why don't we continue this adventure alone, together?"

With a little more discussion, we outline a plan. We will travel to Greece where I hope my non-existent E.U. health card entitles me to free medical care. From there, we have the option of heading south, east, or back to England.

Me, my twenty-two pounds, and a little Monkey.

38. Belief

Early in the morning, Jakub left as we slept. He cooked us breakfast, put it on the table, and wrote a short note. 'I would have been too sad to say goodbye.'

In several weeks of being together for every waking minute, the three of us have grown to be good friends. While three have become two, I have no doubt that we will one day meet again, although I have no idea where or when that will occur.

Our first night out of Istanbul is spent in the truck of a cab. In an isolated field, the trucker pours glasses of whiskey accompanied by bread and cheese. Leah and I sleep on the top bunk, he on the bottom. A few hours later, he starts up the engine and we are on our way again. A little illegal fiddling of the tacho device ensures that he will have no problems with exceeding his maximum daily driving limit. Anxious to keep moving, to get to a doctor, to find out what is wrong, this time-saving tweak pleases me.

All I know of Greece is the three sun drenched isles I visited during my time at university. Soft beaches and white cliffs, it was the closest thing to an idyllic paradise that I had ever seen in Europe. Thessaloniki however, leaves much to be desired. We walk for hours in a town so wet that even the sea itself complains of too much water. Our night is spent in a tiny squat, a crooked stone structure only avoiding demolition because it is attached to a historic wall. One of the permanent squatters tells us that when the police tried to kick them out, they couldn't because the real owner of the building didn't care what happened to it. The only light in the bedroom is a weak desk lamp powered by stolen electricity. It offers just enough visibility to make out the mattress lying on the floor and the hoard of ants that cycle across it, collecting spilt honey. Outside the bedroom is a small hallway with a filthy white sink and ice cold running water. The only toilet is through the other tiny bedroom and we have to excuse ourselves as we pass. During the night, I walk outside to pee in the rain because it's easier.

"I just got into the CIA system," one of the squatters laughs in the morning. Judging by the heavy music that played all night, it took him a fair few hours to do so.

I gasp as I throw my head under the freezing water to try and wash myself. If I am going to hospital, I will at least look respectable.

It is several kilometres walk to the hospital, but at least the rain has stopped.

When I arrive, I am ushered from desk to desk until finally an English speaking nurse directs me outside and points me towards a hospital where I can be seen. He signals for a taxi, but I wave it away, too embarrassed to tell him that I can't afford it.

"I like walking, it's a nice day." It isn't a nice day, I don't want to walk.

At the second hospital, I provide no details except my first name. Every couple of hours, I am moved from one waiting room to another.

"This is the worst hospital I have ever seen," Leah confides. "It's so dirty." We have been walking in and out without being questioned for several hours. We both shy away as a badly injured man is wheeled past us in the corridor. His face is so mangled that it's impossible to tell if it is the result of a terrible impact, fire, or maybe even both.

"It's free. You can't put a price on that." I usher Leah away from the dying man, my arm around her waist.

Finally I meet with a doctor. He is a tall man in his early thirties with dark hair, typical of the Greeks. I like him, I want him to be my friend. I want him to tell me that everything is OK.

He asks what my problem is and I explain as best I can about the pain. I say where it hurts, although I can't pinpoint it exactly, but it hurts and I am worried.

He takes a blood sample from my arm and asks me to pee in a bottle. I do as he asks.

I sit and wait a little more.

"Come again tomorrow," I am told.

"Tomorrow? Can't you tell me anything tonight, please?"

"Tomorrow, test." Tomorrow is so far away.

I trudge along the waterfront for several hours, holding Leah's hand. Am I sinking or falling? I can't even tell anymore.

In drizzling rain, I watch as the waves break upon the sea wall. Harsh, cold spray whips into my face.

The world, warm and welcoming, has turned on me. I am held in suspended motion, my own fate ripped from my hands. My very freedom itself is now in question.

I pick up a stone and throw it into the water. It disappears beneath the surface, never to be seen again. Again and again I throw stone after stone, the rain soaking my clothes, Leah watching, asking me to come into the dry of a bus stop.

"What does it matter?"

I buy a two litre plastic bottle of wine and a box of crackers.

I can barely summon the energy to walk home.

I give in. We sit in the bus stop, Leah comforting me, me with my eyes closed.

Back in the dark squat, I drink wine from the bottle and allow crumbs to fall from my crackers. Let the ants feast.

By morning, the rain has ceased once more. Back we walk, the many kilometres to the hospital, that doomed walk, the same heavy steps I felt on that day I walked Leah to the airport, but this time they are heavier and forever means forever.

"Hello, my name is Jamie. I was here yesterday, I had some tests." Unsuccessfully, I have already tried this line at five different places in the hospital. Fortunately, this receptionist speaks English and finds an envelope with handwritten Greek symbols on the front that she gives to me. I have no idea what they say, but take the envelope as she points down the corridor, indicating that I should return to the same doctor as the day before.

The dull corridors remind me of years earlier when I lay in hospital, dreading the impending doctor's diagnosis, knowing that he would tell me I had fractured my vertebrae. This time around, I do not know what the doctors will tell me, I do not know what their diagnosis will reveal. I open the envelope and study the paper inside. Two graphs and a series of numbers. I try to decipher what it all means, but the curious squiggles contain no comprehensible information. In the waiting room, I take a ticket, just like the ones that you get at a cheese counter. I wish that I was only waiting for cheese. I really like cheese, why can't I only be waiting for cheese?

Another ticket called. I wait, I wait, I watch the clock and I sit and I wait. I've been here forever. I ask Leah to leave me for a bit. This time it is I who needs to wallow in my sadness.

Without Leah beside me, there is no one watching. What if I just got up and left? What if I didn't bother to wait for the diagnosis, if I just went out and said that everything is OK, that this will pass, that there is nothing to worry about? If nobody else knows, does that make me OK?

My number is called. One of the assistants comes over to me. I sit motionless, my ticket in hand.

If I ignore this situation, maybe it will all go away.

The assistant touches my arm to get my attention, then leads me to the doctor's room.

Don't leave me…

She leaves me with the doctor.

I take a seat. It's not the same doctor as before. This guy speaks better English.

"So you had some tests yesterday?"

Why is he so happy? "Yes. Here." I hand him my test results.

"What was the problem before?" I explain everything all over again. The pain, how it started one day without warning, how it comes and goes, how it can't be placed, how I don't want to explain it anymore I just want it to be OK.

He studies the magic graphs. I feel as if I am being sentenced in court. What will the jury decide? Will I hang?

He scribbles something illegible on the paper and hands it back to me, smiling. A smile, so kind, am I OK?

"I would like you to see a radiologist and have a scan."

I feel the glass floor shatter beneath me. The shards rip my skin as I fall, tumbling helplessly. Everything will be OK. Everything is always OK. Until it's not. Now it is not. "What... what is wrong?" I try to sound brave, but my voice falters. I try to sound like I could hitchhike alone to every far flung corner of the Earth, I try to sound like I'm not the boy who was afraid of the world. But I am. I am a small boy and I am falling. I am Angel Gabriel on the stage, I am crying in the forest, I have been caught by the spitting dinosaur, I am running from the little pink ghost. I am burning for eternity and I want it to stop.

I need my family. I need them to keep me safe, to let me lie in bed and bring me hot chocolate and warm peanut butter croissants. Crunchy peanut butter and raspberry jam, yes that would be...

"Nothing is wrong," he smiles, trying to reassure me. "I just want to make sure."

I want to believe him. With all of my heart and all of my soul, I want to believe him.

But I don't.

39. Freedom

I need to get back to my family. I need to get back to them as soon as possible. Between them and the English doctors, they will make everything OK.

All of this is nearly two thousand miles away. Two thousand miles by the fastest, most direct route. Two thousand miles over which I will hitchhike with less than twenty pounds.

I tell the Monkey. She says that she will still come with me.

"Thank you. You make me feel less alone right now."

On this day, I am walking hand in hand with my fear, my little pink ghost, attempting to deal with it. Leah holds my other hand, driving me forward, supporting me, giving me the comfort I need.

Despite this, there is nothing that she can do.

Yet I am eternally grateful.

We catch a bus to the outskirts of the city. One hour, two, three, four, they race by. We walk seven miles without a single car stopping for us and night falls.

Seven hours after we started hitchhiking, a car picks us up. Why does this happen on the time I want to hurry?

"I see you three time, I go, come, go." The man drives us back the way we walked and leaves us under a motorway bridge, warning us to be careful of unexploded land mines. "This way Bulgaria."

We struggle up the steep bank and find ourselves beside the motorway. Marching alongside the railings in absolute darkness, we have neither food nor water and it is desperately cold. I didn't know Greece got this cold. The buses have finished for the day and the city would take all night to return to. We have to keep moving. I can barely face the walk, but Leah urges me on, forcing me to keep up. She waves at every passing car, desperate for a ride. People can't see us on the side of the motorway in darkness and even on the smaller road when we were visible, no one picked us up. For the first time I know that we are both in real, immediate danger. Yet this time I am neither falling nor sinking. I am hopelessly marching on.

Is it that fear is a luxury, afforded only to those who have a chance of escape?

Or is it that our desire to keep each other safe outweighs everything? I promised to keep her safe, I will not break that promise. On she stomps, ahead of me, powering along the rough terrain.

I can see the headlines: 'Two unidentified foreigners found frozen to death alongside motorway.' A more dramatic end than most. Or how about this one: 'Two people blown up on the side of the motorway by a land-mine.' Surely there can't be explosive devices this close to the road? The article would question our intelligence, muse as to how we ended up where we were and why we were travelling without warm clothes or supplies. That's assuming our belongings don't get burnt beyond recognition.

"I'm sorry. I'm so sorry. I didn't mean for this to happen."

"Don't be sorry. I'm not." She drags me on through the darkness, never ceasing to leap up and down for each passing vehicle, waving the feeble light of a single mobile phone screen.

It might have been ten minutes, it might have been an hour. Time is irrelevant right now. All that matters is putting one foot after the other, keeping moving, not giving up.

A lorry brakes hard and pulls onto the hard shoulder, the following cars having to swerve around it. I don't care where it's going or who is driving or how they managed to see us. All that matters is that someone might be able to take us somewhere, somewhere safe, anywhere but where we are right now. To be far from civilisation is a glorious experience. To be far from civilisation at the start of winter with inappropriate clothing and a severe lack of food or water is a considerably less wonderful thing.

We bow, clasp our hands together, offer every symbolic gesture of gratitude that we can.

This man may have just saved our lives.

Later in the night, an erratic driver twitches and swerves, eating hamburgers with only one hand on the wheel. On a different day I might ask to get out, but today is not a different day and I do not have the luxury of wasting time. The police stop us and hold us for over an hour, running drug searches all over the car and breathalysing the driver twice. Finding nothing, they realise that his only offence is being a bad driver.

We get to Sofia in the early hours of the morning and message Sarah, our friend with whom we stayed before. Kindly, she invites us to her house and we spend Halloween there. It's a simple sixteen hundred mile road left to traverse. We will not stop, we will not sleep, we will do it all at once, one great long ride. It is I now who is full of energy, eager to go, to cover huge distances.

By evening, we are at a Slovenian petrol station being gifted free teas. The girl behind the counter pities us and our hopeless plight in the cold November night. Two hours of shivering ensue before a lorry drives us a little further down the road. There we stand for twelve hours. Twelve hours! In all my time of hitchhiking I have cruised around Europe with ease, rarely waiting more than thirty minutes. Now on the time to make haste, people turn me down. Again the staff let us stand inside, supplying us with sandwiches and hot drinks. I try to convey my gratitude to the workers, but they have no idea how truly grateful I am.

By the following evening, we are on the border of France in the town of Strasbourg, over one thousand miles from Sofia. The rain beats down relentlessly and we shelter under a bridge. Each passing car sprays us with water and slowly we become damper and colder. A kindly gentleman goes out of his way to drive us to the motorway and drops us at a large service station.

The service station door is locked and we have to buy chocolate bars through the small night-window to keep our energy up. I approach each driver, asking as nicely as I can for a ride, anywhere west. They turn me down again and again. The rain is relentless and the two of us press ourselves against the front of the garage to escape it. As if the whole world is choosing to conspire against us, the wind blows the rain onto our cowering bodies.

Leah begins to shiver and I wrap her in my sleeping bag as she sits upon the floor. I remove every piece of clothing from my bag and cover her with them all. I will keep her warm.

Her feet are soaked, so I take off her wet shoes and socks, then give her mine.

Standing with my feet exposed to the elements, I am getting desperate. My phone is dead and I no longer have any clue as to how many hours we have been standing out in the rain.

"Please," I plead to the woman in the locked petrol station, "can my friend come inside? She is very sick and I need her to get warm." No says the woman behind the window. She moves away to clean the floor. "Is there anything nearby that we can go to: a hotel lobby, a police station, it doesn't matter, just something to get out of the cold?" The woman shakes her head as she cleans. Nothing she can do.

I shake Leah, trying to rouse her. She barely opens her eyes, lost somewhere between sleep and unconsciousness. With every passing car she becomes harder and harder to wake, her face pale.

Never before have I seen someone this sick, this close to the edge. And this is not any someone, this is one of my best friends in the whole world, My Monkey.

My someone.

Still I rush from driver to driver, begging them to help. No one will.

As I shake her, My Monkey barely regains consciousness…

I will find a way.

"How about a taxi?" I finally ask the woman behind the glass window. She picks up the phone.

We might be miles from anything and I know that I don't have money to pay for it, but it doesn't matter, I will deal with the consequences later. I'll get arrested if

I have to, if that's what it takes to keep Leah safe.

When the taxi pulls up, I drag her into the car and ask the driver to turn up the heat. Within minutes, life is restored to her. That wide eyed wonder, big dark disks forming the pathway to her soul. She looks at me, thankful. I feel my breathing return to a normal rate. Like the warmth now flowing through her body, my heart is warmed to see colour returning to her face.

"Take us to a youth hostel," I tell the driver. I am keeping her safe.

"I have never been so cold in my life," Leah concedes towards the end of the taxi ride.

The meter rings up thirty-three euros.

"Do you have any cash?" Inside her wallet she has forty euros, the last of her money. She hands it to the taxi driver as I run inside to see if they have any rooms available. A miserable receptionist tells me that they do have rooms available, but he is reluctant to let us stay. Outside, Leah struggles to get the change from the French speaking driver.

"Where is the change?" I ask.

"There is a seven euro charge for bags," the driver retorts.

"No, that isn't true."

"Life's tough." The guy turns his back and walks off as I cuss him in the few offensive French words that I know. He returns a volley of insults far beyond my comprehension. Why is it that when you're down, people choose to kick you in the face and steal your broken teeth? I wish a curse upon him, a plague of awfulness and harm. It's the sum of a series of unfortunate events that are out of my control at a time when I need the world to be as kind to me as it has been for the past half a year. Between Leah and I, we now have no money.

Sighing, the receptionist turns on his computer to manage our booking as if we are the most inconvenient people in the world. I want to grab him and shake him and demand to know what it is that makes him so unpleasant. Instead, I ask politely how much the room will be and if I can pay on card. It is eighty euros for two dorm beds. I must have less than ten euros in my account if I had just twenty-two pounds in Turkey a week ago. It has been years since my overdraft was revoked by my bank, the result of continually exceeding my personal limit, but I pretend that my card will work anyway. I hand it over.

Just a few seconds until my card is declined, then we'll have to try and sneak into the common room to sleep. Maybe we could just stand here at reception all night.

My card is handed back to me with a receipt. I look in amazement, no idea how it went through. No doubt that means I am soon due another thumping overdraft charge. We are told that we have to leave the hostel by ten in the morning. It is now after three. Ten euros an hour to sleep on plastic sheets, how wonderful.

With less rain the next day, we move at speed across France and sleep through Luxembourg, courtesy of a pleasant young Belgian couple. They drop us at a service station in Belgium, less than fifty miles from the nearest ferry port. Inside the service area I am disappointed to find two young hitchhikers failing to get a ride. They are both nineteen, part of a charity hitch, and have been waiting for several hours after taking a few trains to help them along their way. I wish them luck and return to the car park.

I spy British number plates.

Leah and I sit by the car, waiting for the owner to return. A tall woman with bleached blond hair approaches the vehicle and I leap to my feet.

"Excuse me, are you English?"

"No, I'm Ukrainian." She is taken aback and threatens to leap for the car and speed away into the night.

"But you are going to England?"

"Yes, I live there." She opens the door.

"I've just hitchhiked all the way from Istanbul to get here and I'm desperate to get back to the UK to visit my family. I haven't seen most of them for over half a year and we're so close, do you think that you could give us a ride to the ferry port? Please." I muster the saddest, most pathetic face I can. Inside, I feel as pathetic as I surely look.

I need you to help me right now.

Hesitantly, she agrees to give us a ride. We put our bags in her spacious boot and lounge comfortably in large leather seats.

"Wait a minute, I just thought, there are two young hitchhikers inside. Do you think you could give them a ride too?"

She throws her hands in the air. "Why not!"

I run into the service station, grab the teenagers, and together we head to the ferry port. The four of us ride onto the ferry for free and on the boat, knowing that I have already expired all of my funds, I order food and drinks on my card, hoping that it works once more. It does. If I'm going all in, I'm going all in. I officially now have less than no money in the world. I'll deal with this later.

Hailing from Norfolk, a rural part of England that leads only to the sea, not one person is able to offer us a lift on the passenger floors of the boat. It has taken a huge amount of time, but we have asked every single person in the passenger lounge.

"There is only one place left to go. The trucker lounge."

Leah hesitates. She knows what I'm thinking. "You want me to go in there… alone?"

I look at her. Slim, tanned, a pretty face, and big brown eyes, if one of us will secure a ride, it will be her. "Do you regret it yet?"

"No."

I kiss her good luck, cross every part of my being, then take a seat and wait.

"It worked," she tells me with a smile. My smile might be even bigger than hers.

The trucker drives us all of the way back to the very first petrol station at which my mother first dropped me.

I have journeyed full circle through twenty-four countries and fourteen thousand miles, only to come back to exactly where I started. I stand at the run down fuel station, admiring how everything is exactly as it was when I left. For the past half a year, people have come and gone, day after day, oblivious to the rest of the world around them, as oblivious to my journey as I was to them. Did I expect everything to have changed?

Except this time, I am heading in the opposite direction. I left alone, dreaming of places unknown. I return with a Monkey, desperate for familiarity.

It is three in the morning when we catch our final ride. By chance, the driver is the father of a guy I went to school with, a kind man who says it isn't a problem to take me home. He'll go out of his way, he likes our story.

At four in the morning, I shake the hand of the two hundred and twenty-seventh stranger to pick me up and I thank him so very much with all my heart.

We stand by the conker tree outside my mother's house, a place I spent numerous days playing as a child.

"How do you feel?" Leah asks.

"I feel as if I never left. Yet I can recall each day of the past half a year. Each day was well spent, each day I lived through something memorable. Each day I met people who have touched my life and that I will remember forever. How often can someone say all of those things?"

The lights are off as I walk down the garden path that I have walked thousands of times before.

What is the great revelation from these six months? That's the big joke. There is none.

If anything, maybe now I understand what it means to be free. Freedom is not an absence of repression, rather it is the choice to exercise one's own free will in spite of all else. Without exercising our right to choose, we are never truly free. Choice may be the choice to do everything or nothing in life. There is no choice too big or too small to represent freedom.

As I raise my hand to knock on the door and unexpectedly wake my mother, I know that I made the choice to be here right now. By the threat of ill health, my hand was forced, but I chose to take action, to walk down this path, to knock on this door. I will never have to regret this because it was my choice and mine alone.

Knock! Knock!

I am the boy who was afraid of the world, yet I set off around Europe on my own, trusting in strangers. That fear does not simply finish, I cannot stop being scared. I can only decide that something else is more important than the fear itself. Maybe it is true that there are two types of fear. There is good fear and there is bad fear. Good fear is the kind of fear that makes you run when faced with an axe-wielding murderer. Bad fear is the type of fear that stops you leaving the house to do anything exciting in case you meet an axe-wielding murderer. It is the type of fear where you worry unnecessarily about bad things that might possibly happen and as a result, live your life in a protective shell, doing nothing that matters to you or anyone else until you silently expire, rolling onto your back and disappearing from the world without so much as a ripple.

I hear movement upstairs.

I never intended to disappear forever. Just for a little bit of time. I will always disappear, then one day, I'll come back, come back again. I hope that the people I care about will always wait for me.

A light comes on inside the house.

I will be afraid when I need to be afraid, go home when I need to go home, but most of all, I will strive to overcome unnecessary fears so that my life can be a memorable one, if only to me. Only this way can I live a life that is true to myself and free from regret.

Beside me, her hand in mine, stands a girl who is exactly the same. She feared, she jumped, she loved the ride. Together we believe in something more, something undefined, in the goodness of people in spite of all else.

I hear someone coming down the stairs.

I am home, but already my feet are itching. This journey is at an end, but this is only the beginning. I cannot wait for what comes next.

I feel like the luckiest boy in all the world.

Maybe, just maybe, it isn't such a great big scary world after all. Maybe, just maybe, it's OK to be a little bit afraid.

We can all be afraid together. We can walk hand in hand with our little pink ghosts.

Epilogue

Four months after I stopped hitchhiking, I learnt of the tragic death of the young Canadian who taught me a juggling trick at Hitch Gathering, the free spirit. His name was Taylor Booth. When I met him, I saw in him a calmness and contentedness with life that I have rarely seen in any other. Although we only met briefly, I remember him well because I aspire to be as free, as calm, as content as he will always be. In his wake, he leaves a great legacy and the numerous messages of tribute across the internet are testament to this and representative of the people's lives he touched. In his twenty-six years, he lived through many more lifetimes than most. I am grateful for the inspiration. I thank you from the bottom of my heart.

You have taught me that when my own time is up, I want not to regret wasting time on trivial matters, I want only to say that I tried, I had a good ride, I remember so many things.

Life, if you let it be, is a daring adventure. I will run far from the path and I will play with the field mice. Somewhere amongst the long grass, I find happiness. Or it finds me. Over and over again. It runs with me through the fields and over the hills, and only on the days that I stop dreaming does it finally disappear. We must never stop dreaming because dreams are the fuel that keeps our souls burning through the darkest hour of the night. Dreams make us free. I choose to choose because I am as free as I choose to be. So too are we all. Live the life you want to live because you are living it for yourself. Everything else will fall into place.

Never stop believing, never stop dreaming, never stop trying.

Impossible is nothing and everything will be OK.

I am twenty-six years old and sometimes I am still afraid, but less so than ever before. What is the scariest thing I have ever done? Sharing this story with you. Thank you for taking the time to read it.

Jamie

P.S. It's OK to be afraid sometimes. We all are.
See you on the other side.

Author's Closing Remarks

Thank you for reading my story. As my nomadic journey through life continues (first inspired by this adventure you just read about), I share my musings and adventures through www.greatbigscaryworld.com. This website is where this book was born and where I will announce new releases. For updates, please check out the website, like the Facebook page, www.facebook.com/greatbigscaryworld, or follow me on Twitter, twitter.com/jamierbw. If you are interested in watching videos from my hitchhiking (and other) adventures, I will share them all on this site. You may also be interested in following along with Leah. You can do so at www.thevegetariantraveller.com.

As this book is a small, independent project, I would greatly appreciate it if you would spread the word. A Tweet, a Facebook share, telling a friend, it all helps. If you liked it, please leave an honest review for others. Amazon, Good Reads, wherever you like, it's just about spreading the word. The success, or lack thereof, of this book, is dependent upon you, the reader.

I hope you found something of substance in these words. If you wish to get in contact with me, please feel free to email me at:

jamierbw@greatbigscaryworld.com

Thank you to everyone who was part of this story, I am grateful for you all. Thank you also to Georgina, Rachel, Jenny, Gill, Mark, Qing, Egle, Andrea, Caoimhe, Lindsey, Leah, my mother, and everyone else who helped to shape this into a story. Your guidance is invaluable.

Thank you, Mr. Tyler, for persuading me to read. It changed everything.

Thank you, Leah, for being ever so brave. You have inspired me.

Printed in Germany
by Amazon Distribution
GmbH, Leipzig